THERAPEUTIC RECREATION
FOR
EXCEPTIONAL CHILDREN
Let Me In, I Want to Play

THERAPEUTIC RECREATION FOR EXCEPTIONAL CHILDREN

Let Me In, I Want to Play

By

AUBREY H. FINE, Ed.D., C.T.R.S.

Associate Professor
Director, Center for Special Populations
California State Polytechnic University, Pomona

NYA M. FINE, M.Ed., C.T.R.S.

Consultant

With Contributions by

Jesse Dixon, Ph.D.   Gus Gerson, Ed.D.
V. Gregory Payne, P.E.D.   Susan Nakayama Siaw, Ph.D.

Foreword by

Peg Connolly, Ph.D., C.T.R.S.

Executive Director
National Council for Therapeutic Recreation Certification

CHARLES C THOMAS • PUBLISHER
Springfield • Illinois • U.S.A.

Published and Distributed Throughout the World by

CHARLES C THOMAS • PUBLISHER
2600 South First Street
Springfield, Illinois 62717

© *1988 by* CHARLES C THOMAS • PUBLISHER

ISBN 0-398-05479-7

Library of Congress Catalog Card Number: 88-8568

With THOMAS BOOKS *careful attention is given to all details of manufacturing
and design. It is the Publisher's desire to present books that are satisfactory as to their
physical qualities and artistic possibilities and appropriate for their particular use.*
THOMAS BOOKS *will be true to those laws of quality that assure a good name
and good will.*

Printed in the United States of America
SC-R-3

Library of Congress Cataloging-in-Publication Data

Fine, Aubrey H.
  Therapeutic recreation for exceptional children.

  Includes bibliographies and index.
  1. Recreational therapy for children. 2. Handicapped
children—Recreation. 3. Play therapy. I. Fine, Nya M.
II. Dixon, Jesse Thomas. III. Title.
RJ53.R43F56 1988   615.8'5153'0880816   88-8568
ISBN 0-398-05479-7

CONTRIBUTORS

Jesse Dixon, Ph.D.
Professor/Associate Dean
San Diego State University

Gus Gerson, Ed.D.
Professor
California State Polytechnic University

V. Gregory Payne, P.E.D.
Associate Professor
San Jose State University

Susan Nakayama Siaw, Ph.D.
Associate Professor
California State Polytechnic University

To

ABRAHAM "ZADIE" SHUSTER

and to

LISA DANIELS

*Two special individuals who inspired our efforts in working
with exceptional children.*

*To the many children who have made a significant impact in our
professional lives. To Gary, Judy, Clay, Theresa, Britt, Tondy, and
John Robert, we thank you for your inspiration and your indirect
teaching. Through your eyes, we have recognized the importance of
play for all children. You have been instrumental in assisting us in
developing and modifying unique recreational services for all and have
demonstrated the worthiness of our efforts.*

FOREWORD

It is a pleasure to introduce this new text, **Therapeutic Recreation for Exceptional Children: Let Me In, I Want to Play.** I have watched this field of therapeutic recreation expand, struggle, and identify itself over the past fifteen years and, despite these necessary growing pains that any profession must face, I am excited and pleased with the developments we have experienced.

Over the past five years, significant advancements have been made in many areas of the field of therapeutic recreation. Yet, there has been a great gap in our literature concerning our work with exceptional children. This book will help close that gap and, at the same time, open our minds to all that remains to be done in this important area of service delivery.

There was a great furor of excitement in the late 1970s regarding the inclusion of recreation as a related service within P.L. 94-142, "The Education Act for All Handicapped Children." As the authors indicate, this was the first major inroad authorizing the provision of recreation services as needed in the education of exceptional children. However, after ten years, we have very little information on this service area and very little evidence of such services in operation. I believe **Therapeutic Recreation for Exceptional Children: Let Me In, I Want to Play** will give us guidance on approaches to instigate the services we have for so long thought to be crucial in the development of exceptional children.

In Chapter 1, Fine provides us with essential background information on who exceptional children are and on their needs and goals for recreation services. They remind us that the primary goal for children in play is to have fun, and they document the developmental and life-enrichment goals that may be achieved. Chapter 2 provides essential information regarding the theoretical underpinnings of play and development and the course of motor development in children. The authors and contributors are to be commended for bringing this summary of literature to the field of therapeutic recreation. Further, I encourage each student and professional in the field to go back to the original literature sources cited in this chapter and to refresh themselves on the rich research and writing that exists on play and development.

Chapter 3 provides information on the field of therapeutic recreation, trends in services, legislation and its mandates for service delivery, and the importance of advocacy. In Chapter 4, contributor Dixon provides a perspective on programming in therapeutic recreation that may be considered a departure from other programming information in the field. Critical information on the purpose, nature, and available tools for assessing the needs of exceptional children are provided in Chapter 5, along with valuable tips on the administration of assessments.

Fine and Fine encourage us to broaden our concepts of service delivery in Chapter 6 and to educate ourselves in some of the so-called "non-traditional" areas of recreation and activity-related therapies. It is important to note that the authors are not claiming these therapies as the sole domain of the therapeutic recreation profession but as legitimate modalities for those in our field who are prepared in their use. A critical element of this text is the inclusion of a chapter on parent involvement in the therapeutic recreation service-delivery process. Professionals and students are encouraged to take serious notice of this information and the benefits of parent collaboration in the delivery of services to exceptional children. The chapter devoted to expanding the concept of leisure education, leisure instruction, and leisure guidance provides valuable information on integrating leisure and therapeutic recreation services within the education system for exceptional children. Accurately, the authors remind us that therapeutic recreation in the schools is necessary but not as yet a reality. Finally, Fine and Fine provide us with their thoughts on future trends for the delivery of therapeutic recreation services to exceptional children.

Overall, the text is made more enjoyable through the use of vignettes, anecdotal, and personalized information, which will aid in understanding the writing and finding meaning in the words. I believe the authors have accurately documented the field and have added their unique ideas and premises to our body of knowledge. As the authors infer throughout their material, we must expand our thinking in service delivery, be creative in our approaches and techniques, and keep foremost in our minds the unique needs and incredible potential of the exceptional children we propose to serve.

Fine and Fine and the other contributors to this text are to be commended for their work. For all professionals and students in the field of therapeutic recreation, I hope this material will stimulate you to action and to the desire for further development of our work with exceptional children. For colleagues from other disciplines, I hope this material provides a greater understanding of the vast contribution of play, recreation and leisure services to the total development of exceptional children and their ultimate opportunities for full participation throughout their life span. For parents, I hope the authors have provided you with more "hope" for all the potential you see in your exceptional children and with greater resources for their development. And, finally and foremost, for exceptional children, my wish is that through access to recreation services, you will someday not have to ask to be "let in to play," but that you will have full opportunity, full involvement, and full satisfaction through your play, your leisure, and your life.

PEG CONNOLLY, PH.D., C.T.R.S.
Executive Director
National Council for Therapeutic Recreation Certification

PREFACE:

A sk any child if he or she wants to play and do not be surprised to see a smiling face. In play, children are being invited to a world where they can call their own shots, a world where they can choose what they wish to do and how to do it. It is by no means simply "child's play." For most children, the opportunities to play by themselves or with others in an organized fashion exist in a multitude of variations and intents.

Play is a child's opportunity to explore his or her inner self. It is a positive outlet for a child's energy, and through these experiences, children learn the ways of life, how to set goals, how to grow up. In short, play is their work, their time to experiment and to enjoy. This is a child's position, but, unfortunately, not every child gets to play the game.

While the need to take part in social activities appears to be universal, if one were to survey all the recreation programs keeping a special tally on those incorporating special children, that tally would be extremely low. Granted, mandatory legislation has drastically changed the focus of attention and services made available to these children. However, they still lack the optimum amount of attention in the area of recreational programs.

The value of recreation is definitely recognizable and, specifically, its participatory aspect. As some may realize, there are a variety of skills that can be easily taught through leisure activities. How many of you can remember learning information through a relaxed conversation than the information being drilled into you by a formal setting? The same applies to children. Their skills of language, sensory motor skill, and socialization may have the opportunity to be enhanced. (Nevertheless, it should be kept in mind that the initial reason the child chooses to play is to have fun. He or she wants to participate on his/her own ground.)

The purpose of **Therapeutic Recreation for Exceptional Children: Let Me In, I Want to Play** is to sensitize the readers to the rationale of play experiences for exceptional children and to illustrate how they and others can learn from their experiences. One major purpose of the book is to attempt to answer some of the basic concerns of educators, recreators, and parents when providing or attempting to locate recreation services for the exceptional.

The chapters are organized logically, exploring the "global" needs of special populations, enhancing their interests, and how practitioners and parents can take an active role in strengthening these experiences. Furthermore, it is hoped that this book will relate to the reader the importance of open communication between practitioners and families. In this way, parents can serve as a positive force to what is being instructed.

This book is intended for people who are planning to use recreation to intervene with handicapped children rather than to justify or define the context of recreation service. The information in this book is based upon the education, service, and research experiences of the authors. Parents will find this book useful for considering ways they can enhance interactions with their children during play. College students may find the framework of ideas helpful to organize the concept of therapeutic recreation services. The writers suggest that educators use this book as one of several resource texts instead of building one entire course around it. Ideally, professionals can use this book to clarify the role of therapeutic recreation as an additional service approach with handicapped children.

Finally, but by no means lastly, it is hoped that this book will offer encouragement to parents and professionals who are involved with exceptional children to continue searching and expanding their own ways of working with children. In today's fast world it is imperative that we recognize the potential value of implementing recreational services for exceptional children. Their goal is to adapt to this rapidly changing and often confusing world.

Too many children have been neglected in the past, and many children have not had the opportunities to develop through their leisure time experiences. This book is intended to offer some solutions.

A.H.F.
N.M.F.

ACKNOWLEDGMENTS

Preparing this manuscript has been a challenging and arduous task. Within the year and a half of our efforts, many colleagues have made significant contributions in encouraging the fulfillment of this project. Through their emotional support and editorial assistance, this manuscript was completed. We would like to recognize the following individuals:

Barney Annoshian, Ph.D.
Laurie Boritz
Susan Batel
Carol Welch-Burke
Peg Connolly, Ph.D.
Victor Coppin, Ph.D.
Ron Deitrick, Ph.D.
George Eisen, Ph.D.
Gus Gerson, Ed.D.
Karen Givens
Don Morris, Ph.D.
Susan Siaw, Ph.D.
George Williams, Ed.D.
Joe Wilson, Ed.D.

We also are indebted to our good friend, Dolores Hernandez, who assisted in the final preparation of this text.

Finally, we would also like to acknowledge our two sons, Sean and Corey. They have sacrificed some of their personal time with us so that we could complete this task. We want them to know how much we love them. Hopefully, over the years to come, we will continue to share our lives, playing and learning together.

CONTENTS

THERAPEUTIC RECREATION
FOR
EXCEPTIONAL CHILDREN
Let Me In, I Want to Play

Chapter 1

INTRODUCTION:
LET ME IN, I WANT TO PLAY

Aubrey H. Fine

The child is there...
Beyond the hurt and handicap...
Beyond the difference...
Beyond the problem and probing...
How can we reach him? How can we
set him free?...

Buck, 1950

EXCEPTIONAL CHILDREN: WHO ARE THEY?

Working with exceptional children can be extremely exciting and fascinating. However, to provide unique and challenging experiences, one must be cognizant of their needs. Haring (1982), as the word implies, defines that "exceptional individuals are those who differ in some way from what society regards as normal" (p. 1). They are children whose performance deviates markedly from the norm, either with higher or lower than average performance or ability in the areas of cognition, emotion and physical abilities.

There are several terms utilized by professionals in the field to categorically classify exceptional individuals. The words **handicapped, impaired, disabled** or **disordered** are at times selected to describe special populations. Disabled persons, as Dunham and Dunham (1978) describe, are individuals who are structurally, physiologically or psychologically different from the normal person because of an accident, disease or developmental problem. At times, the term **disabled** is more commonly applied as a descriptor of physical problems. The term **impaired,** on the other hand, is frequently utilized to characterize sensory deficits such as hearing or sight.

Heward and Orlansky (1988) point out that the term **handicap** refers to

3

the problems or difficulties a person encounters because he or she is different. Their deviations may at times inhibit or for that matter prevent achievement or acceptance. A person who is handicapped may feel less adequate than others (Dunham and Dunham, 1978). One must understand that not all disabled people have to feel handicapped, for example, an individual who is blind can modify his home to compensate for his disability. This individual may not feel disadvantaged in that specific environment. He knows where everything is and therefore can readily adapt. However, place the same man in a new setting and he may feel handicapped until he is more acquainted and comfortable.

In regards to special populations, the term **handicapped** is more restrictive than exceptional. The term **exceptional** has a broader concentration and includes the gifted, i.e. individuals whose skills and performance can be considered above the norm. In general, exceptional children can be classified into one or more of the following categories:

1. visually impaired
2. hearing impaired
3. mentally retarded
4. learning disabled (learning disabilities which are not caused by any visual, hearing or motor handicaps as well as mental retardation or emotional problems)
5. communication disorders (speech and language problems)
6. physical handicaps and other health impairments (including neurological, orthopedic, and birth defects such as cerebral palsy and spina bifida, as well as diseases such as leukemia and kidney disorders)
7. behavior disorders (emotionally disturbed)
8. multiply handicapped (for example, cerebral palsy and mental retardation)
9. gifted and talented

In reference to the special populations focused within the text, a general concentration will be given to the first eight categories noted. Attention will not be given to the gifted and talented, because their programming concerns normally do not fall under the domain of therapeutic recreation.

Many of you may be curious in knowing how many exceptional children live in the United States. Stating precisely how many would be extremely difficult, because accurate data at the present time does not exist. The United States office of Special Education and Rehabilitation believes that 11 percent of all school-age children may be classified as handicapped. However, the present findings are much lower. Data collected indicates that approximately 4,300,000 children receive special education services. Furthermore, it was estimated by the National Center for Health Statistics (1975) that there are approximately 25,868,000 persons within this country (at all ages) who may be considered disabled to some degree.

The Office of Special Education and Rehabilitation, Department of Education has projected figures representing by category of exceptionality the number of nationwide children who received special education within the 1984–1985 academic year. Table I displays the recent government estimate. This data was compiled from the **Eighth Annual Report to Congress** which was prepared by the Office of Special Education in 1986. For the interest of the reader, the table also incorporates the number of children with disabling conditions who received special education services in 1976–1977. This will allow the reader the ability for comparison.

TABLE I
HANDICAPPED CHILDREN BY EXCEPTIONALITY

Type of disability	*Estimate number of children age 3–21*	
	76–77	84–85
Mentally retarded	969,547	717,785
Behaviorally disordered	283,072	373,207
Visually impaired	38,247	30,375
Learning disabled	797,213	1,839,292
Physically handicapped	87,008	58,835
Multihandicapped	50,722	71,780
Speech impaired	1,302,666	1,129,417
Hearing impaired	89,743	71,230
Deaf-blind	2,330	1,992
	3,620,548	4,293,913

Adapted from the Eighth Annual Report to Congress on the Implementation of the Education of the Handicapped Act (p. 4), 1986, U.S. Department of Education.

SOCIETY'S RESPONSE TO EXCEPTIONALITY

People who are disabled may encounter a wide variety of prejudicial experiences. Howard and Orlansky (1988) point out that society has responded towards the exceptional in virtually every human emotion and reaction—from extermination and ridicule to respecting them as human beings first and handicapped persons second.

Gleidman and Roth (1981) state that "to grow up handicapped in America is to grow up in a society that, because of its misreading of the significance of disability, is never entirely human in the way it treats the person within" (p. 301).

Society establishes the means of categorizing persons. People who fall short of our expectations (those exhibiting a stigma) constitute a special discrepancy between virtual and actual social identity. In his classic book, Goffman (1974) classifies three characteristics of stigma: stigma developed due to (1) physical deformities, (2) blemishes in character, and finally (3) stigma of race, nation and religion. Although each of these variables differ, the end result is similar. Society appears to construct a stigma theory to explain inferiority. The stigma in itself causes a variety of discriminatory acts. Unfortunately, persons with disabilities are frequently confronted with many of these deplorable instances.

Handicapism is a term utilized frequently to refer "to the prejudice, stereotyping and discrimination against the handicapped" (Kelly and Vergason, 1978 p. 65). In fact, Biklen and Bogden (1976) prepared an extremely interesting and relevant article on this topic, entitled "Handicapism in America." They defined handicapism as a set of practices that promote unequal and unjust treatment of people because of an apparent or assumed disability. They noted that many individuals in the general public are often uncomfortable in relating with handicapped persons. They listed several of the following common reactions:

1. Presume sadness on the person who is disabled.
2. Pity the individual.
3. At times focus so strongly on the disability that it is sometimes difficult to remember that disabled individuals are **people** first.
4. Disabled adults are often treated as children and are not given mutual respect.
5. People are uncomfortable being around disabled individuals and therefore avoid an interaction. They conclude by noting that if you are labeled "handicapped," handicapism is your greatest disadvantage. You are not treated as an ordinary person.

Many of these reactions are personally echoed in the collection of articles in Brightman's (1984) **Ordinary Moments.** Within this book, unique accounts of the everyday experiences associated with being disabled are openly discussed. **Ordinary Moments** explores with readers how individual's make it in a society which has difficulty accepting them. What makes the book so unique are all of the personal accounts incorporated. For example, an interesting title for one of the articles incorporated was "If I Were a Car, I'd Be a Lemon."

There are many other books that have been written over the years that sensitively portray what it is like to grow up being disabled or, for that matter, parenting a child who happens to be handicapped. Greenfield's books about bringing up a son with autism (Noah) demonstrates vividly the love and frustration a parent may encounter (Greenfield, 1970, 1978). Other books such as Brown's (1976) **Yesterday's Child,** Crews's (1979) **A Childhood: The Biography of a Place,** and Jones's (1977) **The Acorn People,** all have sensitive and critical statements to share. The following are a couple of quotes from the books noted:

> Right there, as a child I got to the bottom of what it means to be lost, what it means to be rejected by everybody. . . . But if I was never able to accept my affliction, I was able to bear it and finally accept the good natured brutality and savagery in the eyes of those who came to wish me well. (Crews, Pp. 171–172)

> You might say she was captured by good intentions. Kids would huddle around her proposing things to do. It was as if she possessed some kind of magic. Well, maybe she did. After all, she stripped those labels off all of us. She gave us back the chance to be children. To dream and play. (Jones, P. 54)

Labeling

It is apparent today that labels are utilized to classify the special needs of an exceptional individual. In the past, derogatory terms, such as moron, idiot as well as imbecile, were clinically utilized to classify individuals with specific levels of mental retardation. At times, these labels prevented individuals from specific privileges that were given to the non-handicapped population. To assist in your understanding of this point of view, I would like to share a simulated experience that I encountered several years ago. I had the fortune or for that matter the misfortune to play a non-published table game which revolved around this topic: labeling.

The game was similar to any general table game. The major objective was to travel around the board without receiving a label and experiencing any devastating life experiences. The winner would be the individual who moved around the board and who would not deviate from the mainstream path. In the simulated experience, the winner was the participant who was the successful person: one with a good academic background, an important occupation and was happy with life's fortunes. In essence, the game simulated life experiences. It began at birth and progressed into middle adulthood.

The game began by dicing on the board to be conceived. A majority of the game players were born as normal, healthy infants. However, there were some who were less fortunate. For example, some were born with serious birth defects and found themselves severely disabled. For those individuals, the game was extremely boring and frustrating. While everyone else was moving around the main parameters of the table game, these individuals followed a very small circular path. They were not able to compete because they were classified as severely handicapped. Throughout the game, other factors were presented which impeded the performance of some. For example, while entering the school-age era in the game of life, some participants were assessed as being learning disabled. It was found that this classification influenced some the players' opportunities for the rest of the game. They were segregated and could never get back on the mainstream track. However, some were fortunate enough to overcome their disadvantage and continued playing competitively. Other obstacles such as accidents or diseases were scattered throughout the game to further complicate attaining the final goal: successful living.

While playing the game, those who experienced the handicapping conditions felt many of the frustrations and prejudices that an exceptional individual may encounter. However, because this was just a game, the players could return to their regular lives when it was all over.

Does labeling have any advantages? There are several arguments that have been made for and against the classification and labeling of exceptional individuals. Heward and Orlansky (1988) and MacMillian (1982) have cited several benefits and disadvantages. The highlights are as follows:

Benefits

1. Categories and labels can assist in the diagnosis and specific treatment of individuals.

2. Labels can allow special-interest groups to promote specialized programs.
3. Labeling can assist professionals in communicating and clarifying specific research findings on specific special groups.

Disadvantages

1. Labels can conceptually cause others to think about the disabled child only in terms of inadequacies or deficits.
2. Labels may cause many to develop certain expectations in reference to the child being categorized. These expectations may actually hinder the potential progress of the individual.
3. Labels may lead to reflection of the labeled child and may cause that specific child to feel inferior.
4. Labels may lead peers to reject or ridicule the labeled child.
5. After being labeled, a child may have difficulty ever again achieving the status of being a regular child.

As can be seen, there are both positive and negative sides to this issue. Labels have disadvantages only because we cause their development. Classification systems are theoretically established to assist in treatment. They allow for more systematic intervention. You must understand that, as potential service providers, it is your responsibility to not misuse labels; furthermore, we need to be more familiar of the potential misuse. If we can treat exceptional persons as individuals first and be cognizant of their differences second, we may find ourselves being more effective practitioners.

Conclusions

Changes in our attitudes and acceptance of children with disabilities has been altered dramatically over the past two decades. Some of these changes have been brought about due to the legislation pertaining to disability. This legislation is based on familiar civil rights such as equal opportunity, non-discrimination, integration and free choice. The apparent thread linking all of these principles is the concept of access: access to education as well as other resources needed to support citizens with disabilities.

Biklen (1985) suggests that we are at a crossroads in regards to integration and a person with a disability. In his article, entitled "Integration in

School and Society," he explores five principles that he believes could help shape fuller integration of the child with a disability in society. Briefly, a synthesis of the principles are as follows:

1. Equity requires support of all of us.
2. Activism and rights, not pity, compassion, and benevolence, will foster the development of integration.
3. Normalization (the treatment of the person with a disability as being as normal as possible) must be accepted as the most optimal format to follow.
4. The success of our ability to promote integration will be determined by our commitment to it.

Now that these issues have been briefly discussed, the role that recreation can provide these individuals will be explored. Understanding who exceptional children are should dramatically assist in your understanding and application of the materials being disseminated.

THE RATIONALE OF RECREATION FOR ALL CHILDREN

In today's fast-moving world, many individuals are faced with an enormous amount of free time. Now more than ever, recreation and leisure activities are being used as outlets for engaging free time in a positive fashion.

It's the same for many children. The time spent outside of school is freely utilized in unorganized or structured-play activities. Children may find themselves participating in a variety of activities. There is athletics, hobbies, reading, informal play or simply watching television. The possibilities are endless. Whatever mode is chosen, a major need is being met by these children. They are attempting to use play as a constructive activity and an outlet for excess energy.

As we begin to explore the complexity of childhood play, we will start to see the importance of these play experiences. Leisure outlets are critical facets in a child's being. Children find themselves pursuing resources which can help them use their free time appropriately. Ellis (1973) pointed out that the time spent playing by a child fulfills a very large element in the child's profile of daily activities. Additionally, he stresses that this outlet "represents a major opportunity for influencing the development of the child" (pp. 3–4).

As we unfold our thoughts within this book, we will all explore with you the importance of recreational experiences for children. Additionally, we will point out that the experiences gained are not merely affective and enjoyable but contribute to the stability and growth of a child. Kraus (1966) stresses that play is an important laboratory for growing up in the lives of various children. Some of the benefits which are consequences of a child's involvement will be explored in greater detail in an upcoming section in this chapter. Nevertheless, it seems important to elaborate that intuitively many people feel that through these encounters with their environment and peers, children explore their own capabilities as well as preparing for leisure pursuits at an older age (Kraus, 1966).

However, let us now focus more specifically on exceptional children. The daily challenges and obstacles presented to them by their various handicapping conditions can, at times, prevent them from fulfilling their leisure desires. The outcome of this situation can be extremely frustrating to a child whose basic needs are no different than others in the pursuit of recreation and leisure (Wehman, 1979). In fact, their involvement in these activities may be of greater importance to them, since along the pathway to play many secondary benefits can occur simply due to their involvement. The areas of socialization, communication, and motor development are just a few end products that could be enhanced.

As stated earlier, there are a variety of reasons why some handicapped children are not given enough opportunities to engage socially with others. This may be due in part to the lack of resources in a community, public attitudes towards the disabled, or, perhaps, just living in a region where there are not many children. The child's possible rejection by his mainstream peers may cause other problems. All of this leads to the exceptional child's failure to realize the potential opportunities existing for him/her. Being handicapped does not include the word **never** when it comes to play. Indeed, how many sports include the word **handicap?** Just like anyone learning a new skill, the child with a disability will also have to be taught.

All of the above-noted problems are distinct and can be handled in different fashions. Attention will be given to these problems in upcoming chapters. Nevertheless, the problems do exist, and frustration can develop both in the parents and in the child. These frustrations are realistic and must be examined more carefully.

In addition to these frustrations, individuals with exceptionalities experience a sense of loss when faced with leisure time. For example, we find many handicapped young adults not properly prepared to deal with their leisure and this causes them a great deal of anguish. Therefore, not only are we attempting to answer concerns for youth, but, by attempting to involve children in play and recreational experiences at a young age, we are also teaching them to utilize leisure skills which can offset future problems as an adult.

One of the major purposes of this book is to eliminate situations where this type of problem occurs, or at least to offset some. The following is an example of a situation that can occur and, if handled differently, could completely change the outcome.

For eight-year-old Billy, that afternoon was like all the other afternoons. He had returned home after attending a specialized school for the physically handicapped and fixed himself a snack. His attention then turned to the television. This time, however, his concentration was distracted. Billy could hear the sounds of shouting and laughing coming from the street. Hands clutched to the tires of his wheelchair, he steered himself to the window to see what was happening. A wave of frustration and sorrow washed over him, for outside was a group of neighborhood children playing catch. Three years Billy had lived in the neighborhood and the closest he had been to interacting with his peers was an occasional hello. Billy lifted his hands. He could play catch, he could laugh, and shout. What was wrong?

Billy has spina bifida; he has been bound to his wheelchair since birth. Because of his birth defect he leads an extremely restricted life, and for Billy, this has sharply restricted his social interaction with his peers.

This example of a child only describes one individual's misfortune. Billy, at this young age, rarely gets the social opportunities that other young boys enjoy. Though it is realized that he has had some very difficult years medically and educationally, his lack of social interaction is crucial.

When looking at a spectrum of activities in which a child should be engaged, the social area seems, in most cases, to receive the least attention. It is not surprising that parents are so concerned with the health and well-being of their exceptional child. Living with a child who is prone to illness can cause a great deal of stress within the family. Without possible realization, parents at times place so much emphasis on the medical area that they do not even realize that they fail to direct some of their energy into other important areas. Thus, no one should be alarmed to find that the area of affective development does not seem to be a priority in many homes.

Many of us overlook this area until the child is much older. If we would try to attend to the child's early life and his/her affective experiences, not only would we be allowing the child to gain useful social and enriching experiences, but we would significantly enhance his/her later development.

For children, play has a variety of purposes. At first glance, play seems to be merely an opportunity to engage in leisure. Actually, play is a mysterious and complex set of interacting behaviors that fulfills a definitive need for most children. Play may be considered intrinsically motivating to the child, a need to be occupied: being with others and, most important, having fun (Fine, 1978; Fine, 1982).

In Billy's case he has not had enough chances to socially interrelate with children his own age. This handicap is not the only barrier that separates Billy from his peers. For many children, play experiences are not recognized as having a very important part in their lives. Some handicapped individuals live very secluded lives and special attention is not given to recreational outlets. The fact that these valuable play experiences are not comprehended completely by those who should understand is unfortunate.

We want children to have the best life possible. So much of our efforts are placed on preserving their health and attempting to develop sound educational experiences. For too long now, we have ignored the right of all children to have access to their leisure. The pity is that it is the child who loses from our shortsightedness. Our efforts to place emphasis on all other areas, while neglecting to ensure that appropriate play experiences are provided, deprives the exceptional child of an alternate route from which to develop. Advocates of play for the handicapped would argue that this is caused by our own upbringing and that we were taught these manners and methods of placing values. Too often, recreation and informal play are viewed superficially. We overlook the therapeutic value and basic importance of play to children. If the non-handicapped (the mainstreamed) can be given these dynamic opportunities, so should all children.

Therapeutic Recreation for Exceptional Children will attempt to emphasize the importance of leisure exploration in the growing child. Hopefully, this will develop a more positive attitude towards the area of leisure. We believe very strongly in the medium of play, not only for its enjoyment value, but as a unique and dynamic rehabilitative force. We also feel that a child must not be deprived of his/her **fun time** and that every effort must be enforced to secure it. Iso-Ahola (1980) contends that play cannot be underestimated in its ability to prepare a child for practical life. Learning that one has self-worth and feeling better about oneself are two qualities which can be enhanced by play. A child who does not play with others may eventually question his/her existence. The child may also become dependent on others to find things for him/her to do.

Another problem occurs when youngsters have the misfortune of being excluded from activities. In most cases, these children are chastised by others and are never really given a chance to engage effectively. For example, there were numerous occasions when Susan, an amputee, was left on the sidelines by her classmates when they went out to play during their recess. Although she wanted to be involved, her handicap caused some segregation.

A poem has been written specifically for this book by Charles Kraus, an individual who has been afflicted with cerebral palsy. We believed that, although this short verse is slightly dramatized, it shares the loneliness that some children encounter when being left out by others. "The child waited at the playground fence today wanting to be let in to play. After the attendant came quite near, upon the child's cheek was revealed a tear. Unable to speak; longing looks did say. Please accept me . . . I want to play."

In just a few words this poem describes what many individuals go through on a daily basis. Feeling left out cannot be described vividly. Perhaps only looking at a child's face and attempting to understand his/her feelings can partially explain this dilemma.

Throughout the book, we will address these problems and answers will be formulated. The authors feel that children must not be deprived of their **free time** and that every effort must be made to allow for their participation.

In the upcoming sections of this chapter, basic needs and benefits from play experiences will be described. The purpose is to ensure that play should be considered important to all individuals. Furthermore, restrictions placed on exceptional children can pose serious threats to their development.

Before moving on to other related topics, it is imperative that we once again reinforce the primary theme of the text. We believe that no child should be disqualified from involvement in leisure activities. We would like to portray, initially, the importance of recreational experiences in the lives of children. After completing this orientation, the focus will be geared to developing unique experiences for exceptional children in formal and informal settings. If people can begin to develop this sense of understanding, we honestly feel that more will be done to ensure the play rights of the child who is disabled.

NEEDS OF ALL CHILDREN
TO EXPLORE THEIR LEISURE

Now let us focus our attention to the general needs of all children to explore their leisure. As we look at this area we may find ourselves pointing out distinctive differences between various age groups, the exceptional population, and the mainstream. Granted, there are differences and special problems that are unique to the various populations of children (i.e. various age ranges, handicapped children, etc.), but that is not to say that similarities do not exist. Too often, many individuals have the tendency to continually point out the obvious differences between the norm and the disabled. Although there are some significant differences between the handicapped and non-handicapped, it must be stressed once again that the disabled must be viewed as individuals first and disabled second. Furthermore, even within the mainstream, all children have their own individual makeups. In effect, everyone is different.

In play experiences, all children have certain needs. The first priority of any child is to have fun. The activities of various children may differ, but the goals are universal. We must assume that the intrinsic drive to amuse oneself is a critical variable in one's pursuit of leisure-time activities. Furthermore, the satisfaction that is gained from playing appears to reinforce a child's involvement. Nevertheless, there are many children who are not exposed to these opportunities and at times their leisure needs are not fulfilled.

Hutchinson (1949) stated that "recreation is a worthwhile, socially accepted leisure experience that provides immediate and inherent satisfaction to the individual who voluntarily participates in an activity" (p. 2). Furthermore, he states that motivation of an individual to take part in the activity could stem from a short-lived or profound interest which defines the motivational desire as one of the most important characteristics of a true recreational experience.

In a similar point of view, Pomeroy (1964) discusses the fact that certain fundamental human desires such as the need to be wanted and understood are important to all individuals and can be satisfied through participation in recreation activities.

Some of the needs Pomeroy discusses are that recreation programs fulfill the human need for: joy of creation, adventure, a sense of achievement, physical well-being, a sense of relaxation, and plain enjoyment. In addition to the qualities noted by Pomeroy (1964), I would like to expand the list and incorporate some of my perceptions. The following represents some additional points of view:

- the needs of belonging to a group
- the sense of personal understanding
- the need to pursue interests that will stimulate enjoyment during leisure time
- the need to develop a sense of responsibility and independence

Before continuing to discuss these needs, the writer needs to point out that the role that play fulfills in the child's world may be comparable to the work life of an adult. Play is the child's career and has as much effect on his or her life as any adult's career. Therefore, recreation for **all** individuals really does, in some way or another, attempt to fulfill all the basic needs and desires required for total human existence.

The Sense of Belonging

The example of Billy discussed earlier in this chapter described a child who is in desperate need of acceptance and friendship. He is lonely and lacking companionship. In addition, Billy is not unique. There are many children like him, both handicapped and non-handicapped, who find themselves without frequent social contact. The reasons for this may be limitless; the response to it is not. A sense of worthlessness can develop when it appears that no one cares. Furthermore, being isolated may instill a sense of boredom.

Recreation activities can be one solution to this dilemma. Through recreation, children can be given the opportunity to meet new individuals and make new friendships. They can be given the chance to socialize and thus develop the feeling of belonging. Knowing that you are an integral part of a group and that you are **wanted** is important to everybody.

The Opportunity to be Creative

Children enjoy the chance to be creative. Most children are inquisitive and enjoy an opportunity to put their mind to work. Although one might find that exceptional children occasionally lack the acquired abilities to complete fine artwork, play and recreational experiences can help all individuals find ways for creative self-expression no matter how small the achievement. During these moments, children may also begin to realize that there is a wealth of activities in which they can learn to be both creative and successful.

Self-Satisfaction and Achievement

The need for self-satisfaction and achievement is prevalent in all children. Have you ever attempted to recall situations in which your own child or another child displayed exuberant pride because he/she has completed a task? Some children are frequently denied these opportunities and become easily frustrated with themselves, thereby developing poor self-images. For example, Danny, a child who was classified as mildly mentally retarded, never really felt good about his accomplishments. He was involved for several years in recreational programs that were integrated. Many of the tasks presented to Danny were too demanding and complicated. To be noticed by others and to be given recognition for personal gain is pleasurable to every child.

In organized recreation programs the area of recognition is continually being addressed, either by the child's own accomplishments or by his/her group's progression. In play situations, where children tend to be less inhibited than in the classroom, a child may begin to attain a degree of success. This usually occurs when activities are organized in advance and a child can successfully compete. Organizing activities that take into account the skill levels of the participants usually enhances the probability of successful involvement. They allow the child to participate in activities that are the most appropriate. It is also important to realize that being able to use their leisure time competently will also bring a sense of achievement to a child. Knowing that one can amuse oneself without the aid of others is an achievement in itself.

When discussing the area of achievement, the relationship between the internal and external feelings should not be underscored. For many children the recognition they receive from others is crucial to their well-being. They are dependent on the thoughts of their peers for motivation. Nevertheless, there is also the intrinsic sense of achievement when individuals feel good about themselves for a specific reason. It would be difficult to ascertain which is more important to children. Yet, the need to obtain a sense of satisfaction is probably one of the most important basic needs for all children as they explore their leisure time.

The Need for Enjoyment and Relaxation

Just because a child is sitting in a wheelchair does not mean the child is always relaxed. For these individuals, wheelchairs are an integral part of their existence, their means of mobility. There is no reason for them to be deprived of the opportunity of reducing stress through play. Leisure is a time for an individual to relax and enjoy. It is an opportunity for all children to smile, laugh, and have fun. That is the reason they are playing!

Many decades ago handicapped individuals had to seek emotional satisfaction as passive observers rather than active participants (Pomeroy, 1964). As times have changed, one can begin to see a general transition where activities have been adapted to allow the exceptional child the chance to be involved. Both organized and unstructured play provides children with unique opportunities.

Too often, we find children who are unaware of the various leisure resources which are available to them. Due to this lack of knowledge or companionships, various children are denied an opportunity. As a consequence of their lack of awareness, numerous youngsters rely on adults to provide them with the experiences and structure needed to acquire and meet their needs. Furthermore, some parents find it necessary to help their child meet these goals, because when a child's needs are being thwarted, resulting frustration may be redirected towards the family.

As adults, our responsibilities should not be merely to provide answers for children so that they can engage in relaxing and enjoyable experiences. We must invest our time profitably by teaching them to discover the resources to develop the skills necessary to participate and function. Depending on the severity of the handicap, this will be accomplished to a greater or a lesser degree. At this point, we develop the child's sense of independence. When children are alerted to the activities that are available to them, they may acquire new skills and thus have more appropriate use of their leisure time.

This whole idea is reminiscent of an old proverb. If we simply feed an individual for life, we develop a sense of dependency. However, if we teach an individual to fish on his/her own (in this case teach them to be responsible for locating one's own leisure pursuits), we permit and reinforce growth and learning.

Responsibility and Independence

A child who learns such responsibility will be less apt to depend on others for entertainment. Most children do enjoy being as independent as possible. This need to be more responsible for one's actions and to become independent is an area of adaptive behavior strongly valued by our society. Children are being taught at early ages the primary steps to obtain goals. Through play/recreational experiences, all children can begin to excel in this area. For example, if a child is going to play later in the day, at that time for play, one has a responsibility to be there at the expected time. Children will learn that if they do not want to disappoint others, they will fulfill their obligations. If they are continually irresponsible, they will not find themselves invited back.

Part of the parent's responsibility to the child is to allow the child opportunities to face these problems. We find ourselves in a peculiar position, because normally we do not want to see our child fail. If we continually pamper our children, they may never learn to stand on their own. The need to have some responsibility and independence appears to be strong in all individuals.

In the chapters that follow, this area will be addressed again from the perspective of how these affective concerns can be enhanced through the utilization of recreation.

Physical and Mental Well-Being

Physical and mental well-being are two general areas which are basic needs of all children. These needs can be fulfilled, in part, by participation in play.

Play experiences are satisfying outlets for physical energy. All children need these opportunities whether they are handicapped or not. They allow a child an appropriate outlet to release excess tension and energy.

The area of mental well-being appears to encompass a majority of the areas previously discussed. Briefly, all children have the need to use their mental capacities. Throughout their leisure time, many hours can be spent pursuing interesting hobbies such as reading, writing, music and art (Pomeroy, 1964). Some children may find these activities mentally challenging and enjoyable.

Areas such as enjoyment, achievement, relaxation, responsibility and independence are greatly important to most children. Through play experiences, these areas can be enhanced (Fine, Lehrer, and Feldis, 1982; Hayes, 1977; CEC and AAPHER, 1966; Shivers and Fait, 1975, 1985).

Benefits from Participation

The premise that this book will continually explore is the importance of play involvement for exceptional children. In the previous section, general needs that can be facilitated through recreation have been discussed. Yet, children not only learn to enjoy their leisure time, but they also gain a great deal from their involvement.

For too long now, recreation has been deprived of its recognition as a general therapeutic tool. Many are unaware that along with sheer pleasure, a child attains many learning skills (CEC and AAPHER, 1966; Tizard and Harvey, 1977; Wehman, 1979).

Information will be shared later in the book not only to strengthen this conviction but also to provide plausible approaches to enhance the experiences. In the upcoming section, goals of play will be discussed. As the reader will soon realize, the goals that will be listed may also be interpreted as the benefits that can be gained by involvement. It is also important to note that all of these goals may, to some degree, be enhanced through recreational involvement. Nevertheless, it is also the role of the recreation leader to implement experiences utilizing activities that concentrate on these goals, which is a skill that will be thoroughly described in upcoming chapters.

Reading the following sections will be helpful in understanding the importance of play experiences for the handicapped. Furthermore, this information will bring into focus one of the primary functions of the book: To highlight the importance of play experiences for the special child and the challenges that are ahead for all of us in providing these services.

GOALS OF PLAY

Just as all of us have both personal and professional goals, goals should also be developed for activity programs. Many of these goals will be similar in nature to those specific goals of children previously discussed. For a child, the primary goal when playing is to have fun. Recreational activities, however, not only provide this outlet but many by-products as well. Among the areas that will be discussed are the enjoyment of play for its intrinsic pleasure and the use of recreation to enhance social adjustment, social development, physical health, language, and cognitive development. Evidence of the benefits that recreation and play experiences can provide seem to encourage many professionals to establish programs that can enable handicapped individuals to participate in recreation (Pomeroy, 1964).

It is important to also realize that the activities selected should reflect the goals chosen. Frequently, one must ask, "Why am I leading this activity?" or "What goals does this activity address?" These questions should be asked periodically to assess the programs implemented and to determine if these programs actually address the needs of the children involved. Activities should also be selected on the basis of a child's development preparation for an activity. A great deal of research has been done by Arnold Gessell and his associates in developing developmental norms for specific age groups (Muro and Dinkmeyer, 1977). These norms provide guidelines that suggest what accomplishments should be expected. Furthermore, the norms also provide guidelines to professionals on what type of activities should be implemented.

The Joy of Playing

As stated earlier, the joy of playing should be the primary aim of any activity. To get children to want to be involved, it must first be determined that they enjoy themselves. From a child's point of view, knowledge of the underlying benefits is unnecessary. They want to enjoy their free time either by playing games, being involved in activities with peers, or completing tasks individually. That is why play can become such a dynamic vehicle to induce change when working with youngsters. If one can provide experiences where enjoyment is not the sole benefit, then the opportunity can become therapeutic as well as fun.

We establish this goal initially because we genuinely believe that fun must come first. Some handicapped and non-handicapped individuals have not had enough opportunities to enjoy themselves due to an unexplained number of misfortunes. We must not destroy this primary intrinsic need to play in order to attempt to teach a variety of secondary skills. This would definitely alter the primary purpose for the interaction; that is, to have fun. All children deserve the right to enjoy their leisure time, and this must be primary on everyone's list if we are to truly classify the activities as play or recreation.

The other goals are generally what one may consider secondary benefits to the child's enjoyment. They are a result of providing useful activities, formulated in advance, which are not only fun but also encompass basic development needs.

Social Adjustment and Social Development

It has been mentioned that recreation can allow a child the opportunity to grow up and learn effective traits to interact. For many special children, there lacks the daily opportunities for realizing personal achievement and to interact positively with other young people their own age. For some, their only group experience with children may be in an academic setting where there is a deficit in the optimum amount of chances to develop self-confidence with others.

One goal of recreation is to provide these youngsters with this basic need: a chance for them to develop skills in interacting more comfortably with others. This point brings out two basic issues. At first, we recognize the need for learning; we recognize how to adjust to group norms and the behavior that is needed to fit in. Throughout a child's experience with others, he or she will begin to realize what behavior is or is not acceptable. He/she will learn this through experience or by people informing him/her. These experiences are of the utmost importance to most children.

The fact that all children have a wealth of leisure hours makes it equally important for them to acquire the necessary skills to afford them adequate use of their time. As a consequence, some of the play skills that are being taught could be implemented during their free time. This could also be helpful in eliminating the feeling of loneliness, boredom, and anger. I recall an experience with a child that dramatically explores this area.

When I first encountered Bob, he found it very difficult to interact with group members. In addition to having a learning disability, he also had a severe speech impediment. He was a sensitive person who wanted to fit in but had a difficult time using the appropriate interpersonal skills. Initially, the group members picked on him by laughing at his speech and not allowing him the opportunity to play freely. After working with him, a strong relationship was developed. With some coaching and guidance, he started to feel more comfortable with the group. He attempted to learn from his mistakes. With this new dimension to his personality, he would confidently perform social encounters correctly when confronted with new situations. For Bob, the turnaround was tremendous. One could begin to see the change in him. Not only was he learning to play more effectively with his peers, he was also beginning to feel better about himself.

Learning to feel better about one's self, learning skills to relate with others, developing a sense of responsibility and independence, and becoming aware of feelings of others, should all be goals of a recreation program. All of these areas, to some degree, are encountered when children are playing, and they can be enhanced and taught through their experiences.

An area that was briefly examined earlier was the feeling of being a part of a group. An important aspect of a play experience is a child's willingness to be with others and to become part of the group. It is also imperative to realize that when interacting with others, a group must function as a whole to be effective.

An example comes to mind to illustrate this point of view. Several years ago I had the opportunity to work with a group of boys in a camp setting. The boys had emotional problems and were constantly fighting with each other. Surprised by this behavior, I responded in the following manner. Immediately I shouted, "Everyone look at your hands." The group members were surprised into silence by this seemingly insane request. Now, I had to quickly think of something to say before I lost their attention. "If I cut away your palms," I continued, "what would you do with your fingers?" Various youngsters remarked that nothing could be done with their fingers, since their palms keeps the fingers together and makes them work. Slowly, the boys then began to discuss how fortunate they were that all of their bodily functions were in order. Some of them related stories about individuals who were disabled and how difficult they thought it was for them.

Eventually, we arrived to the desired point. A group, like the palms of our hands, is what keeps individuals working together. A disjointed group whose members continually fight with each other is one that is ineffective. It also would be an unpleasurable experience. Just as a palm gets the fingers to work in unison, so does a group with its members. After discussing these issues, it was pointed out that if they could not work together, they would probably spend more time doing nothing than having fun. The end result was positive and the boys attempted to work hard on relating to each other.

One goal of play, then, is not only to work on individual social adjustment but also to allow children to become more comfortable in working and playing with each other. Group recreational experiences represent prime opportunities to work on these skills and definitely merit our attention.

Physical Well-Being

Participation in a variety of recreational experiences can contribute to healthier physical and motor development. For some exceptional children, there may not be ample opportunities to release this physical energy. Since a goal of play is to expend excess energy in a constructive fashion, handicapped individuals also need this outlet.

Activities can be adapted to provide physical enjoyment. In the chapters that will follow, effective ways to adapt activities will be discussed in more detail. Furthermore, play experiences can also enhance motor development (sensory motor and gross motor skills). Since a variety of activities involve both fine motor and gross motor skills, recreators can try to enhance these areas by providing activities that are suitable for the child. Activities can also have several purposes for specific children. For example, an activity can be used to develop social skills along with motor skills.

Additionally, certain youngsters may not enjoy certain activities. Perhaps it is not the task that is upsetting them but, rather, they lack prerequisite skills necessary to complete the activity. That is the reason why they are frustrated! For example, in the making of a puppet, a child with poor fine motor skills may find it extremely difficult to manipulate the scissors or to place buttons as eyes on the puppet. If we are able to realize this in advance and select an activity that is more suitable, then the frustration will be diminished. Provisions then can be implemented not only to make a child's experience more satisfying but also effective in enhancing physical and motor abilities.

Language and Cognitive Skills

An important area that we continually face when developing programs for special children is the improvement of language and cognitive skills. Though enjoyment is the primary goal of play, there are many underlying traits that can be incorporated. While a child is playing, he/she is usually in a situation where communication is necessary. If it is determined that communication skills should be developed with a specific child, there are ways to implement an approach that would strengthen this area. At times, activities may pose challenges to the child where he/she will find himself/herself in a problem-solving situation. In addition, many activities also make use of the child's memory. Card games such as Concentration are good examples. With games, a child may incorporate visual and auditory discrimination skills. Therefore, although the child is on the surface simply playing, all of these skills are being used and hopefully stimulated.

It is imperative, then, to realize that a host of skills are being used in a child's world of play. They should be considered goals that recreators can focus upon when working with children. In the following chapters, sections will be presented illustrating recent findings on how play can be used as a dynamic facilitator of these basic skills.

SUMMARY

The literature reviewed in this chapter points favorably towards the critical importance of recreational experiences for the exceptional child. Indeed, it can be seen that all children seem to have the same basic needs and drives so important for their development. The exceptional child has in the past been deprived of his academic and social rights. We must realize that these children deserve a chance to explore their leisure. Furthermore, the writers believe that not only will the child gain satisfaction with himself/herself due to his/her involvement, but the experiences gained may be helpful in improving the developmental skills of the handicapped child.

The critical importance of recreational involvement for all people has been emphasized. With increased knowledge of the effectiveness of this resource, we may begin to appreciate it more fully and tap into it more carefully. We may also begin to carefully examine the provisions made for our children and place play experiences as one of our priorities.

REFERENCES

Biklen, D., and Bogden, R (1977). Handicapism in America. In B. Burton, D. Biklen and R. Bogden (Eds.), *An Alternative textbook in special education.* Denver: Love Publishing.

Biklen, D. (1985). Integration in school and society. In D. Biklen (Ed.), *Achieving the complete school.* New York: Teachers College Press.

Brightman, A. (Ed.). (1984). *Ordinary moments.* Baltimore: University Park Press.

Council for Exceptional Children, American Association for Health, Physical Education, and Recreation. (1966). Recreation and physical activity for the mentally retarded. Washington, American Association for Health. Physical Education, and Recreation.

Crews, H. (1979). *A childhood: The biography of a place*. Boston: G.K. Hall.

Dunham, J., and Dunham, C. (1978). Psychosocial aspects of disability. In R. Goldensen (Eds.), *Disability and rehabilitation handbook*. New York: McGraw-Hill.

Ellis, M. (1973). *Why people play*. Englewood Cliffs: Prentice-Hall.

Fine, A. (1982). Therapeutic recreation: An aspect of rehabilitation for exceptional children. *The Lively Arts*, 4.

Fine, A., Lehrer, B., and Feldis, D. (1982). Therapeutic recreation programming for autistic children. *Therapeutic Recreation Journal, 16*, 6–11.

Fine, A. (1978). Therapeutic recreation: The new boy on the block. *Alabama Inserve Project Newsletter, 1*, 4, 3.

Gliedman, J., and Roth, W. (1980). *The unexpected minority: Handicapped children in america*. New York: Harcourt Brace Jovanovich.

Goffman, E. (1974). *Stigma*. Englewood Cliffs, Prentice-Hall.

Greenfield, J. (1970). *A child called Noah*. New York: Holt Rinehart and Winston.

Greenfield, J. (1978). *A place for Noah*. New York: Holt Rinehart and Winston.

Haring, N. (1982). *Exceptional children and youth*. Columbus: Charles Merrill.

Hayes, G. (1977). Recreation and the mentally retarded. In T. Stein and Sessoms (Eds.), *Recreation and special populations*. Boston: Holbrook Press.

Heward, W., and Orlansky, M. (1988). *Exceptional children*. Columbus: Charles Merrill.

Hutchinson, J. (1951). *Principles of recreation*. New York: A.S. Barnes.

Iso-Ahola, S. (1980). *The social psychology of leisure and recreation*. Dubuque: William C. Brown.

Jones, R. (1977). *The acorn people*. New York: Butan Books.

Kelly, L., and Vergason, G. (1978). *Dictionary of special education and rehabilitation*. Denver: Love Publishing.

Kraus, R. (1966). *Recreation today: Program planning and leadership*. New York: Appleton-Century-Crofts.

MacMillian, D. (1982). *Mental retardation in school and society*. Boston: Little, Brown.

Muro, J., and Dinkmeyer, D. (1977). *Counseling in the elementary and middle schools*. Dubuque: Wm. C. Brown.

Pomeroy, J. (1964). *Recreation for the physically handicapped*. New York: MacMillian.

Shivers, J., and Fait, H. (1975). *Therapeutic and adapted recreational services*. Philadelphia: Lea and Febiger.

Shivers, J., and Fait, H. (1985). *Special recreational services: Therapeutic and adapted*. Philadelphia: Lea and Febiger.

Tizard, B., and Harvey, D. (1977). *Biology of play*. Philadelphia: Lippincott.

Wehman, P. (1979). *Recreation programming for developmentally disabled persons*. Baltimore: University Park Press.

Chapter 2

PLAY—A CHILD'S WORLD FOR LEARNING

SUSAN NAKAYAMA SIAW, AUBREY H. FINE, AND GREG PAYNE

The events of childhood do not pass
but repeat themselves like seasons of the year.

ELEANOR FARNJEON

INTRODUCTION

Play is not only enjoyable but rather a serious and significant pursuit of children. In fact, if we want to understand a child, we need to take the time to understand his play (Bettelheim, 1987). Play represents a key to opening up the doors of life. While playing, children discover the roots of their civilization, learn how things work, as well as how to interact and socialize with others. Play and learning are truly bound together. Aristotle said that learning is pleasurable, and one could say that learning is play.

It is apparent that the more opportunity a young child, disabled or non-disabled, has to enjoy the richness of play in all its aspects, the more solidly will the child's development proceed. Constructive play activities put the child in the driver's seat, and through these experiences, the individual can become much more of an active learner. Bettelheim (1987) suggests that the process of play is the method by which children acquaint themselves with the sets of realities, both inner and outer, and learn how to satisfy their own needs and those of others. Play magically transforms a child into anything s/he desires; from a fireman to being a clown in the circus. Additionally, within their fantasy, children can conjur up phenomenal instruments to play with, even with the crudest resources. Play can reduce the obstacles facing children, and allow them to become the rulers of the world. Consequently, children who are not able to walk, can become noted marathon runners while those who are visually impaired can uncover the treasures of the universe.

The following chapter is divided into two components. The first section will be geared to an explanation of theories of play while the latter section will be designed as a basic overview of motor development. Both are strongly grounded on theoretical research. It is the intentions of both of these authors to provide the reader with an overview of theories of play and motor development. Both of these sections are basic and try only to integrate and develop some conclusions on aspects of the previous research conducted within these two distinct and critical areas. It is believed that a firm understanding of the issues incorporated within this chapter will assist the practitioner or parent in understanding the true meaning of a child's play behavior as well as offer insight into practical methods of enhancing this phenomenon.

Part I—Theoretical Explanations of The Functions of Play

SUSAN NAKAYAMA SIAW AND AUBREY H. FINE

Overview

Imagine four distinguished scientists observing a child cranking the handle on a musical jack-in-the-box. Each observer, having been trained in a different school of thought, interprets the child's play from a unique perspective. When asked, "Why is the child doing that?" the first observer, a staunch Piagetian, says, "The child is trying out his cranking scheme, and he is gaining logicomathematical experience regarding the cause-effect relationship between cranking and the clown popping out of the box. He's asking himself, "What happens if I crank fast? Slow? At an irregular pace? Will the clown still pop out?" The second observer, particularly observant of the child's behavior, is a learning theorist, and he suggests that "The child is merely repeating a response that previously led to an interesting and rewarding consequence, i.e. turning the handle leads to the reinforcement of having a clown pop out of the box. So of course he's going to repeat this response." The third observer, trained in the psychoanalytic school, is obviously uncomfortable with the two previously offered explanations. "I disagree! You two are merely focusing on the cognitive and behavioral aspects of this situation. It is clear to me that the child's actions reflect his need to protect his emotional well-being. Given his age, the child is dependent upon his parents. Thus, he has a need to prove mastery and independence. He's obviously enjoying this activity because for once he is running the show. He's in control of the cranking and the clown popping out of the box." The fourth observer, entertained but not convinced by these previous interpretations, fidgets in his seat and complains that his three companions are thinking too deeply about the purpose of the child's activities. "It's highly likely that the child is alleviating boredom." He continued, "The child's interaction with the jack-in-the-box is merely a means of arousal."

29

A fifth scientist, observing the other four through a one-way mirror, is excited by all four previous explanations. Although he sees weaknesses in each of the explanations, he also realizes that each has merit. He is reminded of the old parable about the blind men who are individually exploring a magnificent elephant. One is at the trunk, another is at an ear, a third is stationed at its side, and the last is at its tail. Each man exclaims that he has discovered what the elephant is. The first exclaims that elephants are round and firm like telephone poles; the second disagrees and says that elephants are pliable and soft like cloth; the third is certain that elephants are flat and rough like rugs; and the fourth, exasperated that the other three are so far off, asserts that elephants are obviously like long, thin ropes! The point being, of course, that no man is absolutely wrong, and no man is absolutely right. Our fifth scholar, in fact, concludes that a child may play for a variety of reasons, and he feels comfortable accepting an eclectic viewpoint.

This chapter is divided into two parts. The purpose of the first part is to examine theoretical explanations of the purpose of play. As suggested in the above fictional scenario, each theory "examines the elephant from a different perspective." Some classical theories that laid the groundwork for later theories will be overviewed. Basic concepts from four major contemporary theories: Piaget's theory, learning theory, psychoanalytic theory, and stimulus-arousal theory will also be presented. Included will be discussions of contributions and limitations of each theory in explaining play and implications for special populations according to each theory. In this first part, the focus is on how play promotes cognitive, social, and emotional development. The second part of this chapter, written by Doctor Greg Payne, will round out the chapter by presenting an overview of motor development in children and its relation to developmental changes in play.

HISTORICAL PERSPECTIVES: FOUR CLASSICAL THEORIES OF PLAY

There were four major explanations of play proposed by early theorists. The first was the surplus energy theory of play, which originated in the writings of eighteenth century philosopher Friedrich von Schiller (1875) and psychologist H. Spencer (1873). According to this theory, humans have a reservoir of energy that is utilized to satisfy primary needs such as the need for food. After primary needs are met, leftover energy in this reservoir is spent on play. Play is motivated by an inborn drive to use up energy within this reservoir. Once depleted, the reservoir is revitalized and the cycle repeats. A major criticism aimed at the surplus energy theory of play is that it is not consistent with predictions of evolutionary theory. For example, if play involves the expenditure of superfluous energy, it would seem that play would be eliminated through natural selection. But analysis indicates that as one moves up the phylogenetic scale, less time and energy is necessary to satisfy primary needs, and more time and energy are available for play. A second major criticism is that there is no physiological evidence that unused energy "backs up and creates a pressure, demanding release" (Beach, 1945, p. 528).

A second classical theory is the relaxation and recreation theory of play, which was proposed by philosophers Lazarus (1883) and Patrick (1916). In contrast to the surplus energy theory, the relaxation and recreation theory characterized play as the result of an energy deficit. After engaging in physically and mentally exhausting work, the body needs to sleep. However, in order to achieve full restoration, the body first needs to engage in play activities that help one escape from the reality-based pressures of work. Patrick (1916) also proposed that play is motivated by **race memories,** which are traces from our evolutionary past. Thus, for example, children enjoy reading books about animals and playing with teddy bears, because our primitive ancestors depended on wildlife for sustenance. One of the major criticisms of this theory is that children do not engage in work to the same extent that adults do, although children do engage in more play than adults do. A second criticism is that there is no evidence to support the existence of race memories.

A third classical theory is the practice or pre-exercise theory of play, which was presented by Groos (1898, 1901). Groos, a neo-Darwinian, believed that play is driven by instinct and has been acquired by natural selection. The purpose of play, according to this theory, is to practice skills necessary for adulthood. Thus, in species higher on the phylogenetic scale which use complex skills during adulthood, there has been a selection for an extended childhood period. The longer childhood period was believed to be necessary to prepare one for the complexities of adulthood via play. A major criticism of this theory is that it is difficult to predict which play activities will prepare one for the tasks of adulthood. Indeed, in the age of **Future Shock** (Toeffler, 1970) and **Escape from Freedom** (Fromm, 1941) in which changes are constant and unpredictable, it would seem increasingly difficult to predict the skills one should practice in anticipation of the future. For example, in the 1960s, high school students struggled to master the slide rule for algebra and chemistry classes, while in the early 1970s, pocket calculators became the rage but were initially too expensive for all students' pocketbooks. In the present computer age, even a preschooler is exposed to the family's personal computer, and the slide rule joins grandfather's abacus in the attic. The rapid technological changes in our society hit home when the university graduate who majored in computer sciences learns that his recent training is rapidly outdated once he reaches the work force. What does this all mean in regard to play? It suggests that play can in no way anticipate or prepare one for every technological skill that will be required in the future.

The last major classical theory is the recapitulation theory of play, which was presented in the writings of G. Stanley Hall (1920) and Luther Gulick (1898). The recapitulation theory is based on the principle that ontogyny recapitulates phylogeny (i.e. developmental changes during childhood reenact the evolution of man through the ages). For example, embryonic development appears to mirror evolutionary development from the protozoan to Homo sapiens. Hall and Gulick interpreted play as a vestige of our evolutionary past. For example, the hard running, the aiming toward a target when throwing, and use of a club in baseball are contemporary versions of the hunting activities of our evolutionary past. There are numerous criticisms of the recapitulation theory. The most significant criticism is the assumption that play must follow a certain developmental course reflecting our past. This has not been supported by empirical evidence. Many changes in our evolutionary past are not represented in the development of play. Moreover, the theory cannot account for the fact that regressions may occur in play. For instance, Sutton-Smith (1966) suggests that adult play is often similar to children's play, which is a finding that contradicts the forward-moving direction predicted by evolutionary theory.

The major contribution of these theories is that they drew the attention of scholars to play, and they influenced the formulations of contemporary theories of play (see Rubin, Fein, and Vandenberg, 1983, for a discussion of the roots of contemporary theories). A discussion will now be presented to four recent interpretations of play: (a) Piagetian, (b) learning theory, (c) psychoanalytic theory, and (d) arousal theory.

OVERVIEW OF PIAGETIAN THEORY

Piaget focused on cognitive development, and as such interpreted play in terms of its relation to the development of knowledge. According to Piaget, our way of thinking about the world is organized into a framework for thinking which he called **cognitive structures.** One's cognitive structure reflects one's way of viewing the world, and this view changes **qualitatively** with development. Table I has been prepared to assist the reader in understanding the major principles related to Piaget's theory. This will then be followed with an analysis of this development perspective and play development in children.

TABLE I
AN OVERVIEW OF TERMINOLOGY AS IT RELATED TO PIAGET'S THEORY

1. Schemes. Is an organized pattern of behavior.
2. Operations. Are the mental equivalents of schemes, and they do not develop until the age of six or seven
3. Assimilation. Involves imposing one's present cognitive structure or framework for thinking on the world. Assimilation involves taking content from the world and molding or bending that content to fit one's cognitive structure.
4. Accommodation. Involves altering one's cognitive structure in order to adjust to information in the outside world that does not fit with one's framework for thinking.

FOUR MAJOR STAGES OF DEVELOPMENT

1. Sensory motor stage (between zero and two years of age). During this stage, infants exercise their schemes and discover properties about objects around them. A major accomplishment of this stage is the acquisition of object permanence, which is the discovery that objects exist independently of oneself.
2. Preoperations stage (spanning approximately the ages of two to seven). Thinking in this stage is intuitive and illogical. The child focuses on salient perceptual features of the world and often ignores other relevant information.
3. Concrete operations (includes the middle-childhood years of seven to twelve). This stage marks the advent of thinking in terms of operations but primarily at a concrete level.
4. Formal operations (12 years and above). An individual can think abstractly and can solve transitive inference problems.

Piaget and Play

Piaget's ideas concerning play are reported in his book, **Play, Dreams, and Imitation in Childhood** (1962). Piaget defined play as pure assimilation. This means that Piaget saw play as imposing one's way of thinking upon the world. But as mentioned above, because assimilation and accommodation cannot occur in isolation, play is a state in which assimilation predominates over accommodation. A child at play is exercising his schemes and operations upon the world just for the sheer joy of exercising them. A child at play might try out a banging scheme on everything encountered, e.g. banging the table, banging the crib, or banging toys.

Qualitatively different types of play are engaged in at different developmental stages, and these are divided into three broad categories of play. The first category, **practice play**, occurs during the sensory motor stage. During this stage, when schemes are especially evident, the infant can be seen displaying **circular reactions**, which involves practicing schemes. Around one to four months of age, babies engage in primary circular reactions in which schemes are exercised just for the sheer joy of it. Babies' first schemes are basic reflexes and are centered on the babies' own body, i.e. they involve interesting things that babies can do with their bodies and involve no interaction with outside stimuli. Later on, around ages four to eight months, Piaget noticed that babies will now repeat interesting actions that involve outside stimuli. For example, a baby may accidentally kick the side of her crib, which causes the mobile above it to jangle. As a consequence of the baby's knowledge of cause-effect relationships, this kicking response is in order to see the mobile jangle. Finally, around 12 to 18 months of age, the infant engages in tertiary circular reactions. By this time, the baby has a better handle on cause-effect relationships and will deliberately try out schemes with a "let-us-see-what-will-happen-if-I-do-it-this-way" attitude. For example, a baby might continually knock her bottle off of her high chair, much to her parents' exasperation. She will knock it hard one time, harder another time, a slight tap a third time, etc. The bottom line is, she is using trial and error by experimenting with her schemes to find out more about the world.

As the child enters the preoperational stage, the predominant category of play is symbolic play. Make-believe play is symbolic, because it involves having one thing represent something else. For example, when five-year-old Kevin pretends that straddling a broom is riding a horse, he is assimilating the broom by making that broom fit his structure of what a horse is. During this period, play is engaged in for the sheer joy of it, and the child will go from solitary play, in which schemes are tried out on one's own, to parallel play and cooperative play. Parallel play is demonstrated by young preschoolers who may play with the same toys (e.g. blocks) sitting side-by-side, but they are not interacting in any way. Finally, during the later preschool years or so, cooperative play emerges. In this type of play, children interact together during play, simultaneously playing with an identical activity. This type of play is probably related to the greater mastery over language in these older children, which facilitates interaction with others. Piaget suggests that during this period, children are very egocentric. They are not cognitively capable of taking someone else's perspective. As such, one may often encounter instances where children are not able to share. This is not a matter of the child being selfish; rather, the child cannot take the other's perspective and does not fully grasp how the other child feels when he will not share.

With increasing age, play becomes more competitive and abstract. The third category of play, involving playing games with rules, emerges during middle and later childhood. During this period, playing is not always for the sheer joy of playing, playing is to win. Even with the advent of computers, where children have an opportunity to play without peers, the goal is still to win. Piaget's examination of moral development, however, indicates that initially children have an inaccurate understanding of rules and how games should be played. At first, in a stage called **moral realism**, children believe that rules are fixed and that the way games are played today are the same way our grandfathers played them and the same way our grandchildren will play them. They are very inflexible and do not realize that rules can be changed by mutual agreement of all players. By early adolescence, children enter a second stage called moral autonomy. By this time, the child has a basic understanding of democracy and understands that rules are not fixed. Piaget would suggest that the opportunity to play games as one grows up would provide an opportunity to accommodate to the fact that rules are changeable. Moreover, the ability to take another's perspective, coupled with the ability to think hypothetically and abstractly during the adolescent period, enables the adolescent to play more complex games such as chess.

Implications of Piaget for Children with Disabilities

Piaget believed that there are three influences on development. The first is maturation, the second is physical and logicomathematical experience, and the third is social environment. Maturation is genetically programmed change, and aside from genetic engineering capabilities that may or may not be considered in the future, there is not much that can be done to affect this influence.

The second influence is physical and logicomathematical experience. Physical experience is the type of experience in which one learns about the physical properties of objects, e.g. rocks are hard, cotton is soft, and ice cream is cold. Logicomathematical experience is the type of experience gained from seeing what one can do with things in the environment, e.g. realizing that five rocks lined up in a row equals five rocks, and that five rocks in a pile still adds up to five rocks, and realizing that five is five in these configurations regardless of whether one is counting rocks or shells or candy or whatever. Learning that a Transformer can be a robot or a vehicle, but that it is always the same toy, is another example of logicomathematical experience.

Some exceptional children may be especially vulnerable in not getting enough physical and logicomathematical experience. Particularly if one is physically disabled, one may not have the rich experiences that a non-handicapped child would. Furthermore, a child who is blind does not get feedback concerning how objects appear from different perspectives. Sandler and Wills's (1965) research on observing the play of infants with a form of congenital blindness found that these children displayed delays in early play experiences, which included exploring in the environment.

In order to gain physical and logicomathematical experience, one must be a participant in development. Indeed, Piaget characterized the child as taking an active role in development. The child who exercises his schemes and operations can be likened to a scientist performing mini-experiments upon the world to discover what the world is all about. Observations of children with mental retardation indicate that these special children do not interact with toys in the same way as non-mentally retarded children do. Their play seems to be less spontaneous. It seems that this special population does not take as active a part in performing mini-experiments upon the world as non-retarded youngsters do. Thus, their understanding of the world is limited and does not develop as rapidly. Furthermore, Barnett and Kane (1985) suggest that the most frequently investigated feature in the play of the child with mental retardation pertains to the apparent absence of symbolic play forms. Several studies have documented that symbolic fantasy play has been severely hampered (Cooper, Moodley and Reynell, 1978; Hill and McCune-Nicolich, 1981). A similar finding has also been noted with children and autism (Rutter, 1978; Fine, Lehrer, and Feldis, 1982).

The third influence on development is social environment. Piaget suggested that one way to advance through his stages is to interact with people who think at a slightly higher stage than oneself. The probability of accommodating to another's way of thinking is greatest if the other's thinking is only slightly ahead of one's own. This is an advantage of being in a setting with slightly older children. One implication is that some exceptional children, e.g. the mentally retarded, should be provided opportunities to interact with peers who are more cognitively advanced. Exposure to ways of thinking that are slightly higher than one's own may be accommodated to, thus providing the means for one's cognitive development. This position has been one of the major reasons why many professionals and parents have advocated for more integrated programming in all aspects of a child's life.

Barnett and Kane (1985) suggest that children with hearing impairments appear to lack some social play skills in comparison to children with normal hearing. These children, in general, appeared to display less cooperative play behavior and favored more solitary participation. It appears that a rationale for the occurrence of this phenomenon relates to insufficient communication experiences.

Limitations of Piagetian Theory

Sutton-Smith (1966), a well-known authority in the field of play, provided two major criticisms of Piaget's ideas about play. First, if play is primarily assimilation, and if by definition assimilation does not involve any changes in one's cognitive structure, then play is not an important factor in development. However, because assimilation plays the role of exercising schemes and operations so that they do not atrophy with disuse, and because assimilation does not occur without accommodation, play does in fact play a role in intellectual development.

Sutton-Smith's second criticism of Piaget's theory of play is that adults engage in play that resembles that of children. If Piaget's ideas about developmental changes in cognitive structure are correct, then it should be impossible for adults to regress to play that is qualitatively at a child's level. Sutton-Smith's concern about the quality of play in adulthood is restated in a different way by Bee (1986). She believes that the major criticism of Piaget's theory is his characterization of development as an invariant sequence of stages in which there is no turning back. Bee cites evidence which indicates that although the basic sequence of development through the stages is correct, the stages are not as discrete as originally suggested. That is, at any given time an individual may perform at levels reflecting thinking at different stages; performance may vary with factors such as fatigue, task requirements, content, etc. An individual does not think at a given level through and through.

Bee (1986) presents a further limitation of Piaget's theory. Piaget formulated his theory with the goal of describing general developmental trends. As such, its applicability to explaining individual or group variability in development, such as with special populations, is limited. However, while Piaget focused on development in normal populations, others, such as his close colleague, Barbel Inhelder (1968), have tested his ideas with mentally retarded samples. Generally, it is believed by some scholars that youngsters with mental handicaps progress through Piaget's stages in the same sequence but at a slower rate than non-retarded children.

OVERVIEW OF LEARNING THEORY

Learning theory views play as a learned behavior just like any other behavior. As such, play should follow learning principles in the same way that other behaviors do. For example, an infant in his crib who continuously flails his arms in his line of vision, continuously kicks the side of his crib, or repeatedly knocks his bottle off of his high chair tray, is merely repeating a response that was reinforcing in the past. It led to a pleasant consequence in the past, so it is repeated. Punishment also affects play. In a series of studies, Lamb and his colleagues (Lamb and Roopnarine, 1979; Lamb, Easterbrooks, and Holden, 1980) found that punishment by peers may contribute to the learning of play with sex-appropriate toys. When three-year-olds encountered a peer playing with a sex-inappropriate toy (e.g. a boy playing with a doll), they ceased playing with the child. This behavioral outcome also occurred with five-year-old children but only after a series of other strategies were attempted (e.g. such as demanding that the child stop playing with the sex-inappropriate toy or manually trying to take the toy away). In most instances, the child playing with the sex-inappropriate toy stopped playing with that object. Reinforcement and punishment would also explain the relationship between activities children seem to enjoy and level of accomplishment. For example, in Chapter 1, Doctor Fine cites an example of a youngster who ceased participation in art activities because his one attempt at art lead to punishment by his father (his father crumpled his artwork and threw it to the ground). Finally, modeling has an effect on play. For instance, a child who is presented with a toy such as a Bo-Bo doll may not initially know how to play with such a toy, but he is readily able to learn to punch and kick the doll after watching a model do so, particularly if the model is rewarded for this aggressive behavior (e.g. Bandura, 1973).

Implications of Learning Theory and Exceptional Children

According to this point of view, one's play behavior is learned behavior that is based on experience. The assumption that play is a learned behavior has three implications for children who do not engage in play behavior to the extent that a therapist would like them to. First, it suggests that a child who does not engage in what is deemed appropriate play behavior may not do so because this play is not reinforcing. A child who fails at a given play activity will not continue to engage in that play activity, because failure can be likened to punishment, and punished behavior is not repeated. Iso-Ahola (1980) suggests that helplessness hinders a person from believing s/he can perform the task successfully. Consequently, as stated earlier, a child gives in. It seems apparent that most children engage in activities that they are good at doing. In fact, those activities where children feel inadequate are usually avoided. The learning theory interpretation of this outcome is quite realistic, and this can be a definite explanation of why exceptional children avoid certain play situations. For example, let us turn to the case of Howard. Howard had developed the basic skills of bowling. However, when his mother attempted to enroll him in a bowling league, he rigidly refused to go. His avoidance in pursuing this leisure activity stems from his inability to interact well with others. Consequently, his previous experiences with failure have discouraged his involvement. This suggests that play and its related variables must be made into a more reinforcing activity for the child, where the individual feels s/he is the master of the outcomes.

Three other theoretical orientations can be reviewed to understand this phenomenon of motivation: (a) attribution theory, (b) locus of control and (c) the theory of flow. A brief discussion will now follow articulating the major principles in each orientation. A more complete elaboration on the implication of these variables will be discussed in Chapter 8.

Attribution

Attribution is a term that is linked with the cause and the outcome of behavior as it relates to success and or failure. Success or failure can be attributed to one of four causal factors: (1) ability, (2) effort, (3) task and (4) luck (Dixon, 1979). Bernard Weiner, a psychologist at the University of California at Los Angeles, has probably contributed the most to the formulation of this theory. He suggests that there are a number of causes that are used to explain success or failure in achievement-related contexts. Weiner (1985) points out that causes are inferred on the basis of several factors, including specific informational cues (e.g. past success history and social norms), causal preferences, reinforcement history as well as communication from others. The attribution theory is an excellent alternative for explaining why some children play in specific activities. The theory implies that these children appear to feel competent and therefore display mastery behavior.

Locus of Control and the Flow Theory

Social learning theory provides us with an alternative for understanding motivation. Learning theorists suggest that situations can be grouped according to the perceived cause of a reinforcement (Weiner, 1985). Locus of control refers to the perceived results of one's efforts as it relates to success or failure. Locus of control pertains to the belief that a response will or will not influence the attainment of a reinforcement. Weiner (1985) suggests that it is considered as a problem-solving generalized expectancy, addressing whether behaviors are perceived as instrumental to goal attainment, regardless of the specific reinforcer. Attributing success or failure to internal factors such as ability or effort is characteristic of internal locus of control, where the individual feels the results obtained were a direct outcome of actions which s/he was responsible. On the other hand, external locus of control is where the child feels that his/her actions had no bearing on the outcome.

Dudley-Marling (1982) suggests that efforts must be initiated to enhance the internal locus of control of persons with disabilities. In fact, there have been numerous scholarly research studies suggesting that many activities are avoided by persons with disabilities (including poorly executed leisure time) due to the individual's external locus of control.

Finally, Czikszentmihalyi (1974) points out that individuals involved in play sometimes experience a cohesion of their self-awareness. He classified this as flow, an interactive concept. Czikszentmihalyi identified this phenomenom while observing people in various work and play situations. Within these observations, he discovered that some people become so involved in the activity, they lose a sense of reality and experience what has been considered as an ecstatic flow. Flow does not just occur due to the child's skills and challenges. These elements (skills and challenges) have to be matched with the situation where the skills have appropriately and objectively matched the challenge, which is an outcome that does not always occur in every play situation. One suspects that flow is a **level consciousness** that many children would aspire to reach, because it represents being in total control.

Scholars have also tried to correlate the flow theory to the potential delays displayed by persons with developmental disabilities. Wade and Hoover (1985) hypothesize the relationship between low intelligence and the ability to experience flow by suggesting that persons with mental retardation may be less able to enjoy traditional flow-producing activities. On the contrary, many activities which demand the use of strategy may be aversive and frustrating.

Learning theory also provides another unique perspective in explaining how the instruction of play can be enhanced within children who are disabled. Play must be broken down into smaller, more manageable units so that children can exhibit mastery in a hierarchical manner. What does this mean? For example, a child who is limited in his/her play (e.g. a child with mental retardation who does not play spontaneously in the manner that a non-retarded child does) can be taught how to play via shaping. Shaping is defined as the rewarding of successive approximations of a desired response. This is a technique that is used when the target response is initially too complex to perform. The therapist should break the play response down into a hierarchy of smaller, prerequisite responses, and then the child should be rewarded for accomplishing each successive step in the response hierarchy. In contrast to depicting development as a series of qualitatively different stages as Piaget did, learning theorists view development quantitatively as a series of small, incremental, and cumulative steps. Every time the child learns something new, more behaviors are added to the child's cumulative repertoire.

A final implication is that since imitation appears to be an expedient way to learn new responses, it is important to provide opportunities for special children to learn how to play from non-handicapped peers. In providing such opportunities, attention must be given not only to enhancing the skills of exceptional children but also to increasing non-handicapped children's knowledge about their special friends. Thus, it can be seen that playing with non-handicapped peers would affect not only play behavior per se but also would affect social interaction skills.

Limitations of Learning Theory

Learning theory is not and was not intended to be a developmental theory. Therefore, there is no specific goal of development but rather a general goal of adapting to one's environment no matter what one's developmental level. Another way of stating this limitation is that the theory provides no guidelines concerning the specific type of play behaviors that should be taught or when they should be taught. This is up to each individual therapist. In fact, in some of the earlier and more extreme versions of this theory, it would have been assumed that any play behavior, no matter how complex, could be taught to any child, regardless of age, provided that all of the underlying prerequisite skills could be identified and trained. The decision of what should be taught and when clearly involves a value judgment on the part of a therapist. On the one hand, a therapist is pulled by a concern to protect our children and let them develop at their own pace, while, on the other hand, a therapist is pulled by a concern to hurry our children along and make them the best they can be (Elkind, 1981).

In summary, learning principles can be used to explain play behavior. Because of its focus on behavior, this theory does not address the effect of play on emotional development. Psychoanalytic theory provides an explanation of play in terms of one's emotional development.

OVERVIEW OF PSYCHOANALYTIC THEORY

The psychoanalytic interpretation of personality has made a major contribution to understanding human development. Freud, the father of psychoanalytic theory, proposed three structures that compete for influence on our personality. Table II has been designed to provide a basic review of each of these dimensions.

Another influential contribution of Freud's theory was his characterization of stages of development. Erikson, a neo-Freudian theorist, elaborated upon Freud's developmental stages, and thus Erikson's and Freud's ideas will be integrated here. The major differences between Freud's and

TABLE II
THE THREE STRUCTURES OF FREUD'S THEORY

Structure and Its Influence

1. Id. Reflects drives accumulated throughout our evolutionary history. The id operates on the unconscious level according to the pleasure principle. The id attempts to have its needs met immediately.

2. Ego. Operates on the conscious and unconscious levels. The ego acts like a judge who overviews the situation and makes the best judgment in light of the situation. The ego develops about the second year of life. Its major responsibility is to mediate between the unrealistic demands of the id and the idealistic demands of the superego.

3. Superego. Is our conscience or the *moral arm of personality*. The superego operates at both the unconscious and conscious levels, but, unlike the ego, the superego operates within the idealistic rather than realistic framework.

Erikson's stages are that Freud placed less emphasis than Erikson did on the role of culture in one's development, and Erikson expanded Freud's five-stage theory into an eight-stage theory that encompasses the entire life span. Freud and Erikson's stages are compared and are presented in Table III. You will note that both Freud and Erikson believed that there is a central issue addressed at each stage of development, which Erikson refers to as **normative crises**. The resolution of the central issue or normative crisis at each stage of development is hypothesized to have lifelong implications.

Psychoanalytic Theory and Play

According to psychoanalytic theory, there are two major purposes of play. First, play provides an avenue for wish fulfillment. For example, the child may yearn to do things that his parents do, such as being able to stay up late at night rather than have an early bedtime. This is especially evident during the period when the child is establishing a superego and is trying to identify with his parent of the same sex. One's motivation for wanting to be like that parent is so that he will be allowed to do those forbidden things. Peller (1952) noted that children also act out roles in play that are beneath their dignity such as pretending to be a baby or an animal. In this way, children can regress to a state that symbolizes comfort and security. In sum, play provides an acceptable (therefore ego-mediated) avenue for acting-out behaviors that the child is normally not allowed to do.

TABLE III
AN OVERVIEW OF THE STAGES WITHIN FREUD'S AND ERIKSON'S THEORIES

Freud	Erikson
1. Oral Stage: Infant relies heavily on others. The infant's unbridled id strives to have its needs met.	1. Trust vs. Mistrust: The infant's experience with life attempting to secure trust in the relationship with caregiver.
2. Anal Stage (second year of life): Gaining greater control over body (e.g., locomotive and toileting).	2. Autonomy vs. Shame: The response the child develops from his/her accomplishments.
3. Phallic Stage (three to five years): Falling in love with opposite-sex parent and being in competition for the love of the same-sex parent. To appease the parent of the same sex, the child identifies with that parent. It is through this process of identification that the child adopts the parent's moral rules and develops a superego.	3. Initiative vs. Guilt: Children are busy exploring their world and learning more about their developing abilities. They also must begin to conform to rules.
4. Latency Stage (school age): This stage allows a period of consolidation, recuperation and a time to focus one's energies inward and to acquire knowledge.	4. Industry vs. Inferiority: The feedback of others provides the potential of leading to feelings of accomplishment of inadequacy.
5. Genital Stage (Adolescence): Sexual urges reawaken. The period where one begins to sever close ties with parents.	5. Identity vs. Role Confusion: Finding yourself and developing goals.

Erikson expanded Freud's theory beyond adolescence and describes normative crises during young adulthood, adulthood and old age. The following are the remainder of his stages:

6. Intimacy vs. Isolation.

7. Generativity vs. Stagnation.

8. Integrity vs. Despair.

The second purpose of play presented by the psychoanalytic school is to master traumatic events as well as express internal feelings. Bettelheim (1987) has suggested that child psychoanalysts have shown how children use play to work through and master quite complicated psychological difficulties of the past and the present. As a consequence, play therapy (an approach which was first developed on the principles of psychoanalytic psychology) has become a significant ingredient in dealing with children who have emotional conflicts. A thorough explanation of play therapy will be incorporated within Chapter Six.

Freud identified the repetition compulsion, which is a drive to repeat traumatic events in order to come to terms with, or master, them. Play is the means by which children repeat traumatic events in order to cope with them. Terr (1985) provides a case example of this type of play. A school bus full of children in Chowchilla, California, was hijacked, and the kidnappers imprisoned the children in an underground vault. Fortunately, the children were able to escape from the vault to safety. For some time after this event, one of the involved children used to repeatedly play a game she called bus. She played the active role in this game and commanded her sister and her dolls to play passive roles as her passengers. Supposedly, with each repetition of this game, a larger and larger portion of the trauma of being kidnapped was mastered. Through repetition, play thus serves as a means for strengthening the ego, which has to protect itself from the destabilizing effects of trauma. The reason why play is more frequent in childhood than later in life, then, is because the child's ego is not as strong as an adult's and because the child, who is more likely to be a passive recipient of events, has a greater need to act out the part of the active participant.

A child's play can attempt to be self-healing, for instance, when children take care of dolls they may be acting out their desires that their parents would take care of them as well and thus try to make up for felt deficiencies (Bettelheim, 1987). Of course, there is a wealth of information of how play can be used with children in hospitals. Children appear to need to act out (play) single episodes of the experience. They appear to integrate other elements only after they have resolved the prevailing feelings. Consequently, play can be used as an alternative for children to cope with internal stress.

Several research studies investigating the psychoanalytic interpretation of play have been conducted by Barnett-Morris and her colleagues. Two well-controlled and implemented studies were implemented by Barnett on preschool children. Barnett initiated her work to try to discount the psychoanalytic interpretation of play. To her surprise, the results of both her studies concluded that preschool age children used play as a method to work through confusing and upsetting behaviors. It appears that the value of free play helps children work through unpleasantness. For example, in one study, they investigated stress in the first day of preschool (for children who had never been formally separated from their mothers). The examiners observed the children to ascertain who appeared to be the most upset from this novel situation. They then gathered those who seemed the most traumatized and collected some data on their stress (e.g. heart rate, informal psychological measures). This was followed with various treatment alternatives (being read a story by oneself or in a small group or being allowed to play with carefully selected toys which appeared to have some relation to their dilemma, by oneself or in the presence of others). The results conclusively supported the position that children (on their own) would use the play experiences as an opportunity to vent some of their anxieties. These children appeared to significantly reduce their levels of anxiety in comparison to those who were read a story. For instance, many children were overheard playing with dolls and pretending that the dolls were their mothers. Consequently, children acted out that their mothers were already picking them up or were soon coming (L. Barnett Morris: personal communication, July 23, 1987).

Implications for Special Populations

Exceptional children are probably more likely to be placed in situations where they do not feel in control. Play would provide an important avenue for feeling in control, thus providing an opportunity to increase one's ego strength. For example, children from special populations may require more medical attention than other children. The belief that undergoing medical treatment often leads to feelings of loss of control has led to a push for preparation programs. Within these programs, hospitalized children are given an opportunity to play with hospital-related toys or equipment in order to master the trauma of the treatment. The children are encouraged to play out the role of administering the treatment rather than being the recipient of the treatment (Azarnoff and Woody, 1981; Elkins and Roberts, 1983).

Children from special populations are also more likely to experience the benevolent overreaction syndrome (Boone and Hartman, 1972). This reaction is a result of parents and others who overprotect the child because of his/her special problems. One result of this overprotection is that the child is not given an opportunity to master situations that he/she has the capacity to master, because others do things for him/her. For example, in a midwestern state, children with cancer are invited to attend a special summer camp. One of the 12-year-old campers, whose cancer had been in remission for years, came to camp and was not able to tie his own shoes. His mother had always tied his shoes for him because of her benevolent overreaction to his cancer. An implication of this phenomenon is that we should be particularly sensitive to not being a benevolent overreactor as well as providing play opportunities for exceptional children where they feel in control.

Finally, the central issues and normative crises outlined by Freud and Erikson should sensitize us to developmental tasks that are faced by special children at different age levels. It is probably not unreasonable to hypothesize that children from special populations are more likely to resolve normative crises in a negative way than non-handicapped children. For example, the aforementioned feelings of not being in control (that are exacerbated by others who are benevolent overreactors) would affect a child's feelings of autonomy, initiative, and industry. The over-involvement of one's family, as well as possible feelings of being different because of one's handicap, might hamper separation from one's family and the formation of a personal identity. The inability to form one's own identity, in turn, may interfere with one's ability to form an intimate relationship with another person.

Limitations of Psychoanalytic Theory

Erikson (1950) suggested that play may often be just play, i.e. he questioned whether play really has meaning beyond itself and thus was uncomfortable with the assumption that play is open for analysis. This, however, is in direct contrast to the wealth of research on play therapy, which has suggested the opposite position.

Ellis (1973) criticizes psychoanalytic theory because it is so subjective and because it lacks empirical support. In his book on **Why People Play**, he wrote: "Psychoanalytic aspects of play have not been treated extensively here. The reason is simply my inability to grasp any essential and rigorous thread to the arguments of the psychoanalysts . . . the essence of psychoanalysis seems subjective rather than scientific. Having revealed my biases, it seems that psychoanalytic theories have been ill-formulated and that there has been almost no attempt to establish ways of testing them."

In summary, although even psychoanalysts (e.g. Erikson) as well as others (e.g. Ellis) question the contribution of psychoanalytic theory to the understanding of play, it is felt that this theory has contributed by focusing our attention to the possible role that play serves in one's emotional development. Other recent theories (e.g. Piaget's theory and learning theory) have not paid much attention to this aspect of play. Moreover, play therapy, which is partially based on psychoanalytic theory, has become nearly standard clinical practice; play is a highly accepted tool for assessment of children's emotional states (Goodman and Sours, 1967).

Arousal Theory and Play

Several versions of the arousal theory of play have been offered: (1) Berlyne (1960, 1966, 1969), (2) Ellis (1973), and (3) Fein (1981). The basic difference between these versions lies in how they characterize what the desired level of arousal is as well as how the direction of arousal (low, moderate, high) is affected by play. A detailed discussion of the distinctions between the three versions is beyond the scope of this chapter; the interested reader is referred to Rubin, Fein, and Vandenberg (1983) for more discussion.

The following is a general overview of this theory that reflects Ellis (1973). According to Ellis, "Play is that behavior that is motivated by the need to elevate the level of arousal towards the optimal" (1973, p. 110). The habituation response and the needs of the reticular activating system are basics of this theory.

Habituation is a type of non-associative learning that is necessary so that we are not bombarded by stimulation. If we are presented with a novel, interesting stimulus, it captures our attention and we display an **orienting response.** The orienting response is reflected in physiological changes such as a change in heart rate. However, after repeated presentations of the stimulus, it loses its novelty and the organism ceases to be aroused by the stimulus.

The second area in need of description is the reticular activating system. This is a system located in the lower portion of the brain that plays a key role in consciousness. The reticular activating system can be likened to a filter or sieve; it filters sensory input and serves as a **mediating center** between stimulation from the higher cortical areas and from incoming sensory stimulation.

According to the arousal theory, there is an optimal level of arousal that one seeks to maintain in the reticular activating system. Schultz (1965) called this sensoristasis (analogous to the biological concept of homeostasis). If one is bombarded with stimulation, i.e. if one is over-aroused, one seeks to reduce the stimulation. Likewise, if one is under-aroused, one seeks to increase stimulation.

According to Ellis (1973), play occurs in situations where one is underaroused. It is stimulus-seeking behavior. Play provides stimulation because it is concerned with characteristics that are associated with stimulation, namely, novelty, uncertainty, or complexity. Not just any stimulus will do. One seeks stimuli that are moderately stimulating, because stimuli that are too novel, too unpredictable, or too complex cause discomfort and neophobia (avoidance of anything unknown), and stimuli that are not novel, not unpredictable, and too simplistic are not arousing.

Arousal Theory and Special Populations

Goldstein and Lancy (1985) proposed a cognitive deficit hypothesis that complements the stimulus arousal theory of play. According to the cognitive deficit hypothesis, one of the problems that may dramatically influence some disabled children is their faulty reticular activating system. For example, autistic children who engage in perseverative behaviors, such as spinning a top for hours, may do so because their filtering system allows too much stimulation in. These children are overwhelmed by all of the stimuli coming through their faulty filtering system, and their way of coping is to structure and order incoming stimuli by engaging in perseverative behavior. Ellis (1973) points out that institutionalized individuals with mental retardation also emit stereotyped, perseverative behavior but for a different reason. He hypothesized that persons with mental retardation emit stereotyped responses, not because there are not enough complex stimuli in their environments, but because they are incapable of systematizing and manipulating the cognitive or symbolic elements that they represent.

Limitations of Stimulus-Arousal Theory

White (1959) suggested that the stimulus-arousal theory cannot account for repetitive behavior. In other words, the assertion that novelty, uncertainty, and complexity are necessary for arousal is inconsistent with the observation that perseverative behavior that presumably becomes old, certain, and no longer complex still continues. By repetitious behavior, White implies that each instance of a repetitious behavior is an identical copy of the previous instances of that behavior. Thus, White proposed a variation of the arousal model which he referred to as the Competence/ Effectance Model. Basically, this model echoes the psychoanalytic school, which proposed that repetitious behavior is engaged in in order to demonstrate control and mastery over one's environment. Supposedly, then, the urge to control and master one's environment explains why an organism would engage in repetitious behavior.

Most scientific research now leads to the convergence that intrinsic motivation is based on the organismic needs to be competent and self-determining. White (1959) referred to effective motivation as the drive by which one's exploration, learning and adaptations through play activities were driven by the intrinsic need to develop competency within the environment.

Self-determination involves the aspect of choice within the particular individual to choose an action. To be truly intrinsically motivated, a person must be free of controls, rewards or contingencies. Research confirms that the opportunity to be self-determining greatly increases intrinsic motivation, while thwarting that behavior certainly undermines intrinsic motivation (Deci, 1985). Thus, it would follow that the development of intrinsic motivation within exceptional children would be desired. Consequently, recreational professionals must program activities that impact this area. This suggests that not only should the activities developed incorporate this emphasis, but other alternatives will have to also be considered (e.g. working with families so they will encourage the transfer maintenance of this behavior in other aspects of the child's life). The data on the impact of locus of control on leisure participation are, at best, unclear. On the one hand, we have findings similar to the Pitmann, Emery, and Boggiano's (1985) study which suggested that those who are highly intrinsically motivated placed a high value on leisure time, in comparison to those who were extrinsically driven who appeared to have opposite conceptions. However, the work of Kleiber (1979) and Kleiber and Crandall (1981) possibly indicates that persons motivated internally are less, rather than more, likely to have a significant commitment to recreation participation. The interpretation given is due in part to the fact that recreation involvement may inconsistently uphold the traditional values of a Puritan work ideology.

SUMMARY AND CONCLUSIONS

Historically, four classical theories were proposed to explain the nature of play. Each of these received little empirical support but were refuted on philosophical grounds. Contemporary theories, whose formulations were probably influenced by classical theories to a greater or lesser degree, each have unique contributions to our understanding of play. Piaget's theory addressed the role of play in cognitive development. An important implication of Piaget's ideas is that opportunities for play between handicapped and non-handicapped children may enhance the intellectual development of exceptional children. Specifically, non-handicapped children may exhibit slightly more mature levels of thinking than non-handicapped children, which may cause non-handicapped children to accommodate to these slightly higher levels of thinking. Also, Piaget's theory draws attention to the importance of providing physical and logicomathematical experience for special children, either in areas that they may have a deficit in, due to their disability, or in areas that may compensate for their handicap.

Learning theorists characterize play as a behavior just like any other behavior. Play serves as a means for learning about the social world. For example, play provides opportunities for learning about sex-role behavior and aggressive or non-aggressive behavior. Learning principles can also be used to shape the play behavior of children who do not play appropriately. This may require breaking down the goal behavior into manageable parts and teaching each of the prerequisite behaviors.

The focus of psychoanalytic theory is on the role of play in one's emotional development. A major contribution of this theory is its highlight of the importance of permitting special children to express mastery through play and to come to terms with things that bother them through this medium. As such, the psychodynamic implementation of play and art therapy are excellent resources for aiding children in self-expression and discovery.

Arousal theory unifies concepts from biology with various concepts from the above-three theories. Its major contribution is this unification. In addition, the hypothesized role of the reticular activating system in mediating arousal and the habituation research on developmental differences in pacers, provides a starting point for thinking about how to provide optimally arousing play activities for special children.

At the beginning of this chapter, it was suggested that the adoption of an eclectic perspective about play may be useful. As can be seen from the above review of the major theories of play, each has its strengths and limitations. It was also pointed out that these theories tend to focus on different aspects of development. It is crucial to be concerned with the **whole child,** i.e. with the cognitive, social, emotional, and physical aspects of a child, and thus it is valuable to consider the contributions of all theories.

In planning any type of program to enhance play in exceptional children, it is important to heed the thoughts expressed by psychologist David Elkind (1981) in **The Hurried Child.** He suggests that children are not allowed to play anymore because play is poorly understood by our society. We are often guilty of robbing our children's childhood; rather than allowing children to play at their own pace, we are sending them to structured activities to fill up their **play time,** such as ballet, Pee Wee baseball (with a goal of winning, not just of having fun), computer camp, etc. The traditional rites of passage come too early for most children. They are constantly confronted with the fear of failure and of living up to someone else's expectations. Unfortunately, the children of the eighties are forced to achieve more as well as earlier than any other generation. With this orientation, our children are cheated out of trying to have fun and explore. Being a dreamer for these children has become a taboo. Along the same line, Brian Sutton-Smith (1985), an expert on play, writes that the technology of our times may be robbing children of important developmental opportunities. The expensive, attractive toys of our age may promote increased isolated play, which may rob a child of the rich social exchanges afforded by group play. It seems that an important avenue for future study is whether the complexity and sophisticated nature of today's toys, from computer simulations to dolls that can become instantly pregnant by donning a special smock, will ultimately enrich or rob our children of so-called developmental opportunities. An important implication is that we want to promote and enhance play without hurrying our special children.

The theories reviewed have focused on cognitive, social, emotional, and biological aspects of play. In the second part of this chapter, the relationship of play to developmental advances in motor development is presented. Considered together, the chapter highlights the major strands of development (Santrock, 1986) associated with play.

Part II—The Motor Development of Children

GREG PAYNE

INTRODUCTION

To adequately and completely study human development a number of domains of behavior must be considered. For the sake of organization, the study of human development is generally subdivided into three areas or domains. These domains are the cognitive, the affective, and the psychomotor. The cognitive domain, which concerns human intellectual development, has been the primary interest of developmentalists. Intellectual development was, of course, the focus of the most prominent of all developmentalists, Jean Piaget. Affective development has also been given considerable attention by experts in the field of human development. Erik Erikson wrote prolifically on this area of human development, which is primarily concerned with the social and the emotional development of the human being. The third domain is equally important and is the emphasis of this section.

Psychomotor, or simply motor, development is a discipline concerned with the changes that occur across the life span in the movement patterns of the human being. Obviously, the movement changes that occur from birth, or even prenatally, to the time of death are substantial. Movement can progress from a level that appears crude and unsophisticated to a level of remarkable precision and control. But why is our knowledge of these movements and their change, or development, important?

THE IMPORTANCE OF UNDERSTANDING CHILDREN'S MOTOR DEVELOPMENT

First of all, we cannot consider ourselves completely educated concerning human development until we understand all aspects of the changes that occur across the life span. We must understand the movement changes that we commonly experience with age as well as the intellectual, social, and emotional. Our knowledge of all aspects of human development is valuable, simply because it contributes to our body of knowledge which enables us to better understand ourselves and the world we live in. However, other more immediately practical applications of our knowledge of human motor development do exist.

Although, for the sake of easy communication and more efficient organization, we tend to subdivide our study of human development into a study of cognitive, affective, or psychomotor development, this organizational schema is not a realistic portrayal of human behavior. Human behavior is a function of a constant interaction of all domains. In other words, what we do intellectually is frequently dependent on our emotions as well as our motions, or movements. A good example is, of course, taking a written test. We require knowledge of the subject matter, an appropriate state of mind, and an ability to manually transcribe the answer. Therefore, if we are ever going to thoroughly understand cognitive development, we must also understand affective and psychomotor development.

Our knowledge of human motor development has, however, more immediate applications. Understanding the way human beings normally develop movement skills enables us to diagnose those individuals who may not be developing **normally**. This, of course, allows early intervention in an effort to improve the abnormality. For example, our knowledge of the infant reflexes enables pediatricians to ascertain at an early age the presence of neurological problems. Since we know that certain reflexive movements normally occur at certain points in infancy, deviations from the normal time line often indicate a need for special treatment.

Finally, movement is a source of tremendous pleasure. Children are wonderful examples of this fact, as they love to be in motion and are eager to participate in movement activities such as games. Movement can also be an excellent source of tension relief and improving self-concept. Although simple participation in movement activities is sufficient to achieve any of the above movement objectives, we often find value in the perfection of movement. Learning to perform a movement well has many advantages. Movement perfection has many potential benefits. For example, the self-concept often improves and one can become much more stable emotionally. Also, as suggested earlier, improvements in the movement domain may indirectly lead to improvements in the individual's intellectual, social, or emotional development. Activities can, therefore, be devised to assist children in the development of their movement potential. To accurately create such a movement curriculum, a knowledge of normal motor development is required so that the child is challenged relative to his/her level of achievement rather than allowed to become frustrated or bored.

THE MOTOR DEVELOPMENT OF EXCEPTIONAL INDIVIDUALS

For all of these reasons, knowledge of normal motor development is also important for individuals working with children who are handicapped. Despite the fact that many handicapping conditions lead to a developmental lag in a child's movement, the sequence or pattern of development generally remains the same. For example, blind babies commonly lag behind sighted babies in the development of early reaching behavior as well as independent walking (Bower, 1977). In both of these cases the sequence for acquisition of movement skills would most likely be **normal** despite the fact that the rate of development would be delayed (McClenaghan and Gallahue, 1978). This phenomenon was also well represented by Williams, Temple and Bateman (1979) in a study investigating learning-disordered and behavior-disordered children and their performance on sensory perception and perceptual motor tasks. These researchers concluded that although the level of development of these children was delayed compared to the **normal** children, the pattern of development was not altered. Wickstrom (1983) supported these findings by stating that mentally retarded children also tend to be retarded in the development of their movement skills. EMR children, for example, generally lag approximately two years behind their non-mentally retarded peers, with this lag increasing in magnitude as the degree of mental retardation increases. These individuals, according to Wickstrom, develop movement skills in a "normal" progression but are limited by their particular handicap.

The plight of handicapped children and their acquisition of movement skills is intensified by their lack of movement opportunity. In many cases, with the appropriate opportunity and instruction, the movement skill of a handicapped child can be elevated to a normal or better level. However, without such opportunity and instruction the child may actually regress as a result of a harmful, but common, cycle. Without sufficient opportunity to improve movement skills, the handicapped child commonly becomes inactive and possibly overweight or even obese. Inactivity decreases social interrelationships and separates the child from his/her peers. Decreasing social experiences may further decrease movement opportunities which, again, decreases activity levels and reinitiates this debilitating cycle. Involving all children in movement programs devised on the basis of our understanding of human motor development is, therefore, critical to the child's optimal development. If a child fails to develop movement skills at an appropriate age, the development of these skills becomes increasingly difficult each year (McClenaghan and Gallahue, 1978).

MOTOR DEVELOPMENT DURING INFANCY

Movement acquisition occurs rapidly during the first year of life. In fact, the neonate, or newborn, progresses from a state of helplessness to a dominance over the skill of walking months later. Among the most interesting and important movements to emerge during infancy are known as the infant reflexes. Also significant in the motor development of the infant is prehension, early attempts at reaching and grasping, and early locomotion. Although other aspects of movement during infancy could be included in this discussion, the infant reflexes, prehension, and early locomotion are considered the most important because of their tremendous influence on the development of movements in later life.

The Infant Reflexes

From approximately four months in utero to six months following birth, movement is dominated by the infant reflexes. A reflex is a movement which is a stereotypical, involuntary response to a specific stimulus. Therefore, when a stimulus is applied, such as touching the infant's palm, a movement response occurs. In the case of the palmar grasp reflex, the fingers close around the stimulating object. Interestingly, these reflexes are relatively invariant and subcortical. The movement occurs with each application of the stimulus without direct involvement of the brain. The stimulus simply creates an electrical impulse which travels to the spinal column. From there, a message is returned to the hand, resulting in a closing of the hand. Since the brain is not directly involved in the production of the infant reflexes, these movements are deemed involuntary. They are not volitionally controlled by the infant. The infant cannot, therefore, voluntarily decide to leave the hand open upon stimulation.

Reflexes are particularly important because of the number of important functions they serve during infancy. Some infant reflexes are crucial for the nourishment and, therefore, survival of the infant. The rooting reflex, for example, is elicited when the cheek near the corner of the mouth is stimulated. The corresponding response is a turning of the head in the direction of the stimulation. This reflex is critical in the attainment of nourishment for the infant as the head turns to seek food upon being stimulated by the mother's breast. The sucking reflex is another well-known reflex of infancy. The sucking reflex is also necessary for the ingestion of food and is elicited by a stimulation of the lips. When the lips are touched, the infant begins to suck. Without such a reflex, the infant could not survive. These **infant** reflexes do not endure throughout the life span, nor even throughout childhood, however. In fact, most disappear within the first few months of life after the child has developed sufficient voluntary control to survive without them. The sucking reflex, for example, usually disappears by the end of the third month of life.

Understanding the infant reflexes is important for other reasons as well. Since the age of appearance and disappearance of these movements is normally predictable, the reflexes are valuable diagnostic tools. If the infant's acquisition of a reflex deviates significantly from the norm, a neurological dysfunction may be present. More specifically, if a reflex is excessively weak or strong, lacks symmetry, perseveres past the normal point of offset, or is completely absent, the infant's movement may be impaired. Therefore, early detection and intervention is possible as a result of our awareness of the infant reflexes.

The reflexes are also important, since they are believed to be linked to the acquisition of more advanced voluntary movements of later life. Examples of reflexes which appear to be especially important in the attainment of the more advanced movements are the palmar grasp that was described earlier, the crawling, and stepping reflexes (Payne and Isaacs, 1987).

The palmar grasp reflex which was mentioned in the introduction of the infant reflex section involves the infant's hand closing tightly upon a stimulation of the palm of that hand. This reflex is observable from birth through the first four months of life and exists for some weeks prenatally as well. This important and well-known reflex is believed to be a precursor to voluntary reaching and grasping that occurs later in the infant's life.

The crawling reflex is another reflex that is easily observable in infancy. This reflex, which also exists at birth through the first three to four months of life, is elicited by stroking the soles of the baby's feet. If done alternately when the child is in a prone position, a crawling action of the legs, arms, and head is initiated. This reflexive crawling may cease as much as four months before voluntary crawling begins. Despite this time lag between the involuntary and the voluntary forms of crawling, involuntary (reflexive) crawling is believed to be an essential element in the eventual development of voluntary crawling.

The stepping reflex, also known as the placing of walking reflex, also plays an important role in the development of a voluntary movement in later life. This reflex is elicited by holding the infant in an upright position, allowing the feet to contact the supporting surface. The pressure of that surface on the soles of the feet is the stimulus which evokes a left-right knee raising action. While the action of the knees is reminiscent of walking, the corresponding arm swing associated with voluntary walking is not observable. This reflex ordinarily appears around the first six weeks of life and disappears four months later. The stepping reflex is apparently linked to voluntary walking. Difficulty in voluntary walking, therefore, could be a function of a poorly developed or negative (unobservable) stepping reflex earlier in life.

Another important reflex is the labyrinthine reflex which is believed to be fundamental to the development of upright posture. This reflex is first evidenced at approximately two to three months of age and generally endures throughout the first year of life. The labyrinthine reflex is characterized by a movement of the head in a direction opposite to a movement of the body. For example, if the child is tilted forward, the head extends back in what appears to be an effort to maintain the original position. This reflex also functions to the side. That is, as the body is tilted to either side, the head responds by tilting in the opposite direction.

The propping reflexes also appear to be related to the attainment of upright posture and also occur when the infant, held in an upright position, is tilted in any direction. The resulting movement response is a propping motion of the arms in the direction of the "fall." When eliciting this reflex, the infant appears to be aware of the potential danger of being tilted into an unstable position and reacts by propping the arms to protect against a fall. However, like all infant reflexes, the propping reflexes are involuntary. They are not the result of a conscious effort on the part of the infant. Forward propping movements occur as early as four months of age, while propping reflexes to the side may not occur until six months of age. Finally, the backward propping reflex occurs as late as ten months of age and like all propping reflexes frequently endures past the first year of life (Payne, 1985).

The reflexes included in this discussion are only a sample of the many reflexes which normally exist during infancy. The palmar grasp, crawling, stepping, labyrinthine, and propping reflexes are, however, particularly significant in the effects they render on movement in later life. Because of this effect on later movement, their utility as a diagnostic tool, and their role in the nourishment and survival of the infant, the infant reflexes are, unquestionably, an important aspect of the motor development of children.

Reaching and Grasping During Infancy

Although the infant reflexes are the dominant movement form during early infancy, the first year of life can also be characterized by many voluntary movements. Among the most important voluntary movements of the first year of life is prehension. Prehension is a relatively crude swiping motion of the arms that precedes the careful visually monitored form of reaching and grasping that eventually will exist. According to Bower (1977), this crude reaching or swiping behavior is actually present at birth. Strangely, this early prehension then subsides or disappears at approximately four weeks of age. It reappears again at around four months of life. The newborn reaching and grasping and the behavior which occurs at four months is described by Bower as Phase I reaching and grasping. At approximately six to seven months Phase I slowly evolves into Phase II reaching and grasping. The differentiation between Phase I and II behavior are interesting and worth consideration.

Phase I reaching and grasping is characterized by a simultaneous reach and grasp. In other words, as the arm extends for a desired object, the hand is opening and closing. This immature form of reaching and grasping is performed with one arm and is visually initiated but not controlled. Therefore, the infant sees a desirable object and initiates a reach based on that sighting. However, once the movement has been initiated, the child does not visually control the reach. Vision again becomes influential in this behavior upon contact with the desired object as Phase I grasping is visually monitored.

Phase II reaching and grasping involves a logical progression in movement behavior from the Phase I technique. For example, the Phase II reach and grasp is not simultaneous. The reach is performed first and is followed by the grasp. This is, of course, a more mature form of movement and is the technique that would be used by an adult. Interestingly, in Phase II, two hands and arms are employed in the reach and grasp. This is unlike the adult reaching and grasping behavior but at six months of age is considered to be a more mature movement since less error is experienced. Furthermore, like Phase I, the reach is visually initiated, but, unlike Phase I, the reach is also visually monitored. Finally, the Phase II grasp also differs from the Phase I grasp. Whereas the grasp is visually monitored in the early form of grasping, in the more advanced Phase II the grasp is monitored by vision and touch.

The progression from Phase I to Phase II reaching and grasping enables the child to be more successful in his/her attempts to control objects in his/her environment. This intentional movement behavior may be linked to the involuntary palmar grasp reflex discussed earlier. From that suspected origin, the reaching and grasping movement will normally evolve into more complex movements of early childhood such as throwing and catching.

Infant Locomotion

Perhaps the movement which attracts the greatest parental concern is infant locomotion. Locomotion, in this case, is simply transporting the body from one location in space to another. The infant uses a variety of forms of locomotion which are all a part of the progression leading up to independent walking. Of greatest concern in this progression are the movements of creeping, crawling, standing, and finally walking. Creeping is the first and crudest form of locomotion attempted by the infant. In fact, the first attempts at creeping may be accidental. When in a prone position and reaching forward for an object the child may be propelled forward when the arms are returned toward the body. This form of creeping is a simple sliding forward of the body and would not normally involve the legs in the production of the propulsion. These first attempts at locomotion often occur around four months of age, although the onset and duration is extremely variable and dependent on the child's environment (Cratty, 1979). If the child lives in an environment that is lacking stimulation or provision for opportunity, creeping may not emerge until much later.

Crawling, a more advanced form of locomotion, generally emerges from creeping. The onset of crawling varies and is dependent on the onset and duration of its predecessor, creeping. Initially, the infant assumes a crawling position which includes a slight bend of the arms and the legs and hips flexed to the extent that the legs are actually positioned under the body. Although early crawling involves slow methodical placement of the arms and legs, with time and practice the child develops a rapid, well-coordinated, efficient mode of locomotion. Crawling is a particularly interesting movement, since much speculation exists concerning the quality of the crawling experience and later intellectual deficits. Could it be that failure to crawl or crawl properly leads to cognitive impairment? This is a theory that was originally proposed by Delacato (1966) but has been highly criticized due to a lack of supporting evidence.

Although not a form of locomotion, standing is a critical link in the locomotion progression. Without the ability to gain and maintain upright posture, walking would be impossible. Standing, according to Gallahue (1983), is first attempted around five months of age. These attempts usually fail, however, and require extreme external support such as some guidance from a parent. By nine to ten months of age this effort has become much more successful as the child has gained sufficient strength and control to pull to a standing position alongside a supporting object such as a chair. As the child progresses, less dependence is placed on the supporting objects until, by eleven to twelve months, the child can stand alone.

Once the child can stand alone, walking becomes possible. Normally, the child walks by the age of one year, although considerable variability exists from one child to the next. This variability in walking acquisition is due, in part, to the varying amounts of stimulation in each child's environment. Regardless of the actual time of onset, certain characteristics are noticeable as the child develops from an immature to a mature state of walking. Since balance is initially difficult to maintain, falls occur frequently. The walk appears wobbly and uncontrolled as the stride is short, choppy, and inconsistent in length. An immature walker often maintains the arms in what is referred to as the "high guard" position. In other words, the arms are raised in a flexed, rigid position rather than hanging and swinging freely at the sides of the body. Young children also frequently exhibit an excessive forward lean and a wide base of support. That is, a considerable distance is maintained between the feet in an effort to improve balance. Also, in this immature form of walking, the legs appear "stiff," as little knee flexion is noticeable. Flexion and extension is also lacking at the ankle which inhibits the young walker from rolling across the heel onto the toe. This creates the appearance of **flat-footed** walking.

In a more advanced walker these characteristics would be greatly improved. The gait, for example, becomes smooth and consistent and the arms are relaxed and swinging freely at the child's side. The mature walker rolls across the heel and onto the toe and maintains a narrow base of support. In fact, the base of support of a mature walker is so narrow that very little space is perceptible between the feet as they pass in mid-stride. Finally, the posture of the walker becomes erect, although not rigid. Most of these mature characteristics are evident by two years of age and by the age of four or five years only very subtle differences are noticeable between an adult and a child walker (Wickstrom, 1983).

MOTOR DEVELOPMENT DURING EARLY CHILDHOOD

After the first year of life, most of the infant reflexes evolve into more sophisticated voluntary movements. The most important movement consideration during early childhood, from one to seven years of age, is these voluntary movements. Although an infinite number of voluntary movements exist, six movements known as the fundamental movement patterns will be included in this discussion. This section has been delimited to these movements, because it is the fundamental movements that are believed to be the basis for the more advanced gross movements of later life. The fundamental movements include: walking, which was discussed in the last section, running, jumping, throwing, catching, kicking, and striking. Although many other gross movements exist such as skipping or hopping, these movements are combinations or variations of the fundamental movements. Therefore, an understanding of the fundamental movements should enable a subsequent understanding of their combinations and variations.

Running

Running development is preceded by the development of walking which was discussed earlier in this section. Since running is an advanced form of walking, the characteristics of these two fundamental movement patterns are quite similar. Running is differentiated from walking for the purposes of this discussion by the presence of a flight phase. More specifically, in running the rear leg propels the body so vigorously that a moment exists when no body part is touching the support surface. Obviously, this takes more strength and balance than simple walking, and for this reason running is not usually experienced by the child until approximately 18 months of age (Wickstrom, 1983).

When the runner is immature, there is a tendency to carry the arms in the **high guard** position mentioned in the discussion of walking. This immature arm position may be an effort to assist in maintaining the equilibrium, since children at this age fall frequently because of poorly developed balance. When in this **high guard** position, the arms do not function in opposition to the legs as they would in a mature running pattern. Also apparent in the running pattern of an immature runner is the short, choppy, inconsistent stride. The stride is further complicated by a **kicking in** of the legs when they follow through behind the body. In other words, the leg, after pushing off, does not continue to follow straight through to a flexed position behind the body. Rather, the foot of the propelling leg actually crosses the midline of the body before achieving a high heel kick behind the body. This immature process creates such excessive body rotation that the arms may begin to **hook** across the midline in front of the body to compensate for the **kicking in** of the legs.

In the mature running technique, which is often evidenced by children as young as five years of age, many differences are observable. For example, the **high guard** position diminishes progress and the arms to a position at the sides of the body. Although initially the arms may function minimally in opposing the action of the legs, they eventually assume a right-angle flexed position and move in perfect opposition to the movement of the legs. Furthermore, the stride begins to lengthen while becoming much more smooth and consistent in length and frequency. The **flight phase,** or time when no body part is touching the surface, becomes more pronounced as the stride is extended. As the stride lengthens, a greater forward inclination also becomes more apparent. Finally, particularly noticeable in the mature runner is the high knee raise in front of the body and the high heel kick in the rear of the body. This high heel kick is achieved by a strong propulsion of the leg followed by a straight backward and upward movement of the foot.

Jumping

Once the child is physiologically capable of generating sufficient force to run, another motor pattern, jumping, is likely to emerge. Many forms of jumping exist, but one of the first forms attempted by young children is a horizontal jump with the feet together. At an early age, a number of immature jumping characteristics can be observed. Primarily noticeable is the lack of any kind of preparatory movement before the actual jump. The child does not crouch to increase the amount of leg flexion in an effort to generate more force. Also lacking is a corresponding arm swing in the direction of the jump which also impairs the child's ability to gain much distance. Further hampering the child's ability to gain distance in this jump is the tendency to jump excessively vertical rather than horizontal. This characteristic gives the jump a choppy up-down appearance. Perhaps the most obvious immature jumping characteristic of all is the child's inability to maintain the feet together and his/her rigidity upon landing. This latter characteristic makes the landing stiff in appearance and jolting to the jumper.

While children as young as two years of age may be attempting some form of jumping, most mature characteristics of the jump will be lacking. Over the next few years these mature characteristics will slowly emerge. The child will begin to exhibit greater preparation for the jump. For example, a semi-crouched position will be assumed to increase the force that can be produced by the legs. Additionally, the arms will begin to whip forward in the direction of the jump. This arm action, which will be synchronized with the propulsion created by the legs, will greatly increase the distance traversed by the child. The mature jumper will also maintain a low trajectory during flight. To keep the trajectory as low as possible, the legs are often **tucked up** under the body during the brief flight phase of the jump. Although the legs are flexed during the jump in the mature pattern, they extend immediately before landing in an effort to reach out and gain as much distance as possible. Following contact with the surface, the legs again flex to absorb the shock of the landing. The child, therefore, gains greater distance and still lands softly and under control.

Throwing

One of the most complex fundamental motor patterns is throwing. Like jumping, many forms of this skill exist. One of the most common is the one-handed overhand throw. Children are often capable of a crude form of this throwing behavior as young as two years of age. However, proficiency is not likely to be apparent until two to three years later, and, in many cases, without proper instruction, proficiency will never be gained.

In watching an immature thrower, a number of characteristics become apparent. As in immature jumping, very little is done in preparation for the actual movement. Preparation preceding the throw is minimized to raising the ball up to the shoulder or, perhaps, slightly behind the head. No rotation of the trunk occurs which hinders a maximum preparation of the arm. Also, the child does not involve the feet in the generation of force for propelling the ball. Consequently, the ball will travel a very short distance. After the throw no follow through occurs as the arm is abruptly and unnaturally halted upon release of the ball.

As the child develops maturity in throwing, arm preparation will improve. The arm will be extended well behind the head prior to throwing. To facilitate this arm preparation the body rotates, or "opens up," so even greater preparation can be achieved. Additionally, the feet and legs become involved in the throwing action. Whereas the most immature thrower would not involve the feet in the throwing action, a more advanced, but still immature thrower would take a step in the direction of the throw with the leg on the same side as the throwing arm. With proper instruction, opportunity, and motivation, this process will evolve into a step taken with the leg opposite to the throwing arm. When this step is synchronized with the whipping action of the arm, the distance of the projection is increased immensely. Finally, following the release of the ball, the mature thrower gradually diminishes the speed of the arm. This action gives the appearance of a much more graceful follow through.

Catching

A skill commonly associated with throwing is, of course, catching. This description is limited to one of the first and most basic types of catching experienced by children: the two-handed catch. This type of catch can be performed as young as two to three years of age, although the form is normally awkward and uncontrolled at that time.

The first attempts at catching may actually be **chest traps.** Immaturity in catching is exhibited as the child cradles the ball in the basket created by the arms and the chest. Initially, failure is common as the ball frequently goes astray. This is, in part, due to an initial fear of the ball which is also a sign of immature catching. In fact, the child may actually close the eyes, turn the head, and arch the back as the ball approaches. Also, the immature catcher is normally seen extending the arms out rigidly in the direction of the approaching projectile. Finally, the legs of the immature catcher remain straight and seemingly uninvolved in the attempted catch.

These characteristics are in contrast to the characteristics of a mature catcher who would flex the legs upon contact with the ball to aid in the shock-absorption process. Furthermore, the mature catcher would contact and maintain control of the ball with the fingers and hands alone. Immediately after making contact with the ball the mature catcher would lower the hands and flex at the waist and knees to further reduce the impact of the ball's arrival. Also, fearful reactions are minimized. The eyes remain open during the catch and the arching of the back, common in immature catching, is eliminated. Finally, while awaiting the approaching projectile, the mature catcher positions the arms comfortably at his/her sides rather than rigidly extended toward the ball. This is, perhaps, indicative of the self-assurance that the mature catcher has developed as compared to the younger, immature catcher.

Striking

Striking is another fundamental movement pattern. In striking, an implement is employed to project an object. Obvious examples of striking are batting in baseball (a two-handed strike) and the serve in tennis (a one-handed strike). Regardless of the type of striking examined, certain characteristics are observable in immature and mature strikers. In many ways, the characteristics of striking are very similar to those of throwing. For example, the immature striker does not involve the legs in the striking action. The upper-body rotation which was so important in throwing is also important in striking and is minimized or absent in the immature striker. Also evidenced in an immature striking pattern is an up-down striking action as young strikers find it difficult to swing an implement horizontally. This, of course, results in much less success, since a horizontally projected object is much easier to hit with a horizontal rather than a vertical striking motion. Finally, the immature striker exhibits excessive stiffness which is especially noticeable in the arms. The arms give the appearance of being inflexible at the elbows and the wrists.

With maturity, however, the child becomes much more relaxed. The mature striker exhibits slightly flexed knees and rotates the trunk around in the direction of the strike. The rotation of the trunk is accompanied by a step in the direction of the strike. The step is taken with the foot opposite the striking hand or side in the case of the two-handed strike. Finally, whereas the arms were rigid in appearance in the immature pattern, the mature striker smoothly coordinates the action of the shoulders and elbows into a sequential striking motion that is culminated with a slight **snap** of the wrists.

Kicking

Kicking is a form of striking in which one uses the leg or foot to project an object such as a ball. Kicking, in an immature fashion, can be observed in children as young as two years of age. Normally, at that level of development the kick is barely recognizable as one of the fundamental motor patterns. With time and practice, however, kicking can emerge into a highly coordinated, effective movement skill.

Like many of the fundamental movement patterns, immature kicking is characterized by a lack of preparation. An immature kicker will not take an approach to the ball, omits virtually all preparatory movement and simply pushes the ball away with the foot when standing next to the ball. No arm swing is observable and the legs remain straight.

As the child matures in his/her kicking ability, more pre-kick motions will be evident. For example, the more mature kicker will run to the ball before kicking. The increased momentum which is generated allows for a much more forceful kick. Also, immediately prior to the kick the mature kicker prepares the kicking leg by flexing at the hip and the knee which places the kicking foot well behind the body. This preparation also contributes to the increased force of the kick. The arm action of the mature kicker is another characteristic which differentiates his/her movement from that of an immature kicker. During the preparation for the kick, the kick itself, and the follow through of the leg after the kick, the arms of the mature kicker work in constant opposition to the action of the legs. This arm action helps generate greater force and also assists the kicker in maintaining balance. Finally, in concluding the kick, the mature kicker follows through with the kicking leg much like a mature thrower follows through with the throwing arm. The speed of the active limb is gradually creating a graceful, efficient follow through.

The developmental characteristics of the fundamental movement patterns can be accurately predicted. The sequence of development of running, jumping, throwing, catching, striking, and kicking are the same for all children, although the rate of development may vary. In fact, many children may never develop mature techniques for these movements. Knowledge of the characteristics of these movements is integral to the creation of programs designed to assist children in their movement development. Without logically designed instructional programs, practice, and motivation, few children would ever achieve a mature level of any of the fundamental movement patterns.

MOTOR DEVELOPMENT OF LATER CHILDHOOD

By the age of approximately seven or eight years of age many children will be performing the fundamental movement patterns at a mature level. Once a child has developed a certain level of proficiency in the fundamental motor patterns, he/she can begin to vary or combine those patterns. Such combining and varying can lead to an endless list of movement possibilities. Such movements as hopping (a variation of jumping) or skipping (a combination of walking and hopping) may be attempted as soon as the movements involved are sufficiently perfected. More importantly, during the later childhood, the fundamental movements are combined and varied for adaptation to games, sports, and dances.

Once the mature level of a fundamental motor pattern has been achieved, very little change will occur in the technique of that movement (Gallahue, 1982). The ability of the performer to combine and vary these movements will, however, continue to improve. Furthermore, as the strength, speed, and related physiological components continue to improve, so will the related movement. These factors combined with an increased social interest make the first two or three years of later childhood a time of movement experimentation, especially concerning group games, sports, or dances. Most children, during later childhood, eagerly participate in a wide variety of such movement pursuits. The child normally places a reduced emphasis on the quality of the movement through approximately ten years of age. During this general or transitional phase of later childhood, the principal motivations to participate in movement activities are fun and social interaction.

This transitional **phase** of later childhood is brief, however, as participation in a variety of movement activities gives way to participation in a selection of favorites. At this same time, an increased emphasis is placed on the quality and the success of the movement. Many children, or even adults, never attain this level of interest in movement participation. From this point in an individual's level of motor development, continued improvement may be dependent on the child's willingness to practice the skill(s) involved.

Occasionally, by the age of ten or eleven years, a child may further specialize his/her movement endeavors. Although this is a condition generally considered to be characteristic of only adolescents or young adults, some children develop such interest or ability in a specific activity that the movement(s) becomes a primary focus in their life. In this case, the movement repertoire may be limited to three, two, or even one movement activity. Furthermore, considerable time and effort may be expended in attempting to perfect the specified movement(s). This occurs despite the fact that considerable movement proficiency is already likely to have been achieved.

SUMMARY OF THE MOTOR DEVELOPMENT OF CHILDREN

Gaining a more thorough understanding of human motor development is an integral facet in increasing our knowledge about the human being and his/her environment. Since motor development constantly interacts with the cognitive and affective domains of behavior, those aspects of our development reflect, in part, the constantly changing movement status of the individual as well as the intellectual and social-emotional characteristics. Knowledge of motor development can also be an important diagnostic tool. By understanding normal movement changes, aberrant development can be recognized early and be treated. Finally, creating age-appropriate movement activities to enhance the motor ability of children is dependent upon our knowledge of human motor development.

Our knowledge of normal motor development can be equally beneficial in programs involving the handicapped child. The handicapped child frequently develops motorically at a slower rate than non-handicapped children, but the sequence of development is generally the same. Application of these concepts may, in fact, be particularly important for the handicapped child, since he/she is frequently deprived of adequate movement experience. Without the appropriate intervention, this lack of movement opportunity can lead to further movement regression.

Particularly important movement changes occur during infancy. The infant reflexes are critical to early neurological diagnosis, survival and nourishment of the child, and the development of important voluntary movements of later life. These reflexes are unique forms of movement, since they are subcortical and involuntary.

Reaching and grasping are important forms of movement during infancy. These early attempts at manipulating objects in the environment are known as prehension. Although present at birth in a crude form, prehension disappears at about four weeks of life. This behavior reappears at approximately four months of life in what Bower (1977) refers to as Phase I reaching and grasping. By approximately six to seven months, Phase I reaching evolves into Phase II reaching. Phase I reaching is visually initiated but not controlled, with the Phase I grasp being visually initiated and controlled. Phase II reaching is visually monitored, while Phase II grasping is controlled by the sense of touch.

The development of locomotion also occurs during infancy. The earliest form of locomotion is known as creeping which initially may resemble a form of **sliding** the body across the floor. Crawling evolves from creeping and is a more upright, efficient form of moving from one point in space to another. Gaining upright posture is important to further locomotor development, since without standing, walking would not occur. By nine to ten months, most children can stand upright when supported. Soon after the child stands independently, the child will walk. The time of onset of all forms of locomotion is highly varied, since the amount of stimulation in each child's environment differs greatly.

During early childhood the fundamental motor patterns emerge. These patterns, which include running, jumping, throwing, catching, striking, and kicking, are extremely important for future motor development. It is these motor patterns that will be combined and varied to form the games, sports, and dances that will become important forms of activity in a later part of the child's life. Some children may never reach maturity in any of the fundamental motor patterns. Others, with instruction, practice, and the appropriate stimulation, may become adept at all of these movements. The developmental characteristics of the fundamental movement patterns can be accurately predicted, as the sequence of development is invariant, although the rate may vary greatly from one child to the next. Knowledge of these characteristics is necessary for the creation of logical developmental activities designed to enhance the child's movement performance.

By the time the child reaches later childhood, attempts may be made at varying and combining the fundamental patterns. To attempt such higher-level movement, a certain level of movement proficiency in the fundamental movement pattern is required. The child uses this new form of movement to experiment in an array of movement activities. During the early phase of later childhood, the child's movement objective is enjoying the movement and the social opportunities that the movement affords.

With continued improvement in movement skill, many children will develop favorite movement activities. Often, the child will then choose to participate in only those activities with a new movement objective. The child's movement focus may change from fun seeking to perfection of the movement. Skill, precision, and accuracy, which were once unimportant to the child, may become the primary movement objective. In some cases, in the latter portion of childhood, one movement activity may be isolated for the child's participation and perfection.

Endnote

Preparation of this chapter was supported in part by an Affirmative Action Faculty Development Award, California State Polytechnic University, granted to S. N. Siaw. Appreciation is given to Doctor Ruth Deich for helpful suggestions in the learning theory and implications sections of this chapter.

REFERENCES

Azarnoff, P., and Woody, P.D. (1981). Preparation of children for hospitalization in acute care hospitals in the U.S. *Pediatrics, 68,* 361–367.

Bandura, A., Grusec, J.E., and Menlove, F.L. (1967). Vicarious extinction of avoidant behavior. *Journal of Personality and Social Psychology, 5,* 16–23.

Bandura, A. (1973). *Aggression: A social learning analysis.* Englewood Cliffs, NJ: Prentice-Hall.

Barnett, L., and Kane, M. (1985). Individuals constraints on children's play. In M.G. Wade (Ed.), *Constraints on leisure,* 43–81. Springfield, IL: Charles C Thomas.

Bettelheim, B. (1987). *A good enough parent.* New York: Alfred A. Knopf.

Beach, F.A. (1945). Current concepts of play in animals. *American Naturalist, 79,* 523–541.

Bee, H. (1986). *The developing child* (4th ed.). New York: Harper and Row.

Berlyne, D.E. (1960). *Conflict, arousal, and curiosity.* New York: McGraw-Hill.

Berlyne, D.E. (1966). Curiosity and exploration. *Science, 153,* 25–33.

Berlyne, D.E. (1969). Laughter, humor, and play. In G.L. Lindzey and E. Aronson (Eds.), *Handbook of social psychology.* New York: Addison-Wesley, pp. 795–853.

Boone, D.R., and Hartman, B.H. (1972). The benevolent over-reaction. *Clinical Pediatrics, 11,* 268–271.

Bower, T.G.R. (1979). Visual development in the blind child. In V. Smith and J. Keen (Eds.), *Visual handicaps in children. Clinics in developmental medicine,* No. 73. London: Lippincott.

Bower, T. (1977). *A primer of infant development.* San Francisco: W.H. Freeman.

Bruner, J. (1970). The growth and structure of skill. In K.J. Connolly (Ed.), *Mechanisms of motor skill development.* London: Academic Press, pp. 63–93.

Chance, M.R.A., and Mead, A.P. (1955). Competition between feeding and investigation in the rat. *Behaviour, 8,* 174–182.

Cooper, J., Moodley, M., and Reynell, J. (1978). *Helping language development.* Bath, England: Arnold.

Cratty, B. (1979). *Perceptual and motor development in infants and children.* Englewood Cliffs, NJ: Prentice-Hall.

Czikszentmihalyi, M. (1974). *Flow: Studies of enjoyment.* Chicago: The University of Chicago Press.

Deci, E., and Ryan, R. (1985). *Intrinsic motivation and self-determination in human behavior.* New York: Plenum.

Dember, W.N., and Earl, R.W. (1957). Analysis of exploratory, manipulatory, and curiosity behaviors. *Psychological Review, 64,* 91–96.

Delacato, C. (1966). *Neurological organization of reading.* Springfield, IL: Charles C Thomas.

Dixon, J. (1979). The implications of attribution theory for therapeutic recreation service. *Therapeutic Recreation Journal, 8*(1), 3–11.

Dudley-Marling, C., Snider, V., and Tarver, S. (1982). Locus of control and learning disabilities: A review and discussion. *Perceptual and Motor Skills, 54*(4): 503–514.

Eimas, P.D. (1982). Speech perception: A view of the initial state of perceptual mechanisms. In J. Mehler, M. Garrett, and E. Walker (Eds.), *Perspectives on mental representation.* Hillsdale, NJ: Erlbaum.

Elkind, D. (1981). *The hurried child: Growing up too fast too soon.* Reading, MA: Addison-Wesley.

Elkins, P.D., and Roberts, M.C. (1983). Psychological preparation for pediatric hospitalization. *Clinical Psychology Review, 3,* 275–295.

Ellis, (1973). *Why people play.* Englewood Cliffs, NJ: Prentice-Hall.

Erikson, E. (1950). *Childhood and society.* New York: Norton.

Fine, A., Lehrer, B., and Feldis, D. (1982). Therapeutic recreation programming for autistic children. *Therapeutic Recreation Journal, 15,* 6–11.

Fein, G.G. (1981). Pretend play: An integrative review. *Child Development, 52,* 1095–1118.

Fromm, E. (1941). *Escape from freedom.* New York: Rinehart.

Gallahue, D. (1982). *Understanding motor development in children.* New York: Wiley.

Goldstein, G.I., and Lancy, D.F. (1985). Cognitive development in autistic children. In L.S. Siegel and F.J. Morrison (Eds.), *Cognitive development in atypical children.* New York: Springer-Verlag.

Goodman, J.D., and Sours, J.A. (1967). *The child mental status exam.* New York: Basic Books.

Groos, K. (1898). *The play of animals.* New York: Appleton.

Groos, K. (1901). *The play of man.* New York: Appleton.

Gulick, L. (1898). Some psychical aspects of physical exercise. *Popular Science Monthly, 58,* 793–805.

Hagen, J.W., and Hale, G.H. (1973). The development of attention in children. In A.D. Pick (Ed.), *Minnesota symposium on child psychology* (Vol. 7, pp. 117–140). Minneapolis, MN: University of Minnesota Press.

Hall, G.S. (1920). *Youth.* New York: Appleton.

Hill, P., and McCune-Nicolich, L. (1981). Pretend play and patterns of cognition in Down's syndrome children. *Child development, 52,* 611–617.

Hutt, C. (in press). Towards a taxonomy and conceptual model of play. In S.J. Hutt, D.A. Rogers, and C. Hutt (Eds.), *Developmental processes in early childhood.* London: Routledge and Kegan Paul.

Inhelder, B. (1968). *The diagnosis of reasoning in the mentally retarded.* New York: John Day.

Kleiber, D. (1979). Fate control and leisure attitudes. *Leisure Sciences, 2,* 239–248.

Kleiber, D., and Crandall, R. (1981). Leisure and work ethics and locus of control. *Leisure Sciences, 4,* 477–485.

Lamb, M.E., Easterbrooks, M.S., and Holden, G.W. (1980). Reinforcement and punishment among preschoolers: Characteristics, effects, and correlates. *Child Development, 51,* 1230–1236.

Lamb, M.E., and Roopnarine, J.L. (1979). Peer influences on sex-role development in preschoolers. *Child Development, 50,* 1219–1222.

Lazarus, M. (1883). *Die reize des spiels.* Berlin: Ferd, Dummlers Verlagsbuchhandlung.

Lepper, M., and Greene, D. (Eds.) (1978). *The hidden costs of reward: New perspectives on the psychology of human motivation.* Hillsdale, NJ: Erlbaum.

McClenaghan, B., and Gallahue, D. (1978). *Fundamental movement: A development and remedial approach.* Philadelphia: W.B. Saunders.

Michaelis, W. (1980). Fantasy, play, creativity, and mental health. In T.L. Goodale and P.A. Witt (Eds.), *Recreation and leisure: Issues in an era of change.* State College, Pennsylvania: Venture.

Olson, G.M., and Sherman, T. (1983). Attention, learning, and memory in infants. In P.H. Mussen (Ed.), *Handbook of child psychology* (Vol. 2, 4th Ed.). New York: Wiley.

Patrick, G.T.W. (1916). *The psychology of relaxation.* Boston: Houghton-Mifflin.

Payne, V.G., and Isaacs, L.D. (1987). *Human motor development: A lifespan approach.* Mountain View, CA: Mayfield.

Payne, V.G. (1985). *Infant reflexes in human motor development.* (Videotape.) Evanston, IL: Journal Films, Inc.

Peller, L.E. (1952). Models of children's play. *Mental Hygiene, 36,* 66–83.

Piaget, J. (1962). *Play, dreams, and imitation in childhood* (G. Gattegno and F.M. Hodgson, Trans.). New York: Norton.

Pittman, T., Emery, J., and Boggiano, A. (1982). Intrinsic and extrinsic motivational orientations: Reward induced changes in preference for complexity. *Journal of Personality and Social Psychology, 42,* (5), 789–797.

Rubin, K.H., Fein, G.G., and Vandenberg, B. (1983). Play. In P.H. Mussen (Ed.), *Handbook of child psychology.* New York: Wiley, pp. 693–774.

Rutter, M. (1978). Diagnosis and definition. In M. Rutter and E. Schopler (Eds.), *Autism: A reappraisal of concepts and treatment.* New York: Plenum.

Sandler, A., and Wills, D. (1965). Preliminary notes on play and mastery in the blind child. *Journal of Child Psychotherapy, 1,* 7.

Santrock, J.W. (1986). *Lifespan development* (2nd ed.). Dubuque, IA: Wm. C. Brown.

Schiller, F. (1954). *On the aesthetic education of man.* New Haven, CT: Yale University Press.

Schultz, D.D. (1965). *Sensory restriction: Effects on behavior.* New York: Academic Press.

Spencer, H. (1873). *Principles of psychology* (Vol. 2, 3rd ed.). New York: Appleton.

Sutton-Smith, B. (1966). Piaget on play: A critique. *Psychological Review, 73,* 104–110.

Sutton-Smith, B. (1985, October). The child at play. *Psychology Today,* Vol. 19.

Terr, L.C. (1985). Psychic trauma in children and adolescents. *Psychiatric Clinics of North America, 8,* 815–836.

Toeffler, A. (1971). *Future shock.* New York: Random House.

Waddington, C.A. (Ed.) (1968). *Symposium on theoretical biology* (Vol. 1). London: Aldine.

Wade, M. (Ed.) (1985). *Constraints on leisure.* Springfield, IL: Charles C Thomas.

Wade, M., and Hoover, J. (1985). Mental retardation as a constraint on leisure. In M. Wade (Ed.), *Constraints on leisure.* Springfield, IL: Charles C Thomas.

Weiner, B. (1985). *Human motivation.* New York: Springer.

White, R.W. (1959). Motivation reconsidered: The concept of competence. *Psychological Review, 66,* 297–323.

Wickstrom, R. (1983). *Fundamental motor patterns.* Philadelphia: Lea and Febiger.

Williams, H., Temple, I., and Bateman, J. (1979). A test to assess intrasensory and intersensory development of young children. *Perceptual and Motor Skills, 48,* 643–659.

Chapter 3

THERAPEUTIC RECREATION—
WHAT IS IT ALL ABOUT?

Nya Fine

Let me be the best I can.... Let me be me.... Let me in,
I want to play....

INTRODUCTION

Therapeutic recreation (T.R.), a viable avenue for providing leisure involvement for individuals with limitations, has grown tremendously over the last twenty years. Consequently, the outcome of these services have helped children, their parents, and other professionals recognize that recreation is a basic human need that must be met.

The purpose, practices, and the impact of therapeutic recreation will be discussed along with a review of legislation as it relates to therapeutic recreation. The following questions will be answered.

1. Therapeutic recreation—What is it all about?
2. What is the philosophical orientation of therapeutic recreation and how did it originate? What are the specific implications of the proposed philosophy on services for children?
3. How has recreation and persons with disabilities been viewed through various stages of history.
4. Where does one find therapeutic recreation programs?
5. What are the distinctions between the types of services provided?
6. How has legislation affected the lives and services of individuals with disabilities?

Back in the late 1950s, recreation theorists warned that due to reduced working hours, people would have to learn how to spend their time wholesomely (Rathborne and Lucas, 1970). As a result, recreation developed into a distinct discipline. Play, recreation, and leisure have been recognized by many as a viable avenue for the development of many skills in all people. All people, including those with disabilities, have the same basic needs for physical release, creative self-expression, social interaction, and to have fun. Thus, individuals with disabilities should have the opportunity to experience recreation. However, these important experiences are often denied (Fine, 1982).

Therapeutic recreation seeks to serve, not ignore, the needs of the physically disabled, mentally retarded, mentally ill, socially deviant, aged, and other populations with special needs.

Throughout the development of therapeutic recreation services, there existed a particular need to have a philosophical frame of reference. The term **therapeutic recreation** created many questions that needed to be addressed. As a result of these queries, there were many definitions, philosophies, and concepts formulated that were based on an individual's own philosophy of recreation, education, and experience. Is the philosophy of therapeutic recreation any different than the philosophy of recreation? Is not all recreation therapeutic in nature? All recreation is therapeutic in nature. However, the application and the utilization of recreational activities are the key elements in the development and delivery of therapeutic recreation services.

Therapeutic recreation harnesses a powerful source (recreation) and channels the energies, benefits, and results within the delivery of services and thus creates a viable avenue for leisure involvement for individuals who have limitations.

It was believed the term therapeutic recreation was first applied in 1938 by the Works Progress Administration to describe all recreational activities intended to serve the disabled, maladjusted or other institutionalized persons. With the growth of recreation programs in hospitals and institutions, recreation activities were based on prescriptions by the medical personnel. "Therapeutic recreation became a term applied to programs of prescribed recreation activities as well as to those programs in which persons with illnesses or disabilities participated" (Shivers and Fait, 1985, p. 7). Hospital recreation, medical recreation, recreation for the ill and handicapped, and recreation for special populations were terms utilized in the developmental stages of the profession.

Doctor William C. Menninger (1948) is one of the earliest professionals who made a statement in reference to the value of recreation with special populations:

It has been the privilege of many practicing medicine in psychiatry to have some very rewarding experiences in the use of recreation as an adjunctive method of treatment. Along with direct psychological help, hydrotherapy, shock, and insulin therapy, many of us have for years used various forms of education, recreation, and occupation in the treatment of our patients. Recreation has not only played an important part in the treatment program of many illnesses, but it has been a considerable factor in enabling former patients to remain well. (P. 304.)

Virginia Frye (1969) provided another perspective view of the impact of therapeutic recreation:

Therapeutic pertains to the art and science of healing. Recreation can be said to be therapeutic only to the extent that specific beneficial efforts of a recreative experience can be identified and predicted. It is in relation to the specific medical treatment that therapeutic recreation becomes a specialized area within the total recreation profession. (P. 12.)

Since Doctor Menninger's thoughts on the value of recreation for the mentally ill and Frye's point of view, many different perspectives have developed. Although diverse, these perspectives contained similar ideas that incorporated both: the value of recreation for fun and rehabilitation purposes. Many professionals have spent countless hours searching, discussing, and developing a conclusive philosophical statement that the entire profession could utilize.

In May 1982, a statement was adopted by the Board of Directors of the National Therapeutic Recreation Society (NTRS), a branch of the National Recreation and Parks Association. NTRS is one of the professional organizations that fosters the development and advancement of therapeutic recreation. The philosophy states:

Leisure, including recreation and play are inherent aspects of the human experience. The importance of appropriate leisure involvement has been documented throughout history. More recently, research has addressed the value of leisure involvement in human development, in social and family relationships, and in general as an important aspect of the quality of life. Some human beings have disabilities, illnesses or social conditions which limit their full participation in the normative social structure of society. These individuals with limitations have the same human rights and needs for leisure involvement.

The purpose of therapeutic recreation is to facilitate the development, maintenance, and expression of an appropriate leisure life-style for individuals with physical, mental, emotional or social limitations. This purpose is accomplished through the provision of professional programs and services which assist the individual in eliminating barriers to leisure, developing leisure skills and attitudes, and optimizing leisure involvement. (NTRS, 1982.)

Therapeutic recreation utilizes three areas of service: therapy, leisure education, and recreation participation. When and where each of the services is provided depends on the assessment of client's needs. A client may need programs from all three areas of services, while another client may need assistance in one area.

The **therapy** service focuses on the improvement of functional behaviors that limit or inhibit leisure involvement. The therapeutic recreation professional determines what individuals require to enable them to be involved in meaningful leisure experiences. In this role, the therapeutic recreator is an integral member of the interdisciplinary treatment team, and with the development of the treatment goals, leisure-related functional behaviors and leisure ability are incorporated.

The **leisure education** service provides individuals with the opportunity to acquire and develop leisure skills and behaviors. This service area is very important, since a majority of individuals with limitations lack the skills necessary to engage in leisure experiences.

The third service area is **recreation participation.** All individuals are entitled to recreation opportunities. The therapeutic recreator provides opportunities which will allow voluntary involvement in recreation skills and activities.

The philosophy adopted by NTRS supported that recreation is an important aspect in everyone's life-style. Therapeutic recreation provides the opportunity for individuals with disabilities to express themselves via the use of recreation. However, the position statement differs from previous definitions, in that the statement incorporates how therapeutic recreation services can be utilized. Assessment of the individual's needs provides the development of the program plan, and the planned utilization of recreation is the key ingredient in the delivery of the services. Whether the process is for fun or a planned therapeutic intervention, all activities are based on the individual being served.

The philosophical base of the profession is and will continue to evolve, resulting in a better understanding which will increase the identity of therapeutic recreation.

PHILOSOPHY OF THERAPEUTIC RECREATION AS IT RELATES TO CHILDREN

The philosophical statement has definite implications to all disabled individuals, including children. It is apparent that the philosophy is a synthesis of where many professionals perceive the focus of therapeutic recreation services should be. Nevertheless, voids do exist when dealing with children. Although the philosophy differentiates between the various areas of services (therapy, leisure education, recreation participation), it does not focus on the process (techniques) utilized in working with children.

Throughout the book it has been discussed that it is important for a child to be involved in fun, productive, free time. Professionally, we feel strongly that play can contribute to the well-being (physical, mental, social, emotional). We must also recognize that a major contribution of therapeutic recreation is that it allows a child to be involved in a fun activity which may enhance learning. Dixon (Chap. 4) suggests that recreation can serve as an important resource for a child by providing accessibility information to leisure opportunities. All the services of therapeutic recreation are valuable, but the main goal for a child should focus on the awareness and acquisition of skills that would enable a child to participate in self-selected activities. Therefore, it is imperative that this goal be incorporated into all programs when working with children.

HISTORY OF RECREATION AND THE TREATMENT OF PERSONS WITH DISABILITIES

Throughout history, it has been documented that even the earliest society had some form of recreation. Dance, music, arts, and games were important aspects of the primitive cultures. From a historical perspective, let us look at how recreation and the attitudes toward the disabled were viewed.

In the primitive ages man lived in an environment that placed a high priority on survival skills. Recreation was utilized as a means of obtaining and improving survival skills through games. Since survival skills were the utmost importance, those who did not possess these skills had no support.

In ancient civilization it was believed that the use of recreational activities was used as a form of therapy. Music, reading, poems, and walks in the gardens were planned or prescribed activities by the medicine men, priests, and healers. In early societies of Egypt, Greece, Rome, and China, they all had well-organized systems of care and treatment for afflicted people (Shivers and Fait, 1985). As time progressed so did the belief that disabilities were caused by evil spirits. Consequently, it became an accepted fact by many that the only way to destroy the spirit was to kill the individual (Beyer, 1979).

The Greek civilization was concerned with the treatment of the whole person, both the mind and body. Music, exercise, and other activities were used to relax the mind and body. Hippocrates was the first to endeavor in understanding disabilities. He taught that illnesses and disabilities were not a form of punishment from God. However, the emphasis remained on treating the well person to being more healthy.

The philosophy of taking care of the sick evolved in the Roman era. A hospital was established to take care and provide assistance to the injured. Music, games, and other activities were used to relax the mind and body. However, at the same time, the Romans did not accept disabled individuals. They frequently placed defective children in baskets which were then thrown into the river or abandoned on a public street. It was quite common for someone to come along and take a child and raise the child as a slave (Beyer, 1979).

A change occurred during the fourteenth and fifteenth centuries. Leisure and play were being viewed as evil and were not to be partaken. The attitudes toward the disabled person fluctuated between acceptance and rejection. The church provided custodial care in the monasteries, but there was an inherent attitude problem. Through various teachings, the birth of a handicapped child was accepted proof that the parents were involved in witchcraft or had wicked thoughts. Consequently, the deformed or abnormal child was regarded with great fear as if a family was being punished by God. It was also during this time when a large number of men and women who were handicapped were burned as witches.

As the Renaissance era began, social events and village activities made a significant contribution to the people of the villages. There were great advances in scientific thinking in which doctors discovered some of the causes and symptoms of physical disabilities. Thus, fewer people believed that the disabled were possessed by evil spirits. Custodial support was to be found which brought an end to confinement for the physically disabled and the mentally retarded. However, the disabled population still remained the outcasts of society. During this time many of the disabled were in constant demand as a court jesters or village fools. In fact, today's view of one who exhibits deviant behavior as either a public nuisance or a sub-human object stemmed from this era (Carter, Van Andel, and Robb, 1985).

During the seventeenth century the highlights of leisure activities consisted of adults and children partaking in festivals and games. Involvement in play promoted an understanding for children in learning their roles in society, while adults used leisure outlets for relaxation and diversion from work (Butler, Gotts, and Quisenberry, 1978).

When the English settlers began their way to the New World, the disabled settlers were prohibited from the journey. Life in the New World for disabled citizens consisted primarily of being farmed out for assistance or for basic board and care. The young government did accept its responsibility for the welfare of the soldiers and civilians who were permanently injured during the Revolutionary War. These individuals were accepted as dependent on the government or the members of the community. It appears that a definite difference existed between the war heroes and the general disabled population.

The negative attitudes and barriers of the disabled also existed in the early days of this nation. However, there were some prominent individuals who did not let their physical disabilities stop their great contributions to society. Peter Stuyvesant had lost a leg during the war and wore a peg leg. He was a successful leader and became the first governor of the Dutch colony of Amsterdam (New York). Stephen Hopkins, an individual afflicted with cerebral palsy, was one of the signing members of the Declaration of Independence.

The Americans and the British began treating the disabled with more consideration in the eighteenth century. This was due to the influence of the Protestant attitude. This attitude reflected that each individual must strive for perfection and acceptance for all. Consequently, this lead to a change towards helping the ill and the disabled.

During the eighteenth and nineteenth centuries the focus began to change from primarily custodial care to attempts of basic rehabilitation. Jean Itard, a French physician, initiated the first documented scientific attempt at habilitating a mentally retarded child. The now famous story of the Boy of Averon was initiated through Itard's efforts. Although his efforts did not demonstrate significant growth in the child's cognitive and language abilities, the boy displayed significant growth in his adaptive behavior. In 1773, an asylum for the mentally ill was established, and a private school for the deaf evolved in the early 1800s. Between

1829–1832, schools were founded in New York, Pennsylvania, and Massachusetts.

Samuel Howe organized the first school for the blind, later called the Perkins Institute. Thomas Hopkins Gallaudet was one of the first involved in working with deaf. He became involved with a neighbor's child who became deaf at the age of four. Through his efforts he taught her how to be independent and self-sufficient. In 1817, he founded the Hartford School for the Deaf, and in 1864, his brother, Edward Gallaudet, opened a college in Washington, D.C. for the deaf. Although services began to develop for persons who were blind and deaf, people with other disabilities still did not have the same opportunities. These individuals remained the responsibility of their family.

Various physicians utilized planned activities such as gardening, reading, and music as a form of treatment for their patients. Florence Nightingale introduced recreational opportunities for hospitalized soldiers. She utilized music and pets as a form of treatment. Before World War I structured recreation programs were virtually nonexistent. Institutions in the early 1900s organized programs directed at alleviating overcrowding and to provide human care and resident services. Activities were utilized to consume time, prevent boredom, and prevent the occurrence of behavior problems (Wehman, 1979).

Various charitable organizations were being organized to assist the disabled. President Hoover in his first year of presidency was involved with the development of a conference for the protection of children. In this conference national goals for children were established. One of these goals stated that:

> [E]very child who is blind, deaf, crippled, or otherwise physically or mentally handicapped, that such measures as early diagnosis, care, treatment, and the training of the child will be evaluated. Through the training the individual may become an asset to society rather than a liability. Expenses of these services should be met publicly when they cannot be met privately. (Dean, 1972)

The American Red Cross headed one of the major thrusts in providing recreation for the disabled in the armed forces. The position relating to leisure services stated:

> [R]ecreation is helpful in sustaining and cultivating morale favorable to treatment and in developing human capacities. We do not consider that recreation is therapy. We do consider that it should be an added constructive force in the recovery of the patient. Perhaps that is what

other people call therapeutic, but that it should be part of the medical treatment is not one of the basic fundamental principles of the American Red Cross. (Rathborne and Lucas, 1979, p. 11)

When World War I began, the American Red Cross established the Division of Recreation. Along with the initiation of these services in the armed forces, recreation programs began to appear in state hospitals. It was at this time that recreation really began to be viewed for its therapeutic benefits. As a consequence of World War II, there was an apparent attitude change toward all disabled individuals. This was due to the many new disabled veterans the country was about to accept.

In 1945, the Veterans Administration established recreation services as part of their programs. Hospitals provided appropriate recreation activities that enabled patients with physical or mental limitations to participate. Recreators modified the activities to meet the special needs (Shivers and Fait, 1985). Doctor John Davis also built into the care system his ideas of sports, prescribed exercises, and graduated activities.

Another historical milestone was the emergence of organizations promoting the development and growth of the therapeutic recreation profession. During the late 1940s and early 1950s three important organizations were formally established. These organizations were the American Recreation Society (ARS, 1949), the Recreation Therapy Section of the American Association for Health, Physical Education, and Recreation (RTS–AAHPER, 1952), and the National Association for Recreation Therapists, Inc. (NART, 1953) (O'Morrow, 1986). These organizations merged to form the National Recreation and Parks Association (NRPA). This change unified the park, recreation, and leisure service movement. In October 1966, the National Therapeutic Recreation Society became a part of the National Recreation and Parks Association. With the birth of this professional organization, a major thrust of the profession evolved. It did not occur overnight and the future direction of the field continued to develop.

The American Therapeutic Recreation Association (ATRA, 1985) is a recently established professional organization concerned with the development and the future direction of therapeutic recreation. Although NTRS and ATRA have different views, they both are very critical to the future development and direction of the profession. Professional societies represent the hearts and souls of the field. Consequently, both of these organizations have attempted to ensure quality as well as to voice the concerns of the field as a whole. The bottom line is that these organizations provide the professionals with the unity and dedication it takes to transform a young, powerful, and ever-growing profession. This will ensure that the profession will continue to evolve as a valuable and prominent profession that can enhance the lives of many.

THERAPEUTIC RECREATION— WHERE DOES ONE FIND THESE PROGRAMS?

Most therapeutic recreation programs do not function independently but operate within a system that provides a specific type of care or service (O'Morrow, 1980). These services are often found in a clinical or a community-based settings. It is imperative that parents and other professionals become aware of these services so that they can tap into all possible resources for direction and assistance.

Clinical Settings

In the clinical settings, the therapeutic recreation specialist looks at the behavioral and functional skills for the individual and how they affect their leisure. Carl Rogers, who developed the client-centered therapy, believed that the helping professional should be supportive, empathetic, and genuine. Through this mode the therapist allows the client to feel secure and to grow at his/her own pace. The client-oriented approach is often applied in therapeutic recreation.

Therapeutic recreation services may be found in the following clinical settings: general hospitals, physical rehabilitation centers, extended and long-term health care facilities, private and public psychiatric facilities, residential or school centers, and community health centers.

The medical-clinical model, a widely accepted approach, is "characterized by a doctor-centered, illness-oriented approach to patient care and treatment. Treatment is directed at just rehabilitating the disease, rather than the whole person" (O'Morrow, 1980, p. 169). In this type of setting the doctor is the one who prescribes the treatment and how it will be done. The professional staff is involved only in the delivery of the services as ordered by the physician.

This model is still adhered to in some settings, but many are incorporating an interdisciplinary approach to treatment. In this approach the entire staff of professionals are involved with the formation of goals and treatment plan for the client. An interdisciplinary team will consist of doctors, nurses, psychologists, therapeutic recreation specialists (may be referred to as recreation therapist, activity therapist), physical therapist, occupational therapists, social workers, and other individuals who are involved with the treatment of the individual.

Each discipline contributes to the various goals that are formulated for the client. The therapeutic recreationist is responsible for incorporating the importance of leisure in the context of the total treatment plan (Peterson and Gunn, 1984).

Several institutions in the United States have demonstrated the utilization of therapeutic recreation services as a key ingredient in the multidisciplinary setting. Casa Colina Hospital, located in southern California, has a national reputation as a rehabilitation institute as well as recognition for their therapeutic recreation programs. Therapeutic recreation programs are part of the overall rehabilitation process.

Community Recreation

Leisure time and recreational activities play a major role in the lives of most community residents, and a large number of these residents are disabled. With the movement of deinstitutionalization and integration, there is a greater need for the expansion of community-based programs. Participation in recreational activities may well be one of the easiest ways a person with a disability can become active in the community.

It is the responsibility of the public, private, and voluntary sectors to provide recreation programs for all persons, including the disabled. Active participation in planned recreational activities in the community can have positive results for all of those involved. These programs should and must be provided. The responsibility is no longer just a moral issue but, in many ways, a legal obligation.

For the exceptional child it is important to be involved in recreation and leisure experiences at an early age. The results from participating in these experiences can foster growth in the physical, cognitive, emotional, and social areas of the child (Piaget, 1962). One of the main goals for a child involved in recreation is to have fun, but the benefits from participating in these activities are limitless. Recreation can provide the child with the opportunity to acquire leisure skills and to function in an integrated setting. The greatest gift we as parents and professionals can give a child is the ability to function as independently as possible. There exists a need for a variety of programs for the disabled population, but the ultimate goal of any program should be that of preparing a person for independent and normative functioning (Wolfensberger, 1972).

The community-based programs must also be based on the individual's needs and must provide opportunities to participate in self-selected activities. When an individual demonstrates the abilities to participate with his/her mainstream peers, integrated services are essential. However, for those who need more structure and assistance, special recreation programs should be provided.

Programs have to exist before the disabled population can participate. During the last ten years there have been many local level recreation programs initiated and expanded, but there still exists a great void in providing community leisure services for the disabled. There are many reasons for this dilemma: funding, lack of accessible facilities, and the lack of transportation. However, the biggest factor appears to be the lack of awareness concerning the needs of the disabled members in the community.

Humphrey (1979) sees the role of a community therapeutic recreation specialist as a catalytic resource leader. The therapeutic recreation specialist may have many roles to fulfill in the community. She/he may function as a consultant, an advocate, an educator-teacher, but the most important role is to provide appropriate recreation programs for the disabled. Understanding the capabilities, determining the activities, and the leadership modifications necessary for participation creates the need for a therapeutic recreation specialist within the community sector.

There are those individuals within the recreation field who believe there is no need for a therapeutic recreation specialist in the community setting. There are recreation professionals who are competently prepared to provide services for the disabled. However, they appear to be a minority. It is essential that colleges prepare all recreation students to serve those with special needs. Thus, more than one course is needed to suffice this great need. The future of providing these services depends on the colleges and professionals that exist now. Now is the time to move in this direction, not merely to discuss it. The end result would be a close working relationship between the community recreator and the therapeutic recreation specialist which would create quality and diverse programming for the community members.

What programs exist in the community? Primary sources should be found in public recreation and parks departments or voluntary agencies. Voluntary agencies such as the Association for Retarded Citizens, Young Men's and Women's Christian Associations, and Easter Seals Societies sponsor recreation programs specifically designed for disabled children. Furthermore, community colleges and universities provide various types of programs ranging from motor development services to special recreation programs for various disabling conditions. Local community colleges offer programs as well.

One should check into the community for additional services offered by religious agencies. One of the services offered by the Jewish community center in Mobile, Alabama, was a social recreation program for learning disabled children. In another community a local group of dedicated college and high school students organized a social recreation group for a wide range of disabled children. The purpose was primarily for fun. In addition to the inherent value gained by the children through these experiences, the community experienced exposure to the disabled children and gained a learning experience which made the community more sensitive and aware.

Another resource may be found in hospitals or special group organizations. For example, a summer recreation program for children with myelomeningocele (spina bifida) was offered to the clients of the Myelomeningocele Clinic at the University Affiliated Cincinnati Center for Developmental Disorders (CCDD). The program provided experiences in many activities that the children had never participated in. Thus, through these experiences the children gained independence and the ability to carry out a leisure life-style.

There remains a void in the provision of recreation programs for the disabled members in the community. Parents, professionals, and the disabled members of the community must voice their needs. It is the community's responsibility to be aware and provide these needed services.

LAWS AND THE DISABLED

*Let us not look back in anger, nor look ahead in fear, but around
in awareness.*

JAMES TURBER

When discussing access to services and activities for children with disabilities, legislation and litigation come into the discussion. Burgdorf (1980) used two words to sum up society's method of dealing with the disabled. The two words are **segregation** and **inequality**. For these two reasons, the disabled community and their advocates have engaged in a long uphill battle for equality.

This section will provide:

1. A historical overview of major legislative actions that have influenced the disabled community.
2. An analysis of P.L. 93-112: P.L. 94-142 and their contributions to the lives of the disabled.
3. The need to promote advocacy.

When reviewing literature pertaining to legislation that has evolved, one can gather that a number of these laws were established solely to assist the disabled. It is also true that a great number of these laws were enacted between 1970 and 1975. Thirty-six federal bills relating to the disabled were passed in the year 1974 alone (O'Morrow and Reynolds, 1985).

Although many federal laws are passed annually, there are still many bills that die in committees. Legal advocacy groups have been formulated to disseminate information in regards to the disabled population. The advocacy groups have been and will continue to be a major factor in the passing of legislative acts pertaining to the disabled.

Constitutional rights are guaranteed to all citizens under the U.S. Constitution. Two of the most important clauses are the right to have equal protection under the law and the right to due process. The equal protection clause of the Fourteenth Amendment requires that the government will treat all of its citizens without prejudice or discrimination. Due process provides that every person has the right to be treated with fundamental fairness; that his/her life, liberty, and property cannot be taken away, except in extreme unusual circumstances (Burgdorf, 1980).

In 1954, in the case, **Brown** vs. **Board of Education**, the Supreme Court decision stated that separate education of the races in public education is inherently unequal and, therefore, forbidden by the equal protection doctrine. This initiated the widespread civil rights reforms. In the 1950s there was an abundance of national legislation passed, much intended to ensure that mentally retarded individuals would receive an education and training (Stewart, 1978).

The government has been involved with the health-related services since the eighteenth century, and, through the years, both the federal and state governments have developed a delivery system for these services. In 1918, the Smith-Sears Veterans Rehabilitation Act became the first nationwide act to provide vocational training and the placement for veterans. This act was the predecessor to the development of services for all of the disabled individuals.

The Vocational Rehabilitation Act (1920) provided the disabled individual with counseling, vocational training, and placement which was funded through federal grants to each state. The government began to take an active role in human programs when the Social Security Act of 1935 was enacted. This act established a permanent pension for the aged and later included the unemployed, young children and the disabled.

In the 1950s and 1960s a great deal of legislation and national support was seen. Many national organizations concerned with various disabling conditions were formulated and, over the next two decades, became engaged in large-scale lobbying efforts to pass beneficial legislation (Burgdorf, 1980).

The Architectural Barrier Act of 1968 (P.L. 90-480) mandated that any public building to be structured, leased, altered, and which was financed by or on behalf of the United States government must meet the standards of accessibility, subsequent to the date of enactment. This law was passed in 1968 but was not enforced until 1973. Although this law has drastically improved the mobility of the disabled citizens, accessibility is still a serious obstacle.

In the 1970s the efforts of the disabled population and national organizations made large gains in equality through litigation. In January 1971, the Pennsylvania Association of Retarded Citizens (PARC) brought a major class-action suit against the Commonwealth of Pennsylvania. PARC and parents of the mentally retarded children were seeking judgment on the statues pertaining to the exclusion of mentally retarded children from programs of education and training in public schools. The court's decision based on the Fourteenth Amendment declared that it was unconstitutional to discriminate against the mentally retarded, solely because of a disability. This landmark case established the educational rights of persons with disabilities (Stewart, 1978).

As the laws were being changed and created, the disabled population were gradually gaining in the uphill battle for equality. The principle sources for rights to service for disabled individuals are Section 504 of the Rehabilitation Act of 1973, the Education of All Handicapped Children Act of 1975, the Developmentally Disabled Assistance, and the Bill of Rights Act (Frakt and Rankin, 1982).

The Rehabilitation Act of 1973 (P.L. 93-112) had a great impact on recreation services. Recreation did not have any real implications until this time. Title VI of the Civil Rights Act (1964), which is often referred to as the Handicapped Bill of Rights, and Sections 504 encompass all aspects of the handicapped person's life, including the right to participate in recreational activities (Shivers and Fait, 1985).

Historically, people have not associated the word **discrimination** with the disabled, but with the Rehabilitation Act of 1973 (P.L. 93-112), the disabled were recognized as a class of people who have the right to education, employment, and access to society.

Probably the most important aspects of the law were: (1) its emphasis on serving the most severely disabled; (2) its emphasis on expanding the freedom of disabled individuals through the removal of architectural, transportation, and employment barriers; and (3) its establishment of a civil rights provision for the handicapped (DeLoach and Greer, 1981).

P.L. 93-112

> **Section 501.** The federal government established an Interagency Committee of Handicapped Employees. This committee is responsible for affirmative action plans for the employment of the disabled. It encourages state governments to hire and promote the disabled and is responsible for an annual report on the hiring and promoting of the disabled person.
>
> **Section 502.** The Architectural and Transportation Compliance Board is responsible for making sure that the federal agencies comply with architectural standards, the removal of architectural barriers in public facilities, and the promotion of barrier-free facilities for public and non-profit organizations.
>
> **Section 503.** Organizations that have contracts with the federal government must take affirmative action in employing and promoting qualified disabled individuals.
>
> **Section 504.** This states that no handicapped individual can be secluded from participating in or be denied the benefits or subject to discrimination under any program actively receiving federal funds.

When the Rehabilitation Act of 1973 was passed, disabled individuals and their advocates knew a major milestone had been reached, but little was known of the implications and how these regulations were to be enforced.

It took four years after Section 504 (P.L. 93-112) became law before HEW (Health, Education and Welfare) came up with the first set of regulations to implement the legislative act. These regulations were established after the disabled and advocacy became visible and vocal. Thus, Congress passed amendments to the 1973 Rehabilitation Act of 1978. Since the state-federal vocational rehabilitation system was required to serve the most severely handicapped, Congress provided procedural conditions regarding complaints filed under Sections 501, 502, 503, and 504. Section 505 provides for the reimbursement of attorney fees under certain circumstances.

The Development Disabilities Act of 1975 stated that persons with developmental disabilities have rights to services in the least restrictive environment. The Comprehensive Rehabilitation, Comprehensive Services, and Developmental Disabilities Amendments of 1978 also included provision for comprehensive independent living services. This law was designed to meet the needs of individuals so severely disabled that they did not have the potential for employment but would benefit from services designed to assist them to independence (DeLoach and Greer, 1981).

There has been gradual and positive gains made by the Supreme Court concerning various litigation cases, but the courts as a whole are still not up to par. In 1979, the **Southeastern** vs. **Davis** case questioned the validity of Section 504 and the regulations that were endorsed in 1978.

The case was concerned with whether Section 504 of the Rehabilitation Act forbids professional schools that are federally funded from imposing physical qualifications for admission to their clinical training programs (Burgdorf and Spicer, 1983).

Ms. Davis, a hearing-impaired applicant to the nursing program at Southeastern College, was not granted admission. The court decided that her disability would prevent her from functioning sufficiently in the nursing program. The court felt that the school's decision to exclude her was not discriminatory based on the meaning of Section 504. It was evident that Ms. Davis's civil rights were not clearly understood. The civil rights movement for the disabled has and will continue to grow stronger, and the struggles for legal equality will continue at all administrative and judicial levels.

The Education Act for All Handicapped Children of 1975, called P.L. 94-142, became a reality in providing education for all handicapped children. All handicapped children between the ages of 3 and 21 must now be included in a free public education program.

It is the responsibility of parents and professionals to be aware of the significant implications of this important legislative act.

P.L. 94-142

Here are six major provisions and procedural safeguards:

1. All handicapped children shall receive a free appropriate public education in an educational setting that is in the least restrictive environment.
2. Individualized education programs will be developed by a representative of a local education agency, the teacher, parents or guardian of the child.
3. In school-placement procedures and in fact in any decisions concerning a handicapped child's school, there will be prior consultation with the child's parents or guardians.
4. The right to due process, which protects the individual from erroneous classification, inappropriate labeling, and guarantees him an education equal to the non-handicapped.
5. Protects against discriminatory testing in diagnosis, tests, and other evaluation material used in placing handicapped children. Tests will be prepared and administered in such a way as not to be racially or culturally discriminatory, and they will be presented in the child's negative tongue.
6. State and local educational agencies shall take steps to ensure that handicapped children have available to them the variety of programs and services available to non-handicapped children, including . . . industrial arts, home economics, and vocational education (Stewart, 1978).

P.L. 94-142 requires that an individualized education program (IEP) be designed for each child. Within this IEP the programs that are needed to ensure the total education of the child are provided including, if deemed necessary, "related services." These services can be therapeutic recreation, physical therapy, and occupational therapy. P.L. 94-142 marks the first time recreation has been included in educational legislation (Reynolds and O'Morrow, 1985).

Coyne (1981) states that "recreation is authorized when assessment determines that leisure services are required to assist the child. After this need is determined, a statement of the specific recreation services to be provided to the child along with related goals, instructional objectives, evaluation procedures, and timeliness which must be included in the child's IEP" (p. 5). One can see how important assessment is in providing the appropriate services for the child. In this act, recreation incorporates the assessment of leisure function, therapeutic recreation services, recreation programs in the school and community, and leisure education (Reynolds and O'Morrow, 1985).

P.L. 99-457

Education of the Handicapped Act Amendments of 1986 emphasize the provision of special education services to handicapped infants and toddlers (both through age 2). This law encourages each state to develop a comprehensive statewide program of early intervention services for handicapped infants, toddlers, and families. Early interventions services will include an individualized family service plan written by a multidisciplinary team including the parents. By the 1990–1991 school year, only those states who have developed a comprehensive program will be eligible to receive federal grants for handicapped infants and toddlers (Heward and Orlansky, 1988).

The legislative milestones that have been accomplished have not been done overnight or without major setbacks. There has been gradual and positive changes. Voices have to continue to be heard, not just by the families and advocates, but by the disabled individuals, themselves. Changes do take time—time to educate and time to make society aware that these needs exist. Not only must we continue to educate the general community but encourage and support the professionals who lobby for laws, create laws, enforce laws, and make decisions concerning these laws.

ADVOCACY

We have reviewed some of the major legislation that has influenced the disabled. What is the next step? It is the parents' obligation to understand, and it is the professional's obligation to inform the disabled and their families. One can see how important it is for all professionals, including the therapeutic recreation specialist, to be aware of these laws and to assist the family whenever possible. Sometimes, families are not aware of the services to which they are entitled. When the services are made known, it is also the parents' responsibility to check into the appropriate resources to find out what services are available. Disabled individuals and their families can become easily frustrated in their efforts to obtain the services and benefits they are entitled to. This is due to the difficulties in understanding the responsibilities of various agencies and the nature and scope of the program they administer (Protection Advocacy, Inc., 1986).

Advocacy may be needed in order to obtain the services and benefits that are entitled to your child. Here are some advocacy strategies which may assist in obtaining these services as well as protecting one's rights.

- Be assertive. You have the right to receive services.
- If you do not understand, ask questions. You have the right to obtain information from the agency in a form you understand. If you do not understand, ask for further explanation and ask as many questions as needed.
- Share information. Your opinions are valuable, so do not be afraid to voice your opinion. You know the needs of your child as well as the professionals who evaluated your child.
- Be prepared. Be sure you know what you want and the reasons for it. Make a list of questions you want answered.
- Be willing to listen. After you have requested a service or asked a question, listen to the response. Make sure that the response answers your question.
- Keep records. Keep all papers concerning your child's case together in a file. Keep a diary or log of verbal contact, and write the name of each person you spoke to and when you spoke to that person.
- Obtain assistance. If you feel uncomfortable about a situation, do not go alone. Take a friend, a relative, or a representative from an advocacy organization. You have the right to take someone with you, and that person is often supportive and keeps you focused on the problem (Protection Advocacy, Inc., 1986).

Look in your local areas for special-interest groups or advocacy groups. In California, there is an advocacy group called the Protection Advocacy, Inc., which protects the civil, legal, and service rights of the disabled. They provide information for and legal representation of disabled persons.

If there is not an advocacy agency within your area, each state has a

(1) bureau of developmental disabilities, (2) state protection, and (3) advocacy agency. Here are a few organizations that are also involved with the advocacy of the disabled.

> National Council of the Handicapped
> Room 3116, Switzer Building
> 330 C. Street, S.W.
> Washington, DC 20005

This council was appointed by the president and confirmed by the Senate. It consists primarily of individuals who have disabilities or parents of individuals with disabilities. The council was developed under the Rehabilitation Law of 1973 and reviews all laws, programs, and policies that influence the disabled.

> Office of Civil Rights
> 330 Independence Avenue, S.W.
> Washington, D.C. 20005

If we are to continue to make progressive gains in the civil rights movement of the disabled, then it is extremely important that we (disabled, parents, professionals, advocates) continue to voice the needs that still exist within our society.

SUMMARY

Therapeutic recreation services are extremely important for disabled individuals, especially children. A major contribution of these services is that it can assist the child in acquiring awareness and skills for engagement in self-selected activities, thus creating a leisure life-style. The philosophy, purpose, and scope have been discussed to inform the reader of the historical development of therapeutic recreation as well as the future of this profession.

Major legislation has assisted the disabled in gaining equality in society. However, there still exists a void in the enforcement of these legislative laws. It is the responsibility of parents, professionals, and the disabled individuals, themselves, to be knowledgeable of the laws which protect their rights. Advocacy is and will remain an important thrust for the protection of equal rights and opportunities for the disabled.

REFERENCES

Beyer, G. (1979). *Physical disabilities.* New York: Franklin Watts.

Burgdorf, R. (1980). *The legal rights of handicapped persons: Cases, materials and text.* Baltimore: Paul H. Brookes.

Burgdorf, R. Jr., and Spicer, P. (1983 supplement). *The legal rights of handicapped persons: Cases, materials and text.* Baltimore: Paul H. Brookes.

Butler, A., Gotts, E., and Quisenberry, N. (1978). *Play as development.* Columbus: Merrill.

Carter, M., Andel, G., and Robb, G. (1985). *Therapeutic recreation: A practical approach.* St. Louis: Times Mirror/Mosby.

Coyne, P. (1981). The status of recreation as a related service in PL 94-142. *Therapeutic Recreation Journal, 15,* 3, 5.

Dean, R. (1972). *New life for millions: Rehabilitation for Americans disabled.* New York: Hastings House.

De Loach, C., and Greer, B. (1981). *Adjustment to severe physical disability.* New York: McGraw-Hill.

Fine, A. (1982). Therapeutic recreation: An aspect of rehabilitation for exceptional children. *The lively arts,* 4.

Frakt, A., and Rankin, J. (1982). *The law of parks, recreation, resources, and leisure services.* Salt Lake City, Utah: Brighton.

Frye, V. (1969). A philosophical statement on therapeutic recreation services. *Therapeutic Recreation Journal, 3,* 11–14.

Heward, W., and Orlansky, M. (1988). *Exceptional children.* Columbus: Merill.

Humphrey, F. (1970). Therapeutic recreation and the 1970's. *Therapeutic Recreation Annual, 7,* 8–13.

Kraus, R. (1983). *Therapeutic recreation service, principles and practices.* Philadelphia: Sanders.

Menninger, W. (1948). Recreation and mental health, 340.

O'Morrow, G. (1980). *Therapeutic recreation: A helping profession.* Reston: Reston.

O'Morrow, G. (1986). The first twenty years. Arlington, VA: *National Therapeutic Recreation Society.*

Peterson, C., and Gunn, S. (1978). *Therapeutic recreation program design: Principles and procedures.* Englewood Cliffs, NJ: Prentice-Hall.

Peterson, C., and Gunn, S. (1984, 2nd ed.). *Therapeutic recreation program design: Principles and procedures.* Englewood Cliffs, NJ: Prentice-Hall.

Philosophical position statement of the National Therapeutic Recreation Society (1982). Arlington, VA: *National Therapeutic Recreation Society.*

Piaget, J. (1962). *Play, dreams, and imitation in childhood.* London: Heinemann.

Protection Advocacy (1986).

Rathborne, J., and Lucas, C. (1970). *Recreation in total rehabilitation.* Springfield, IL: Charles C Thomas.

Reynolds, R., and O'Morrow, G. (1985). *Problems, issues, and concepts in therapeutic recreation.* Englewood Cliffs, NJ: Prentice-Hall.

Shivers, J., and Fait, H. (1985). *Special recreational services: Therapeutic and adapted.* Philadelphia: Lea and Febiger.

Stewart, J. (1978). *Parents of exceptional children.* Columbus: Charles E. Merrill.

Wehman, P. (1979). *Programs for the developmentally disabled persons.* Baltimore: University Park Press.

Wolfensberger, W. (1972). *Normalization: The principle of normalization in human services.* Toronto, Canada: National Institute on Mental Retardation.

Chapter 4

THE DEVELOPMENT OF AN EFFECTIVE THERAPEUTIC RECREATION PROGRAM

JESSE T. DIXON

Seeing all possibilities, seeing all that can be done,
and how it can be done, marks the power of
imagination. Imagination turns into reality....

WYNN DAVIS

INTRODUCTION

Programming therapeutic recreation services for handicapped children will involve considerations for: (a) their motivation, (b) their self-concept, (c) their growth, (d) their awareness, (e) their access to recreation participation, (f) the intervention necessary to influence their level of independence, and (g) practical measures for documenting progress. This chapter addresses these considerations with an emphasis on the development of recreation activity skills. The information is intended for problem solving in service settings with handicapped children.

A CONCEPTUAL MODEL OF SERVICE

Developing a plan for action and programming activities for handicapped children requires a framework of therapeutic recreation service. For the purpose of discussion in the remainder of this chapter, the Gunn and Peterson model of therapeutic recreation service will be used to distinguish the emphasis of program planning. The model identifies three phases of service: rehabilitation, leisure education, and independent recreation (Fig. 1). Rehabilitation programming emphasizes the need to address the functional abilities of the child as a part of "therapy." This would include developing a rapport with a child to ensure effective communication and the development of physical and social skills that are prerequisite to many recreation activities. Once prerequisite skills are demonstrated and the child's awareness and knowledge permit informed choices, leisure education is planned to develop physical and social skills, develop a knowledge of leisure resources, and develop attitudes for independent leisure participation. Leisure education includes the use of instruction, practice, opportunities, and counseling to facilitate the child to move beyond the therapy phase of service. The service phase, entitled Independent Recreation, is realistic when a child has some level of independence with regard to activity skills, opportunities for socialization, and has a repertoire of activities to choose from for a personal leisure life-style. The recreation professional can serve as an important resource to a child who is independent by providing accessibility information for leisure opportunities. An accessibility guide for community recreation settings, innovative adaptive devices or strategies for recreation activities, and opportunities for integrating leisure experiences into personal growth plans are possible contributions. Recognizing these three phases of service can help to establish a linear contribution of service in the development of programs serving handicapped children.

COMMON ORIENTATIONS FOR PARTICIPATION

Understanding Abilities, Likes, Dislikes, and Needs

One goal of the therapeutic recreation process is to increase the awareness and ability of a handicapped child so that he or she will make self-directed choices for independent recreation participation (Peterson and Gunn, 1984, p. 51). Gold (1980) attributes informed choices to the "content influence" of activities. That is, the handicapped child has a knowledge of, belief in, or awareness for the value of recreation participation. Recognizing alternative preferences for recreation participation may expand the content influence of activities for handicapped children. Four preference orientations are frequently observed for recreation participation and can be labeled as follows: acquisition, prevention, maintenance, and serendipity. In addition, the issue of certainty and the use of evaluation concepts are considerations which influence the preferences for recreation participation.

FIGURE 1

COMPREHENSIVE LEISURE SERVICE MODEL
(Peterson and Gunn, 1984)

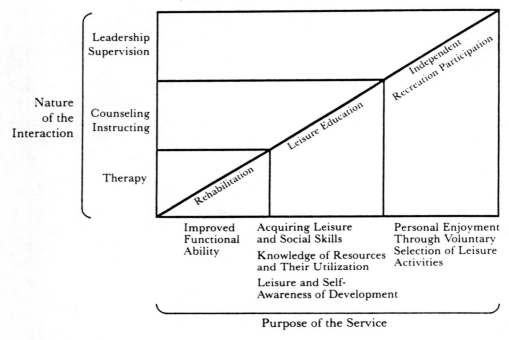

Carol Ann Peterson/Scout Lee Gunn, *Therapeutic Recreation Program Design: Principles and Procedures,* 2/e, c 1984, p. 12. Reprinted by permission of Prentice-Hall.

Acquisition

The concept of acquisition involves gaining something by one's own efforts (Guralnik, 1975). Commercial advertisements for recreation frequently suggest the acquisition of fitness, quality entertainment, and interesting information (Dixon, 1986). Children may be motivated to select recreation activities to develop art, music, or physical activity skills as well as to acquire new experiences. When acquisition is the focus of participation, there is a degree of uncertainty due to the level of skill and the amount of effort necessary to achieve or complete an objective. For example, people frequently participate in recreation activities to acquire a level of fitness. Following an assessment, this could include a desire for weight reduction, an increase in cardiovascular endurance, or a change in muscle tone. Acquiring a level of fitness that is beyond the participant's assessed status would probably require skills in nutritional planning, exercise selection, and performance. When fitness programs are appropriate, the degree or rate of acquisition are influenced by the participant's perception of their goals and their ambition for improvement. In therapeutic recreation service settings, professionals can provide leisure education to develop activity skills and influence the expectation for success of acquisition strategies. Human service efforts aimed at the rehabilitation of handicapped children frequently use the concept of acquisition.

Acquisition and Rehabilitation

Rehabilitation is an individualized process that is intended to reduce or eliminate the effects of disability and restore the functional capacity of a person (Rosen, Clark, and Kivitz, 1977; Shivers and Fait, 1985). The concept of rehabilitation assumes that a person lacks a significant ability and must acquire this ability to achieve a normal state of health. The rehabilitation process is designed to compensate the individual for functional problems following disease, illness, or injury (Shivers and Fait, 1985). For example, the child who experiences a visual impairment will require training in orientation and mobility skills in order to be aware of the environment and achieve some level of independent functioning. Otherwise, an extreme dependence on others may result in a very limited life-style. Similarly, the institutionalized child may need to acquire specific coping strategies to resume living in the mainstream of society.

Therapeutic recreation is a supportive service designed to contribute to a rehabilitation plan. For a child with a physical disability, recreation participation may be encouraged to develop the fitness or motor skills necessary for self-help tasks, social opportunities, and meeting the requirements of academic or vocational placement at a later date. In psychiatric settings, recreation participation may be oriented to developing social skills, positive attitudes, and identifying personal life values (Shivers and Fait, 1985). For rehabilitation settings, the use of recreation experiences to acquire skills and awareness can contribute to the physical and/or psychological strength of children and their ability to demonstrate a level of independent living in society.

Prevention

The concept of prevention suggests the need for activity or experiences to avoid negative consequences (Avedon, 1974; Glasser, 1976). Shivers and Fait (1985) recognize the concept of prevention as part of a healthy life-style for individuals to avoid dysfunction or illness. These authors recommend a balance between tension and relaxation with recreation opportunities. That is, recreation is considered to have preventive value for dealing with pressures that result in physical/mental illness or other forms of deterioration (Avedon, 1974; Shivers and Fait, 1985).

Therapeutic recreation programs frequently use a prevention orientation to motivate people to participate in activities and preserve a state of health. For example, warm-up exercises are recommended to avoid possible injuries and prepare children for excelling in active participation. Special diet plans and food information are presented to avoid problems with physical appearance, nutrition, and weight control. Handicapped children may encounter numerous media sources which promote nutritional items, cosmetic products, and activity programs with suggestions to avoid injury, illness, or being unattractive. In addition, community recreation sources are frequently promoted to discourage social isolation and encourage children to be "where it is happening" (Burt, Meeks, and Pottebaum, 1980). In terms of prevention, therapeutic recreation programming may be a valuable resource for handicapped children who are concerned about physical health, appearance, and social opportunities.

Maintenance of Motivation

The concept of maintenance involves a **continuation**, rather than a termination of experience, and a satisfying process or outcome (Ellis, 1971; Kelly, 1982). Media sources may suggest a maintenance orientation for the repeated use of a vacation site or the pleasurable use of beverages or foods. A maintenance orientation with regards to recreation can be described as participation for the fun of it; that is, people seeking activities which provide pleasurable experiences (Havighurst and Feigenbaum, 1974). Perceiving recreation activities as pleasurable may help to explain the enthusiasm of individuals who repeatedly plan or seek opportunities for participation (Kelly, 1982; Shivers and Fait, 1985).

Some authors view recreation for pleasure as a basic human need that is vital to the life-style of well-adjusted and healthy people (Burt, Meeks, and Pottebaum, 1980; Peterson and Gunn, 1984). Therapeutic recreation professionals frequently encourage a maintenance orientation as the **emphasis of participation** for handicapped children. Recognizing the process of recreation participation encourages children to be more aware of the play experiences and not be limited to outcomes such as winning, losing, or completing an objective (O'Morrow, 1980, p. 123). Although the concept of maintenance is not limited to commercial sources of recreation, useful program ideas and alternatives may be learned from successful recreation businesses. For example, popular amusement parks appear to be very successful at providing unique and challenging environments, rides, and experiences that people rate as exciting, fun, thrilling, and educational. Apparently, such commercial recreation enterprises are designed to provide positive, entertaining experiences for patrons and encourage return visits for repeated participation. Overall, the use of novelty and complexity to stimulate the human senses may be important factors for attracting and maintaining the future interest of children in entertaining recreation (Ellis, 1973). The application of novelty to recreation programming can include planning activities that have not been experienced recently, as well as "new" activities. Assessing handicapped children for their recreation history will provide insights into the maintenance of program novelty for professionals or parents who are seeking alternative ways for planning new activities. The use of complexity in programming recreation activities involves adding information to the recreation experience to make participation more stimulating for handicapped children (Ellis, 1973, p. 92). The use of complexity can include increasing the task difficulty of one activity skill to make it more challenging or increasing the number of skills required for participation to expand a game and prevent boredom.

Serendipity

The concept of serendipity involves the discovery or awareness of desirable things not sought for (Isaac and Michael, 1971, p. 178). The term **serendipity** is derived from a Persian fairy tale about the three princes of the Isle of Serendip (Ceylon) who repeatedly travel to the mainland to complete specific tasks. During their travels they never complete their missions, but they always have other valuable discoveries or experiences. Hence, the term serendipity implies unplanned discoveries of a positive nature. Chubb and Chubb (1981, p. 250) discuss quality recreation experiences in terms of serendipitous conditions. That is, individuals who participate in recreation without long-term goals or preconceived notions allow the elements of surprise and spontaneity to influence the experience. For example, the unexpected sighting of plants or animals during nature outings or discovering the aesthetic use of a utility item for decorating the home could be serendipitous experiences (Chubb and Chubb, 1981, p. 250; Dustin and McAvoy, 1984, pp. 14–15). Serendipitous conditions require handicapped children to be perceptive of opportunities and to take advantage of them when they occur.

In therapeutic recreation service, serendipitous conditions can encourage handicapped children to make spontaneous decisions as part of participation. Encountering a crowded restaurant or movie theatre could lead to the discovery of a restaurant, type of food, movie, or another source of new recreation that would have otherwise been ignored due to planning. A trip to a shopping center could lead to the discovery of an unexpected bargain or merchandise item. A movie outing may provide children with insights for coping with daily living within an entertainment experience. The use of serendipity as an orientation for participation can be stimulating for handicapped children. Serendipity requires the professional, parents, and the children to be comfortable with the **uncertainty** opportunities for positive experiences.

In summary, recognizing orientations for motivation in recreation participation provides parents and professionals with alternatives for increasing the awareness of handicapped children and encouraging some level of independence (Fig. 2). It is possible that the four orientations may be used in combination or alternately depending on the preferences of the children involved. In addition, parents and professionals need not be limited to the four orientations described here. Ideally, increasing the awareness of handicapped children may result in motivated choices for independent participation in recreation activities.

Discussion of Limitation

Intuitively, the concept of acquisition appears to require a child to be ambitious. In rehabilitation service the patient is encouraged to restore or develop personal abilities which are reduced by a handicapping condition. The use of an assessment may clarify the absence of a specific ability. Wheelchair sport activities may be attractive to a child with

FIGURE 2

MOTIVATION ORIENTATIONS

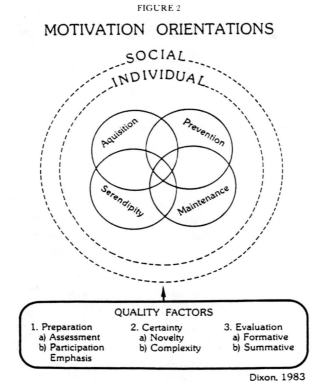

SOCIAL

INDIVIDUAL

Aquisition

Prevention

Serendipity

Maintenance

QUALITY FACTORS

1. Preparation
   a) Assessment
   b) Participation
      Emphasis

2. Certainty
   a) Novelty
   b) Complexity

3. Evaluation
   a) Formative
   b) Summative

Dixon, 1983

paraplegia who desires wheelchair mobility skills and seeks participation in wheelchair sports. Recreation programming can represent an opportunity for children to resume or develop activity skills as well as provide structure for socialization. In contrast, it is possible for a child with paraplegia to show no interest in skilled sports participation and see no application to his or her personal life-style. Similarly, a child in a psychiatric setting may be subject to group program planning to develop interaction skills and experience social opportunities. Such programming can provide model experiences for a transition or return to community settings. An individual child, however, may elect a life-style that is isolated compared to the objectives of parents or a treatment program. Parents and professionals may want to suggest prevention, maintenance, or provide serendipitous conditions for individuals who are not oriented to acquisition.

The prevention orientation appears to be dependent upon the strength of a fear for motivating active participation. For example, a child's fitness efforts at reducing excess body weight may be motivated by avoiding the disapproval of a friend. If a child's feelings of affection terminate, however, the motivation for fitness may also decline. Similarly, in service settings for young legal offenders, a child may be motivated to participate in group recreation activities to avoid feelings of loneliness and develop social contacts. A child's motivation for group interaction may diminish, however, if he or she decides that a misunderstood and disruptive loner is a romantic and desirable image to project. In other words, a prevention orientation for recreation participation can be useful but is limited when fearful concerns diminish or can be rationalized by a child.

A maintenance orientation for recreation can be useful in therapeutic service settings where children are motivated to participate in recreation for **the fun of it**. Emphasizing the pleasure associated with preferences for recreation is reinforcing for continued participation. In describing **Positive Addiction**, Glasser (1976) suggests that people may enjoy certain recreation activities so much they crave future opportunities for participation. Hence, it is essential for parents and professionals to be aware of the use of choices and opportunities to facilitate handicapped children to repeat recreation experiences. It is possible, however, for individual beliefs about recreation to inhibit the pleasure associated with participation. For example, there may be children who believe that too much pleasure is undesirable or an undeserved reward (Havighurst and Feigenbaum, 1974). In this event, recognizing the concepts of acquisition, prevention, and serendipity may provide alternatives for motivation.

A serendipity orientation can be useful in situations where opportunities for spontaneity occur. Discovering new sources of interest, objects to observe, activities to experience, or changing a child's level of awareness can be positive benefits from recreation participation. Due to the spontaneous nature of the serendipity orientation it is likely that a summative approach to evaluating recreation participation would be useful (Peterson and Gunn, 1984, pp. 141–142). One potential drawback for the use of serendipity as an orientation is that a child may choose to perceive opportunities as being externally planned by fate, powers, etc. The positive value of serendipity is related to the awareness of the child in responding spontaneously to experiences or making discoveries. To suggest that serendipity involves preordained events changes the role of the child and implies an external locus of control (outside the person in participation). It is possible that a child could reduce his or her awareness for discovery and rely on external forces to establish positive discoveries or heightened awareness. For individuals who demonstrate a need for preplanned objectives and the certainty of outcomes, the use of acquisition, prevention, and maintenance could be emphasized with formative (progressive) evaluation strategies.

Distinguishing orientations for motivation in recreation participation is intended to suggest alternative ways handicapped children may recognize content influence. In addition, parents and recreation professionals can identify different values for activities which may contribute to the motivation of children with impairments. Ideally, planned intervention can increase the awareness of handicapped children and result in motivated choices for independent participation in recreation activities.

RECOGNIZING ABILITIES AND ENCOURAGING DEVELOPMENT

Common goals of therapeutic recreation include improving the self-image of the participant and the way the participant is perceived by others (Kraus, 1983; Stein and Sessoms, 1977). In view of these goals, it would seem important for parents and professionals to be aware of the conditions and factors that influence the perceptual process when people systematically infer personal attributes on the basis of observable performances by themselves and others in recreation activities (Heider, 1944; Hastorf, Schneider, and Polefka, 1970). Perceived attributes can be personal qualities or conditions outside of the person which contribute to the outcome of participation in recreation activities (Hastorf, Schneider, and Polefka, 1970). Based on an analysis by Heider (1958), causes for success or failure can be attributed to one or a combination of factors, including (a) ability, (b) effort, (c) task difficulty, and (d) luck. The factors **ability** and **effort** have been viewed as originating internally in the person performing, whereas **task difficulty** and **luck** appear to be factors external or outside of people (Rotter, 1966). In terms of stability, the causal factors **ability** and **task difficulty** can be considered unchanging over time within a performance, whereas **effort** and **luck** appear to be subject to unpredictable variance (Weiner et al., 1971). Hence, these causal factors can be viewed as internal and external as well as stable and unstable. Figure 3 illustrates the dimensions for these four causal factors.

The use of causal attributions appears to be learned (Katz, 1967; Coleman et al., 1966). In addition, the use of these causal factors as they are arranged in the figure suggests a relationship between them. Perceiv-

FIGURE 3

DIMENSIONS OF CAUSAL ATTRIBUTIONS

Locus of Control

	Internal	External
Stable	Ability	Task Difficulty
Unstable	Effort	Luck

ing failure as due to lack of ability (a stable factor) indicates that effort cannot reverse the performance outcome. However, failure attributed to effort, an unstable factor, suggests that the future outcome can be modified by exerting more effort. When success is viewed as due to high ability (a stable factor), the probability of future success is supported. When success is attributed to effort (an unstable factor), any future outcome is subject to the variance of this trait (Bar-Tal, 1975). For example, a person who fails to return a volley in racquetball and feels that he or she did not have the racquet **skill** to accurately hit the ball will not believe that running faster during a volley could enable successful hitting. In contrast, a child who feels that he or she did not hustle for correct body position in making skilled return volleys is likely to believe that if they had exerted more effort their skill could have been better utilized to succeed. Success can also be viewed in terms of stability. A child whose racquetball skill is considered to be superior will likely be **expected** to succeed in future volleys with previously defeated players. However, when a child's success is attributed to someone else's fatigue or an unlucky break ("my foot slipped"), the outcome of future encounters will not be certain.

The usefulness of these attributions depends upon the insight gained concerning recreation service as it relates to handicapped children. The causal attributions ability, effort, and task difficulty are subject to the influence of therapeutic recreation intervention and have implications for a child's observed recreation satisfaction, self-concept, and the way they are perceived by others (Ellis, 1973; Weiner, 1974). Within the context of rehabilitation and leisure education, the use of successful intervention techniques suggests that training or education could be considered as additional external causal factors when explaining the recreation participation development of handicapped children (Dixon, 1979). When independent recreation participation is demonstrated by a handicapped child, he or she should receive credit in terms of personal abilities and efforts. The external use (outside of the child) of therapeutic recreation intervention as a causal factor should serve to reflect on the role and responsibilities of the parents and the professionals in the service phase of recreation.

REMEDIAL REFERENCES, RECREATION SKILLS, AND PROGRAMMING

Children who experience a handicap often do not exhibit appropriate recreation behavior (Ellis, 1973; Kraus, 1983). Some of these children have not had the same developmental experiences as "normal" children, nor have they been effectively facilitated through the developmental progression of motor skills (Wehman, 1977). As a result, handicapped children can appear to be slow or behind in their participation skills (Moran and Kalakian, 1977).

Motor activity, within the context of recreation, is viewed by many educators to be a potential medium for promoting skill development, fitness, social interaction, and intrinsic satisfaction (Bradke, Kirkpatrick and Rosenblatt, 1972; Kraus, 1983; Shivers and Fait, 1985). Therapeutic recreation programming sources typically include planning activity-related approaches which can serve as references in planning motor activities for remedial use with handicapped children. These remedial reference areas for motor skills and recreation participation include (a) perceptual motor efficiency, (b) functional basic skills, (c) physical and motor fitness, and (d) rhythmic development (American Alliance for Health, Physical Education, and Recreation (AAHPER), 1977; Council For Exceptional Children (CEC) and AAHPER, 1966; Institute For Physical Education, 1975; Moran and Kalakian, 1977). All four of the content areas involve physical movement and have a separate definition and rationale indicating their value as therapeutic recreation program content. Each of the four remedial reference areas are briefly defined and described as they appear in the literature.

Perceptual Motor Efficiency

The capacity to perceive sensory information from motor experiences when a child is participating in recreation activities includes the abilities to hear, see, and feel. Perceptual motor ability is helpful to the individual in organizing and systematizing the environment and making appropriate motor responses to sensory stimulation (Moran and Kalakian, 1977). The following concepts are included in perceptual motor training programs (Bradley, Konicki, and Leedy, 1968):

1. Body image
2. Space and direction
3. Balance
4. Hearing discrimination
5. Visual discrimination
6. Form perception
7. Large muscle movement
8. Fine muscle movement
9. Symmetrical activities
10. Eye-hand coordination
11. Eye-foot coordination
12. Rhythm

During a perceptual motor training program one or more of these concepts may be emphasized during participation. For example, movement around the body's center of gravity (balance) and visually monitoring foot placement (eye-foot coordination) could be stressed while walking on a balance beam, a line on the floor, or playing hopscotch. Similarly, identification of body parts (body image) and moving correctly on command (space and direction) could be emphasized and developed during a game of "Simon Says."

Functional Basic Skill Efficiency

The ability to exhibit motor skills which ordinarily develop instinctively (phylogenetic skills) and to learn additional motor skills necessary for participation in desired games (ontogenetic skills) can complement activities of daily living. A repertoire of basic skills has a strong application for functioning in an academic, a vocational or daily living situation, e.g. walking, pulling, pushing, lifting. In addition, recreation activities often include variations of learned skills such as running, throwing, catching, swinging, dancing and marching. Two major categories of basic skills are identified in Table I.

TABLE I

PHYLOGENETIC SKILLS (INSTINCTIVE)

Crawling	Jumping
Walking	Running
Kicking	Hopping
Throwing	Climbing
Pulling	Swinging
Pushing	Squatting
Rolling	Catching
Kneeling	Hitting
Hanging	
(The Illinois Program, 1972)	

ONTOGENETIC SKILLS (LEARNED)

Marching	Surfing
Dancing	Skating
Bicycle Riding	Sailing
Car or Motorcycle Driving	
(Moran and Kalakian, 1977)	

NOTE: The skills listed in the two categories are intended to be representative rather than definitive.

A knowledge of basic skills is particularly useful for analyzing recreation activities and identifying the prerequisite skills necessary for participation. The demands of daily living and opportunities for recreation are oriented to the phylogenetic and ontogenetic skill categories.

Physical and Motor Fitness

Fitness refers to a bodily state which characterizes a person's ability to function in daily life (Wheeler and Hooley, 1976). Physical (organic) fitness represents the quantitative capacity of the body tissues. For example, the strength or flexibility of the body are measures of organic fitness. Motor fitness involves the body's qualitative capacity to move. For example, demonstrated balance or agility are measured within the category of motor fitness. The components that are categorized under the organic and motor fitness headings are identified in Table II.

The value of physical and motor fitness relates to the efficiency of

TABLE II
PHYSICAL AND MOTOR FITNESS CATEGORIES

Organic Fitness	*Motor Fitness*
Strength	Balance
Flexibility	Agility
Muscular Endurance	Speed
Cardiovascular Endurance	Coordination
Reaction Time	
(Moran and Kalakian, 1977)	

bodily function or movement and has desirable implications for self-concept, e.g. feeling good with one's own body (Wheeler and Hooley, 1976). The fitness level of children is often measured and developed during participation in recreation activities.

Rhythmic Movement

The concept of rhythm is a connection of parts into a whole. Rhythmic **movement** involves energy, action, and control, as well as relaxation and release. Rhythm in action is demonstrated by coordinated movement patterns where parts of the body move in a timed sequence that appear smooth and controlled (Godfrey and Thompson, 1966). Music and sound can also represent expressions of movement, in that a person can respond to the rhythm he or she feels in his or her body through a musical instrument. Rhythm, in relation to motor performance, is classified into three categories distinguished by the character of the movements and the use of apparatus.

Non-Locomotor Rhythm

This category includes bodily movements that are made while the feet are stationary. This type of movement includes bending, stretching, swinging, twisting, swaying, and raising or lowering the upper parts of the body.

Locomotor Rhythm

This category involves bodily movement or travel from place to place. Locomotion requires a relocation or change of the body's base of support and includes walking, running, jumping, hopping, leaping, and handsprings.

Manipulative Rhythm

This category includes the movement or manipulation of items such as ropes, balls, wands, hoops, and musical instruments in relation to time. The physical manipulation of objects is observable and can be performed in a stationary position or in locomotion. The size and the nature of the objects will determine whether the movements utilize large or fine muscles. Sound or music can be used to assist or guide the participant in manipulative rhythms. When musical instruments are used, the sound or music created can be used to judge the quality of the motor involvement. One value of rhythmic training is the efficient and skilled movement that results when a person is able to sense and accurately express rhythm.

It should be noted that although the same movement or activity can be used in different remedial reference approaches, there will be a different purpose emphasized for participation. For example, an individual may be asked to hop on one foot for a given distance as quickly as he or she can (fitness-speed). In contrast, a participant could also be requested to hop, in time, to the beat of a selected piece of music as part of rhythmic training (locomotor rhythm).

Each of the four remedial reference approaches identify different motor abilities. These skills contribute to an individual's capacity to function in daily life situations, as well as participate in and experience recreation activities.

The Use of Remedial Reference Approaches in Programming

The four remedial reference approaches may appear in the literature as separate content areas or be combined within selected recreation activities (Braley, Konicki, and Leedy, 1968; Hackett, 1970). In therapeutic recreation service to handicapped children, any one of the remedial reference approaches could be justified as a module within an activity program. For children who experience a severe handicap, all four of the remedial reference approaches may be valuable and a necessary part of long-range programming. For parents or professionals who are programming, establishing priorities or recognizing a hierarchy for these approaches may be helpful. Projected long-range use of the remedial references could help to guide the professional or the parent in systematically sequencing behavioral objectives and facilitating transitions in activity skill training with handicapped children.

Based upon the nature of the content described for the remedial references, there is a logic for sequencing the four approaches in a therapeutic recreation program (Fig. 4). Perceptual motor ability is fundamental to a child's awareness of his/her own body, the ability or inability to move, the body's relationship to objects, the environment, and other people. It is important for any handicapped child, in the context of recreation or other daily living situations, to initially perceive and process stimuli correctly in order to make an appropriate motor response. If a handicapped child does not perceive stimuli during participation in recreation activities, then the personal feedback necessary for intrinsic motivation would be unavailable (Dixon, 1980). A handicapped child cannot be expected to efficiently perform basic functional movements if he or she does not perceive and correctly interpret information from other people, the environment, and movement experiences.

Given that a handicapped child can make the appropriate motor responses to sensory stimulation, a number of fundamental motor skills have been identified for the play behavior of normal children (The Illinois Program, 1972). Therapeutic recreation service goals include teaching appropriate or normal play behaviors to handicapped children (Council for Exceptional Children and American Alliance for Health, Physical Education, and Recreation, 1966; Ellis, 1973; Wehman, 1977). Ideally, a repertoire of functional basic motor skills could be readily applied within the context of playing a game or a fitness activity. Children who experience a handicap should be competent in the necessary **basic skills** before he/she is encouraged to perform them in a quantitative or skilled manner during a fitness program.

A reasonable amount of both physical and motor fitness is essential for handicapped children in educational opportunities and recreation activities where physical stamina and skilled motor ability are necessary for independent participation. A functional level of both motor and physical fitness should facilitate a feeling of well-being in the handicapped child and add to their quality of life (Wheeler and Hooley, 1976). The promotion of physical fitness in both the organic and motor categories is commonly programmed in terms of basic motor skills. For example, running is frequently used to develop cardiovascular endurance, lifting a weighted object can be used to develop strength, and walking on a line can be used to develop balance (Hackett, 1970; Moran and Kalakian,

FIGURE 4

REMEDIAL REFERENCE MODEL
FOR THERAPEUTIC RECREATION SERVICE
(Dixon 1980)

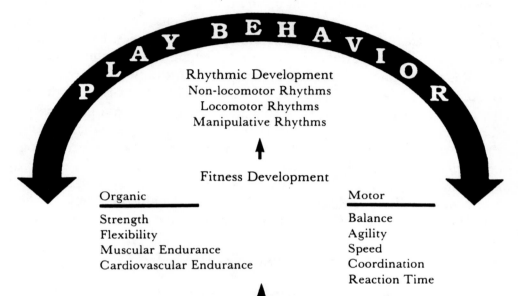

Rhythmic Development
Non-locomotor Rhythms
Locomotor Rhythms
Manipulative Rhythms

Fitness Development

Organic	Motor
Strength	Balance
Flexibility	Agility
Muscular Endurance	Speed
Cardiovascular Endurance	Coordination
	Reaction Time

Functional Basic Skill Development

Walking	Rolling	Squatting
Marching	Jumping	Catching
Kicking	Crawling	Kneeling
Throwing	Hopping	Hitting
Pulling	Climbing	Running
Pushing	Swinging	Hanging

Perceptual Motor Development

Body Image	Symmetrical Activities
Space and Direction	Eye-Hand Coordination
Balance	Eye-Foot Coordination
Hearing Discrimination	Form Perception
Large Muscle Movement	Rhythm
Visual Discrimination	Fine Motor Movement

1977). Ultimately, the degree to which handicapped children can be successfully integrated into society will depend, in part, on their physical capacities and their competencies demonstrated to the public (Dixon, 1979). The demonstrated quality of movement often characterized as smooth or graceful is dependent upon the timed sequence of movements in accordance with the appropriate rhythm (Arnheim, Auxter, and Crowe, 1973). In recreation events such as the Special Olympics, participation may include running, throwing and jumping and develop the rhythmic abilities of the participants. For informal group situations the rhythmic use of music and dance is popular and offers leisure choices for children during unobligated time. It should be noted that the programmed use of rhythmics does not have to follow perceptual motor, basic skill, and fitness training, since it could be encouraged at anytime for facilitating creativity with children. If motor proficiency is a long-range treatment goal, however, the other previously described approaches would complement and facilitate the success of handicapped children in rhythmic activities by first establishing prerequisite skills and physical capacities.

A Remedial Reference Hierarchy

A hierarchy has been illustrated which suggests a sequence for programming the four remedial reference approaches for use with handicapped children in recreation programming (Fig. 4). One feature of the model presented is that play behavior is a conceptual umbrella component. This is very important, in that therapeutic recreation service should emphasize fun and facilitate intrinsic motivation during an activity period for each of the remedial reference approaches. This can be accomplished through the use of effective intervention techniques which involve skill training without total mastery and an informal atmosphere where enthusiasm and an emphasis on fun are clearly demonstrated (Ellis, 1973). Leisure education may use the hierarchy as a reference in planning programs and facilitating independent participation in a recreation activity.

It is intended that this hierarchy be applied where an overall deficiency in motor performance ability is noted with handicapped children. The hierarchy presented is a suggested sequence for systematically presenting the four remedial reference areas in a long-range therapeutic recreation program. The sequence emphasizes the value of having recognized prerequisite skills and abilities for active recreation or daily living situations in order to plan for progressive and successful experiences. Ideally, each remedial reference approach would be programmed by the professional or parent to encompass both the treatment (participation) goals and the intrinsic needs (preference) of the children involved. The author assumes that the completion of each approach would be planned in accordance with specific objectives identified prior to implementation. Where handicapped children are considered to have an overall deficiency in motor performance skills, the sequence of remedial references should help the professional or the parent to make program teaching decisions and to establish specific measurable objectives for therapeutic recreation content.

TEACHING RECREATION SKILLS TO HANDICAPPED CHILDREN

Recreation professionals are expected to develop effective approaches for presenting recreation activities to special populations (O'Morrow, 1980). In the leisure education phase of therapeutic recreation service, teaching procedures help to communicate information about an activity to a handicapped child. It is important that the interaction between the teacher and the learner result in a mutual sharing of information. The learner can develop a greater awareness of the motivating characteristics of the activity or experience while the professional gains insight into the learning preferences of the handicapped child. A teaching-based activity analysis procedure can help to prepare the professional or parents to present recreation activities to children who experience a handicap with participation.

Activity analysis has been described as a procedure for examining an activity to understand motivational factors and qualities that complement professional treatment goals (Peterson and Gunn, 1984; Kraus, 1983; O'Morrow, 1980). This includes dividing an activity into component or behavioral requirements for participation and planning a systematic evaluation. However, activity analysis could include specific considerations for the professional or the parent actually teaching or presenting recreation activities effectively (O'Morrow, 1980). The author wishes to recognize the contributions of materials on task analysis by Gold (1980) and kinetic analysis by Shivers and Fait (1985). Both approaches contribute information which applies to the teaching of recreation skills to handicapped children (Carter, Van Andel, and Robb, 1985; Shivers and

Fait, 1985). This author applies many of the concepts of task analysis and kinetic analysis within the concept of activity analysis. This author feels it is appropriate to plan the intervention necessary for leisure education within the process of activity analysis. In addition, the distinction between the terms **activity** and **task** suggest that recreation activities involve skills within the context of play rather than the context of work (Guralnik, 1974). For these reasons this author will refer to activity analysis for use in teaching recreation skills to handicapped children.

The identification of a teaching-based activity analysis procedure may encourage professionals and parents to be flexible in their teaching techniques. The concept of teaching flexibility includes consideration for the skills of the teacher as well as the handicapped child. Developing teaching alternatives should encourage the identification of techniques that ultimately result in successful interactions when recreation activities are presented. The three phases for developing a teaching-based activity analysis procedure include: (a) the demonstrated **method** of recreation participation, (b) the identification of recreation participation **content** which defines the method, and (c) the **process** of designing strategies for teaching the participation content.

The Method of Recreation Participation

The demonstrated method of recreation participation is an important consideration for ensuring access for the handicapped child. Different methods for participation are illustrated by the following approaches.

The Use of a Functional Device

The purpose of a functional device is to serve as a tool for assisting the handicapped individual to perform a recreation activity. Handicapping conditions can often be negated in recreation participation through the use of a handle, holder, an extension, or bracing materials. For example, the use of a wheelchair facilitates mobility for the child with limb paralysis or motor spasticity. Handles attached to puzzle pieces may allow a handicapped child who is lacking in fine motor skills to manipulate the pieces with an open hand. An extended handle can be designed for push-and-pull toy cars, trucks, etc., so the child using a wheelchair can have access to and control floor toys. It is important to emphasize that the use of a functional device within the concept of method refers to use by the participant rather than the professional or the parent during recreation participation.

The Use of an Alternative Stimulus

The purpose of using an alternative stimulus is to direct the feedback from recreation participation through the accessible senses of the individual. A handicap may be experienced in participation if the physical sense required for an activity is inaccessible. For example, the visually impaired child may be excluded from games that utilize color, knowledge of position and other visual cues. For example, toys or puzzles may be adapted by using tactile fabrics on colored areas or playing boards. This adaptation is intended to motivate the visually impaired child to use the sense of touch to solve puzzles, manipulate toy component parts, and to monitor changes on a game board. Target games may be adapted with materials that provide distinctly different auditory cues which reflect the accuracy of attempted throws. This strategy is intended to encourage visually impaired children to participate and to monitor their changing scores independently. The use of an alternative stimulus in adapting recreation activities represents a service approach which emphasizes the abilities of handicapped children.

Changing the Participation Technique

The purpose of changing the participation technique for a leisure activity is to acknowledge alternative methods of performance. The changes in participation technique may or may not involve a functional device but should reflect a level of independent recreation participation. There are occasions when changing the method or technique for doing an activity can facilitate the participation of children who would otherwise experience a handicap. Participating in games and athletic sports from a sitting position has been a successful adapted insight for individuals in wheelchairs. Rule changes have accompanied this adaptation, and the result has been international participation in recreation and sports activities by individuals who use a wheelchair. For example, the method of holding a tennis racquet with two hands instead of one may result in a more functional backhand stroke for individuals who experience difficulties due to their strength and range of motion. Mouthwriting and footwriting represent alternative methods for pursuing artistic painting for individuals who do not have the use of their hands. Changing the participation technique for an activity requires the professional or the parent to have an understanding of the requirements of an activity and how the skills of the child can be substituted.

Creating Transitional Recreation Experiences

The purpose of creating transitional adapted recreation experiences is to provide an opportunity for the handicapped child to learn useful prerequisite knowledge and subskills within the context of a program. For some children, a handicapping condition may be accompanied by a lack of prerequisite information or skill training necessary for independent participation. Independent participation can be facilitated in some cases by creating an adapted experience as a transition for learning information and developing awareness. For example, a fishing game can be useful for teaching children the prerequisite skills and purpose of using a fishing rod and reel. This can occur as a part of leisure education prior to the introduction to an outdoor recreation environment. The objective of such a game parallels the fishing experience and allows for the introduction of safety rules and other concepts in preparation for a fishing trip. Stuffed toys can also serve as transitional toys for teaching body-part identification to handicapped children. The features of such toys are typically enlarged, easily identified, and can be associated with the child during a play session. Macrame could be introduced to handicapped children by initially teaching the prerequisite knot skills for using rope which would later be used for making plant hangers, wall decorations, etc. A teaching guide could be constructed to illustrate, with a picture or a sample, how each knot is tied. This teaching guide could be particularly useful with children who initially prefer not to interact with the professional or parent in a teaching situation. In addition, a teaching guide could expand therapeutic recreation service when there is a large number of children in relation to the number of professionals. Creating transitional experiences through adapting activities is a useful strategy where the concept of recreation is balanced with an emphasis on education.

During recreation participation it is the feedback a person receives from an activity that is reinforcing and increases voluntary movement at an independent level (Dixon, 1981; Shivers and Fait, 1985). Considering different methods for participation provides the professional or the parent with alternatives for making feedback more accessible to a handicapped child. In addition, the use of an alternative method for participation may reduce the need for instruction.

Recreation Participation Content

Participation content refers to the demonstrated behaviors that are required of the person to complete the method of participation. For example, in bowling, the content can be listed as:

1. The grip of the ball
2. The three-step approach
3. The backswing
4. The delivery
5. The follow-through

The strategy of dividing an activity into parts so that each one can be learned separately and then integrated into the whole activity again has received mixed support in the research literature. Apparently, the nature of the activity can influence the way an activity is divided into parts for instruction. Schmidt (1976) provides a summation for use of the part method in teaching motor skills. Continuous skills such as swimming or riding a bicycle involve a time-sharing of movements. That is, there is an interaction between the movement components. To learn the timing and interaction, Schmidt (1976) recommends that continuous skills be taught and demonstrated as a whole. In contrast, a serial activity has number of discrete or separate steps and allows the isolation of movements for teaching and practice. Assembling a puzzle, playing a game of chess, or operating a television set require a sequence of skills that can be isolated and taught as separate parts in a forward or a backward chaining procedure.

When the part method of instruction is used, the functional level of the child determines the **number** of steps or behaviors in participation content. For example, if the child's comprehension is severely impaired, the three-step approach in bowling can be divided into single steps or smaller units of learning. In contrast, a child with a high level of motor skill might allow the backswing, the delivery, and the follow-through of bowling to be combined into one step as a larger unit of learning.

Recognizing potential problem areas in the list of content behaviors can be useful in preparing for the teaching process phase of activity analysis. Gold and Pomerantz (1977) have identified two characteristics of learning situations that can help the parent or the professional to recognize and avoid confusion during leisure education. The authors make a distinction between bits of learning that are **informational** and **judgmental**. A leisure activity is considered judgmental if there are a variety of correct responses or non-specific feedback for completing an objective. For example, in archery the bow-string can be drawn at different lengths to release the arrow and hit the target, depending on the different procedures used for aiming. Similarly, a strike in bowling can be achieved by using a straight or curving roll of the ball. When an activity is **introduced** to a child, the objectives of leisure education can be clearly understood if the teacher identifies informational learning cues. A recreation activity is informational for teaching if correct participation can be clearly identified and all other responses can be recognized as incorrect. For example, drawing the bow in archery might include touching the bowstring to the lips before releasing the arrow. Specifying this condition allows the participant to have immediate feedback on this aspect of their performance independent of the parent or the professional. That is, a handicapped child can recognize the objective and evaluate directly from his or her participation without intervention. In teaching bowling, the use of a straight throw instead of a curve can focus initial attention on one method for throwing and making corrections in hitting the pins. Modifications of skilled attempts at rolling the ball should be more successful if there is consistency in the method used for throwing and fewer variables for the handicapped child to address in participation. In addition, the arrow markers in the lane near the foul line provide participants with early feedback regarding the accuracy of their throw and makes the learning process more informational. When learning is informational, it will be easier for the handicapped child to isolate the learning objective and to recognize guidelines for participation. The purpose of making judgmental aspects of content informational is to clearly identify what is right or wrong for achieving learning objectives.

In practice, the parent or the professional will find more resources for teaching and evaluating activity content that is informational. Limiting activity elements that are judgmental to clearly right or wrong decisions will provide the handicapped child with direct feedback from participation. As an impact of service, the handicapped child will be more independent and the likelihood of participation within a correct range of behavior (normalcy) will be increased (Gold and Pomerantz, 1977).

Planning the Process

The process of activity analysis refers to the planned interaction between the teacher and handicapped child when activity content is presented. Designing strategies for teaching activity content involves:

- Identifying desirable feedback for the learner
- Organizing and presenting the activity content
- Planning the type of interaction that will occur during the teaching process (Gold, 1976).

Recreation activities are motivating because of the desirable feedback the handicapped child receives during participation (Dixon, 1981; Shivers and Fait, 1985). Feedback from participation can include the demonstrated completion of an objective, the perception of stimulus such as music or a movie, and the nature of a social interaction with other participants. The feedback provided from recreation participation can be a reinforcer during the leisure education process. Hearing the song to be learned on an instrument, seeing art projects that belong to others who have completed instruction, or noting the degree of skilled improvement across a period of time are examples of using activity feedback from participation to motivate a learner. The motivation of handicapped children in a treatment setting will be directly affected by the accessibility of feedback during the leisure education process. Organizing the content and using an efficient format for presenting information should be planned around the motivation of the handicapped child.

Organizing and Presenting Activity Content

Organizing and presenting the content of an activity will include selecting a group or individual setting for teaching (Gunn and Peterson, 1984; Kraus, 1983). Whether the setting is cooperative or competitive should depend upon the learning preferences of the handicapped child. Selecting a teaching format is also important. The use of forward- or backward-chaining techniques will depend on the nature of the activity. Activities that provide the most motivating feedback upon completion should utilize a backward-chaining format whenever possible. For example, using a record player and assembling a puzzle are activities that permit the use of a backward-chaining format and emphasize the objective of the activity at the beginning of the learning process. There are many activities, however, that require a sequence of skill acquisition and logically require the use of a forward-chaining format. For example, throwing games such as darts or sequential movements in dancing are activities that require prerequisite skill to complete the objective of the activity. Social interactions or affective experiences that require social skills are probably taught most efficiently in the actual setting where the behaviors will be required rather than in artificial or practice situations. Ideally, the parent or the professional should use a strategic intervention that is supportive and constructive when identifying personal feelings and skill development in relation to the learning objectives.

Planning the Instructional Interaction

The interaction planned for the activity analysis process identifies how the parent or the professional will communicate information directly to the handicapped child. The teaching stimuli that can be used include visual, auditory, tactile, kinesthetic, and abstract cues (Dixon, 1981).

Visual Cues

Visual feedback is a common form of stimulus in recreation participation. When used to introduce a new leisure activity, the professional often demonstrates the activity to a child so that he or she can see what participation would look like. The visual demonstration is a valuable stimulus for communicating the nature of the intended activity as well as modeling appropriate behavior.

Auditory Cues

Auditory feedback is typically experienced when listening to records, tapes, or the radio. When used to educate a child about a recreation activity, verbal explanation or direction as well as the sounds in the activity communicate information and feedback.

Tactile Cues

Tactile feedback is a valuable part of activities such as woodworking, making pottery, finger painting and other crafts or artistic pursuits. The ability to receive information through the sense of touch has proven to be of immense value for visually impaired children and offers an additional stimulus by which the professional or parent can communicate information about a recreation activity to special populations.

Kinesthetic Cues

The awareness of the body's position in space is easily experienced in swimming where the water element and its properties of resistance gives the individual sensation as he or she moves. Duplicating a basic movement in dance also requires a sense of body positioning as it relates to space. By assisting and guiding an individual's body through space or by calling attention to the position of the body (e.g. tying a ribbon to the body part), a stimulus for kinesthetic awareness is provided.

Abstract Cues

Abstract stimuli involve the role of the cognitive process in conceptualizing the recreation activity as a whole. If an individual has difficulty performing a physical skill in an activity, it is sometimes helpful to break it into parts and teach each phase or movement separately. After an individual learns an activity by the part method, it may help him or her to see the parts performed together as a whole and in the correct sequence. For example, bowling consists of the grip, the approach, the swing, the delivery, and the follow-through. Helping an individual to understand how these parts fit together might include showing him or her these parts in their correct sequence and at a comfortable body rhythm. These kinds of cues show the individual how the separate parts of an activity fit together and help to convey a sense of timing necessary to ensure a smoothness or quality of movement.

These cues can be used separately or in combination. For example, auditory, tactile, and kinesthetic cues are appropriate for teaching the visually impaired child. Visual demonstration is a commonly used cue for hearing-impaired children. The selection of teaching cues depends on the learning preferences of the handicapped child. That is, the cues that are clearly perceived by the child should be used to communicate the teaching objectives.

In addition to effective communication, the teaching process should provide for a transition to a level of independent participation in the activity. The transition can be planned by identifying teaching cues which range from strong to light intervention. For example, physically manipulating a child's arm while teaching a swimming stroke is a stronger intervention than verbally guiding the rhythm of the movement. Similarly, physically moving a child's hand to the appropriate puzzle piece can be faded to a gesture of pointing to the correct vicinity. Planning a transition from strong to light teaching cues allows the instructor to avoid a "sink-or-swim" feeling in the participant. The teacher does not convey an abrupt testing of the participant but promotes the mutual sharing of information and progression of skill development as a positive demonstration of learning acquisition. The degree of learning or level of independence will depend on the **criterion** used in the teaching process.

Criteria are described within performance measures and are used to evaluate learning (Gunn and Peterson, 1984). Determining criteria for learning one part of content or all of an activity is arbitrary. Peterson and Gunn (1984) suggest the least amount of the behavior that is still representative of the teaching intent for determining criteria. Gold (1976) suggests repeated performances of the skill in the setting where the activity will ultimately take place, e.g. in the community or the residential setting. In two separate studies by Dixon (1983, 1984) a 50 percent criterion level was used to teach a recreation activity to participants labeled as mentally retarded. Both of the studies yielded significant improvement in the skilled participation of the clients. The 50 percent level was selected in an attempt to create an intermediate level of novelty during the teaching process (Ellis, 1973). Negative effects on motivation were not observed in either study for this criterion level.

In general, the criterion level for teaching should be strict enough to ensure a level of independence and transition to other skills required for participation. To promote mainstreaming, a criterion level should go beyond sheltered situations and include the environment where the handicapped child is evaluated by society. For further information on alternative criteria, the reader is referred to materials by Gold (1976) and Peterson and Gunn (1984).

Distinguishing Content and Process for Programming and Evaluation

Leisure education programs for developing activity skills can directly affect the motivation of handicapped children during therapeutic recreation service. Gold (1980) has distinguished the content of skill development programs from the process used to communicate information about activities in order to clarify the impact of intervention in programming. In addition, recognizing the content and the process of leisure education can lead to a mutual sharing of information between the professional and the child during instruction and evaluations.

Recognizing Activity Content

Activity content refers to the list of observable behaviors that are required for the child to demonstrate a level of independent participation. For example, the activity of bowling includes (a) the grip, (b) the approach, (c) the backswing, (d) the delivery, (e) the ball release, and (f) the follow-through. Four benefits of identifying activity content are listed.

1. **The professional can recognize behaviors the child must demonstrate and identify teachable components.** For example, in bowling the grip of the ball and the approach steps are skills that can be taught separately without completing the objective of bowling. The backswing, the delivery, and the follow-through may need to be taught together in a timed sequence with an emphasis on rhythm. Communicating specific activity skills can increase the understanding of both the professional and the child for the requirements of participation.

2. **The professional can plan the sequence of steps the child will complete and target potential problem areas.** For example, in bowling the professional may prefer to teach the backswing, the delivery, the release, and the follow-through before teaching the approach to the foul line. This would allow the objective of the activity to be communicated early during instructional efforts and possibly heighten the motivation of the child. If accuracy is a problem, the professional may prefer to focus on teaching a straight roll rather than a curving delivery. In teaching situations, the sequence for presenting information can complement successful participation and emphasize the motivational factors of an activity.

3. **The professional can recognize the child's ability level through the percentage of activity skills completed.** For example, if a child successfully demonstrates three of the six activity skills needed for bowling, the professional may record that 50 percent of the activity has been learned. Indicating that a child has learned 50 percent of an activity within sixty minutes of instruction may be more meaningful to administrators, adjunctive staff, and parents than recording that "he/she is doing better today." In measuring ability, the activity content list allows a percentage of competency to be determined and discourages ambiguous charting.

4. **The professional can develop an awareness of how the activity parts fit together as a whole.** In other words, instruction may emphasize the sense of timing or rhythm necessary throughout participation to reflect coordinated movement and appropriate body positions. Dividing an activity into a list of skills is useful, but participation must ultimately be evaluated within the context of the completed sequence or whole activity.

A knowledge of what is to be learned provides the specialist with content behaviors for criterion-referenced instruction. As an additional part of leisure education, the how of instruction includes considerations for the skills of the specialist, the motivation of the child, and developing a level of independent participation. The term **process** refers to considerations for instructional intervention (Gold, 1976).

Recognizing the Process

Planning the process of leisure education involves anticipating the interaction between the specialist and the child when an activity is presented. It should be noted that if a child is highly skilled and adaptive, the teaching process may appear to be of little significance. That is, the child may be able to participate successfully with a minimum of verbal instruction and visual demonstration. However, an emphasis on the teaching process used by a parent or the professional is intended to address problems that occur with a child's ability to understand and participate in recreation. Five benefits for planning the process of leisure education are listed.

1. **The professional can develop a lesson plan for communicating information about an activity to a child.** A complete plan for learning is intended to clarify what is expected for the child as well as the professional. In addition, specifying clear goals and objectives may enhance the child's cooperation during the teaching process.

2. **Planning the process provides an opportunity for the professional to match his or her own teaching style and skills with the requirements of an activity.** For example, if performing a strike in bowling is beyond the skill of a professional, a competent demonstration by another staff member or child may be arranged. An accurate demonstration can serve to focus a child's attention on specific information. In contrast, any problems the professional may have with an activity can distract or even discourage a child from participation.

3. **In planning the teaching process, many decisions can be made in advance of the interaction with the child.** For example, in bowling, a three- or a five-step approach may be used and the delivery may involve a straight or curving roll of the ball. In introducing bowling, the professional may choose to teach one approach and one method of delivery to clarify what is expected of the child. Eventually, the child can use selected fundamental skills to develop his or her own style of participation. Specifying learning objectives in advance clarifies the teaching process and the evaluation criteria for both the professional and the child.

4. **In planning the teaching process, the professional can anticipate transitional learning environments for the child.** For example, tape marks on the approach lane are vivid cues for teaching a footstep pattern used in an

approach. Physically guiding a child's arm through the backswing, the delivery, the release, and the follow-through without the ball is a strong cue for communicating kinesthetic sensation in movement. Strong physical cues can usually be faded to a visual demonstration and verbal cues as a child's level of skill improves. Planning transitions from strong to light cues in the teaching process allows the professional to avoid the abrupt testing of a child. The mutual sharing of information and progression of instruction can represent a positive demonstration of learning acquisition.

5. **Identifying learning objectives for the teaching process can help the professional to evaluate levels of independence and influence expectancies for client participation.** For example, specifying a number of successful trials can be used as an objective in terminating instruction for a skill (Peterson & Gunn, 1983). If a child repeatedly demonstrates the ability to knock down bowling pins in 80 percent of his or her trials, then he or she can be expected score in most frames. The degree of accuracy for striking bowling pins may also serve as an objective during the learning process (Peterson and Gunn, 1983). If a child maintains an average based upon similar scores, then he or she can expect outcomes in the near future to be within a small range of scores. As part of leisure education, a child can learn that criterion levels are intended to reflect a level of independence in participation. In essence, the use of realistic objectives identifies learning acquisitions and makes children aware of their abilities in participation.

In summary, the distinct characteristic of a teaching-based activity analysis is the planning of the interaction between the recreation professional (or parent) and the handicapped child. The practitioner should be aware of alternative methods for participation to develop accessible leisure activities. In order to introduce and actually teach activities, the professional or the parent should understand the content of the method for participation and plan strategies for teaching that content. This includes considerations for the motivation of the child, potential feedback from participation, the learning preferences of the child, and an effective teaching format and interaction. An outline of this activity analysis procedure is included in Appendix I for assistance in preparing the presentation of activities to handicapped children.

The emphasis on professional preparation in therapeutic recreation service is motivated by three assumptions identified by Gold (1976).

These assumptions about teaching are supported by Hayes (1971), O'Morrow (1980), and the research experience of this author.

- First, the more a child experiences a handicap in recreation participation, the more the professional must know about teaching the activity.
- Second, the more the professional knows about teaching an activity, the less prerequisite skills are needed by the handicapped child. For example, the effective use of verbal, tactile, and kinesthetic cues in teaching an activity can eliminate the significance of a visual impairment.
- And third, the decision to teach or not to teach a recreation activity to a handicapped child must be based on whether or not that activity can be analyzed and effectively taught rather than on labels of impairment.

EVALUATION

The concept of evaluation in therapeutic recreation involves the collection of information in order to make useful judgments concerning:

1. The selection of leisure activities for program content.
2. The degree of intrinsic motivation and satisfaction demonstrated by the handicapped child during participation in recreation activities.
3. The benefits of recreation activities for children who experience a handicap (Peterson and Gunn, 1984; Kraus, 1983; O'Morrow, 1976).

Ideally, the evaluation process should be an integral part of a therapeutic recreation program. That is, the therapeutic recreation professional or parent should plan activities and design the conduct of a program with the intent of recording information about the children participating. Evaluation procedures can help to identify and clarify the role of the leisure experience in a remedial setting. The way handicapped children are portrayed in the evaluation process of a therapeutic recreation program will subsequently influence their independence in a recreation setting, their self-concept, and the way they are perceived by others. Thus, the professional or parents should determine the purpose of the evaluation process carefully during program planning.

The Purpose of the Evaluation Process

The evaluation of a handicapped child involves collecting information during an interaction with a professional, parent, or observing the child in a solitary or group recreation experience. The purpose of the evaluation process may be normative, functional, or emphasize the education and awareness of a handicapped child.

Normative Evaluation

Normative evaluation generally compares the performance or behavior of a handicapped child with cultural or developmental standards representing the majority of society. In essence, this is a social comparison and reflects any deviancy from the norm. Normative evaluation is frequently used in recreation programming with mentally retarded children to determine age-appropriate behavior, etiquette, and desirable social or activity skills which are useful for achieving normalization and mainstreaming (Fig. 5).

Functional Evaluation

Functional evaluation does not use a social norm as a standard for making judgments about a child's level of participation in recreation. The demonstrated physical and mental skill of a child can be measured in relation to the physical and mental requirements in a recreation activity. Functional evaluation is frequently used with the physically handicapped child who does not have the use of a body part. For example, an above-the-elbow amputee may require an adapted prosthetic device in order to operate both flipper buttons on a pinball machine. A functional evaluation would not focus on the physical difference of the individual from the majority of society. Instead, the evaluation information would be used to determine if the prosthesis was satisfactory for independence in the activity (Fig. 5).

Education-Awareness Evaluation

Education-awareness evaluation involves teaching and facilitating the handicapped child as part of recreation programming before judgments are made about his or her participation. The evaluation procedure does not use a social norm or a list of activity requirements for criteria. The programmed leisure experience is compared with the remedial needs and personal interests of the handicapped child. For example, the use of

FIGURE 5

THE PURPOSE OF EVALUATING A PATIENT OR CLIENT
IN THERAPEUTIC RECREATION SERVICE

Type of Evaluation Purpose	Comparison/Measure	Evaluation Result
Normative Evaluation	$=\dfrac{\text{Patient or Client Behavior}}{\text{A Cultural or Developmental Standard}}$, e.g., Age appropriate behavior, etiquette, social skills.	Identifies patient or client deviances from the norm.
Functional Evaluation	$=\dfrac{\text{Patient or Client Behavior}}{\text{The Physical and Mental Requirements of an Activity}}$, e.g., The ability to kick a ball in a soccer game.	Identifies skill deficiencies and competencies specific to an activity or situation.
Education-Awareness Evaluation	$=\dfrac{\text{Necessary Professional Teaching or Facilitation Skills}}{\text{Needs, Interests, and Abilities of the Patient or Client}}$, e.g., Evaluate cardiovascular fitness in a group mile run. Client prefers competition with other runners.	Identifies a facilitative basis for intervention with a patient or client in therapeutic recreation service.

a running program to develop cardiovascular fitness and provide activity for the emotionally disturbed child should be conducted in accordance with his or her motivational needs. During evaluation, some individuals may prefer to run alone, whereas others may prefer a group for socializing or competition. Without consideration for a child's orientation to motivation, an evaluation of self-directed competencies is not accurate. For example, in evaluating a visually impaired child's participation in a clay-modeling art class, it is important to know his or her preference for teaching methods. Some children may prefer more kines-thetic and tactile cues for learning about shapes, whereas others may only require verbal direction. Preferences for learning are determined by the individual and can influence the participation in recreation activities if the motivation is recognized by the professional or the parent (Fig. 5).

Since the evaluation process in therapeutic recreation is a direct reflection of the person who experiences a handicap, it is important for the professional to clearly identify the evaluation purpose. This may involve isolating or combining the normative, functional, or education-awareness orientations to evaluation with respect to agency service goals and the individual needs of the child.

Developing Evaluation as a Part of Therapeutic Recreation Service

The following is a list of guidelines for developing the evaluation component of therapeutic recreation service for handicapped children.

A. Determine whether the patient or client is in need of the therapy, leisure education, or independent recreation phase of service (Peterson and Gunn, 1984).
B. Determine the intended purpose for conducting an evaluation of the handicapped child (normative, functional, education-awareness level).
C. Select the recreation activities to accurately reflect the purpose of the evaluation. (This is an intuitive process for the professional or the parent.) For example, determine whether the activities are desirable for encouraging social integration and normalization, developing functional mobility, or to satisfy the program requests of the individual child.
D. Select the procedure for implementing the evaluation.
   1. Identify your own strengths and preferences for evaluating the child.
   2. Identify the strengths and preferences of the child.
E. Interpret the implications of the information collected in terms of the evaluation. This would include considerations for child's awareness of evaluation purpose, the conditions of the evaluation, and the evaluation procedure.

These guidelines are intended to emphasize the role of the therapeutic recreation professional or the parents in the evaluation of a handicapped child. There is insufficient standardized evaluation material for collecting information and making judgments about the recreation participation of handicapped children. The very nature of individual preferences for participation in recreation activities requires professionals and parents to make the evaluation procedure unique to each individual and a part of the recreation program.

Implementing Evaluation Within Recreation Activities

Ideally, evaluation can be a part of therapeutic recreation service if the process complements treatment goals and encourages the handicapped child to participate. This includes making the evaluation process a positive experience for the children being served. For example, a standardized procedure for evaluating mentally retarded children may ignore individual differences in perceptual abilities. Some children may require more verbal direction or physical demonstration than others in order to clearly understand what is sought in the evaluation.

Enthusiasm should be exhibited and the spirit of fun should be promoted as a part of the evaluation process. The therapeutic recreation professional or parents can model such an attitude and interact with the participants to make evaluation personal and non-threatening.

It is important for the handicapped child to have an awareness of the evaluation process and its purpose for him or her. This will encourage both positive and negative feedback regarding the evaluation process.

Finally, the result of evaluating children does not have to be interpreted as negative, unless the instruction or counseling provided does not facilitate them to adapt when they experience a handicap in recreation participation. For example, visual impairment may not be restrictive in a recreation activity if sufficient auditory, tactile, kinesthetic, and abstract cues are provided. The above-the-elbow amputee need not be excluded from activities that require two hands if a functional device can be substituted. Similarly, a hearing-impaired child can be included in activities that utilize auditory commands by including visual cues for participation, e.g. touch football. Interpreting evaluation information can identify considerations for facilitating independent participation in recreation activities rather than emphasizing individual differences. Ideally, therapeutic recreation programming should encourage the handicapped child to participate in evaluation rather than be subjected to it.

In order for therapeutic recreation professionals to be accountable for programming and administrative funding, evaluation procedures need to be well planned and implemented. The role of evaluation in therapeutic recreation service will be directly affected by the purpose of the evaluation process. Evaluation can provide a social comparison, indicate a functional level of skill, contribute to the education, awareness, and growth of an individual, or be a combination of all of these factors. It is important to know what you want, because if you try hard enough you are going to get it (Cox, 1979). This perspective on life has a strong implication for the role of evaluation. The way handicapped children are portrayed in evaluation of their recreation participation will influence their self-perception and the way they are perceived by society. Therapeutic recreation professionals and parents should determine evaluation purpose carefully, incorporate the evaluation process into program planning, and implement evaluation as a part of the recreation experience for handicapped children.

CONSIDERATIONS FOR COMMUNITY PROGRAMMING

Artificial Reinforcement and Motivation

If a child's level of independent participation is measured in an evaluation, the use of artificial versus natural motivators will be a concern. It is sufficient to recognize that when artificial motivators are used to influence participation behaviors, e.g. token rewards, they will have to be phased out at a later date for independent participation to occur. Ideally, professionals or parents can identify motivational factors that are part of real life rather than service settings in order to encourage mainstreaming and normalization.

Zero-Order Behaviors, Normalcy, and Recreation Participation

Zero-order behaviors exist with minimal outside support or no social reinforcement from external sources. The explanation for these behaviors is that they are expected by society and, therefore, receive little or no attention unless they are terminated. Zero-order behaviors usually become a remedial concern when they are absent from a person's routine of daily living (Gold, 1980). The behavior of wearing clothing and personal hygiene maintenance skills are examples of zero-order behaviors. Appearing naked in public, failing to inhibit perspiration odor or neglecting to clean teeth prior to socializing attracts negative attention from other people. The purpose of clarifying zero-order behaviors is to emphasize the absence of external social reinforcement in daily living. People are expected to value these behaviors without ongoing reinforcement. If the value of recreation participation is treated like a zero-order behavior with handicapped children, it may be difficult to sustain long-range development of recreation skills and integrate recreation values as a quality-of-life issue during adulthood. For parents of handicapped children, recreation may be a quality-of-life issue. That is, parents may want their child to initiate play. If normal play behavior is a treatment goal, parents and professionals may want to avoid treating the opportunity for recreation as a zero-order behavior. Recreation participation, like zero-order behaviors, is expected to be intrinsically motivated rather than externally directed. In treatment settings, however, appropriate recreation behavior may be programmed with remedial expectations. When the treatment goals are reached, parents and professionals can avoid the zero-order status of recreation participation by continuing to reinforce the **value** of recreation in the life-style of handicapped children.

A Least Restrictive Environment: The Most Appropriate Site

A least restrictive environment is probably best defined in terms of the handicapped child's ability to participate in recreation activities he or she prefers. Determining the least restrictive environment for a child's participation is crucial to a successful outcome. Understanding a child's abilities, likes, dislikes, and needs are all factors that influence program decisions regarding recreation participation. The decision to program segregated recreation experiences or mainstreamed recreation experiences will depend on the treatment goals of the professional, the parents, and the personal needs of the child. Examples of segregated therapeutic recreation programs include wheelchair athletics and the Special Olympics. Wheelchair athletics provide opportunities for physically handicapped individuals to compete in adapted sports, experience success, and to demonstrate their motivation and abilities. The Special Olympics program provides individuals labeled as mentally retarded with opportunities to participate in adapted sports and games within the forum of an organized event. Participation is the emphasis of the Special Olympics, and everyone is considered a winner. In segregated participation, the participants in these programs do not compete with individuals who are not labeled as impaired. One of the major contributions of these programs is that the participants are able to explore and to clarify the nature of their impairment. In other words, a handicapped child can determine the nature of their own limitations through their own participation, observe the adaptations of other children with impairments, and seek to improve their capabilities for participation within the context of the programs. Such programs represent new experiences for many handicapped children and expand their awareness for activity and the benefits of an active life-style. Segregated programs may call attention to the special characteristics of handicapped children (Wolfensberger, 1972), but they can provide a strong basis for the transition to mainstreaming experiences and achieving normalcy. Wheelchair athletics and the Special Olympics program may have been considered to be very unusual and outside of the mainstream when the programs were founded. Both programs, however, are currently conducted on an international level of participation and receive widespread media attention.

Mainstreaming implies success in the present system of therapeutic recreation services and other human services (Frein, 1976). It implies that all people can adequately develop and use leisure skills and opportunities regardless of their place in society or the handicap they experience. Successful mainstreaming requires effective recreational services which result in adaptations or modifications to facilitate independent leisure participation for handicapped children. The concept of mainstreaming can be applied to therapeutic recreation service through the use of a continuum, with the conditions for independent leisure participation and impaired leisure behavior identified. Powell (1979) specifies five desirable conditions that would facilitate recreation participation of the handicapped child into the mainstream of society. These conditions are:

1. The elimination of misconceptions about persons who experience a handicap, with an emphasis on their acceptance and individual abilities.
2. The reduction of segregated settings and services, with an emphasis on more integrated settings and services.
3. The conscious development of a less restrictive environment.
4. The movement of the client from a state of dependency to a state of independence.

5. A reduction of the emphasis on disabilities while increasing the
potential and abilities of handicapped individuals.

It is doubtful whether any of these conditions can be achieved
independently of each other. For example, achieving independence will
require the development of ability. Acceptance of individual differences
will be directly related to an integrated setting. Furthermore, the development of a less restrictive environment will depend on public attitudes,
client abilities and interests, and the opportunity for integrated settings.

In graphically representing these five conditions on a continuum for
therapeutic recreation service, it is necessary to include descriptions that
relate to leisure satisfaction and independent recreation participation.
Figure 6 illustrates the concept of facilitating a handicapped individual
from a state of impaired recreation behavior to independent recreation
participation. As an outcome, the handicapped individual demonstrates
his or her independence, recreational abilities, and intrinsic motivation
in a least restrictive environment. Thus, society can recognize and become
more familiar with special populations, and the potential for integration
in recreation settings is increased.

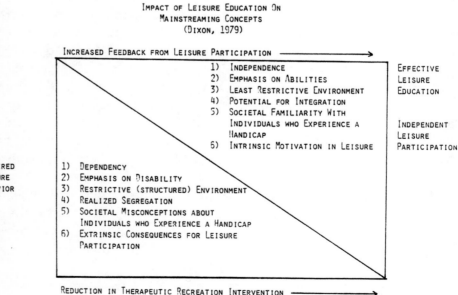

FIGURE 6

IMPACT OF LEISURE EDUCATION ON
MAINSTREAMING CONCEPTS
(DIXON, 1979)

INCREASED FEEDBACK FROM LEISURE PARTICIPATION ⟶

1) INDEPENDENCE
2) EMPHASIS ON ABILITIES
3) LEAST RESTRICTIVE ENVIRONMENT
4) POTENTIAL FOR INTEGRATION
5) SOCIETAL FAMILIARITY WITH
   INDIVIDUALS WHO EXPERIENCE A
   HANDICAP
6) INTRINSIC MOTIVATION IN LEISURE

EFFECTIVE
LEISURE
EDUCATION

INDEPENDENT
LEISURE
PARTICIPATION

IMPAIRED
LEISURE
BEHAVIOR

1) DEPENDENCY
2) EMPHASIS ON DISABILITY
3) RESTRICTIVE (STRUCTURED) ENVIRONMENT
4) REALIZED SEGREGATION
5) SOCIETAL MISCONCEPTIONS ABOUT
   INDIVIDUALS WHO EXPERIENCE A HANDICAP
6) EXTRINSIC CONSEQUENCES FOR LEISURE
   PARTICIPATION

REDUCTION IN THERAPEUTIC RECREATION INTERVENTION ⟶

CONCLUSION

Programming therapeutic recreation services for handicapped children involves the selection of appropriate activities, considerations for motivation, and the efficient use of intervention to develop activity skills and participation. This chapter was developed for practical application in programming recreation services for handicapped children. The information is intended for the parent, professional, or student who intends to develop activity skills and encourage recreation participation. Ideally, play behavior will occur spontaneously in treatment settings with children, but parents and professionals may recognize that intervention can improve the accessibility of recreation activities. The author has made an attempt to present material that is sequential and consistent with a theme of recreation skill development. The selection and development of material for this chapter has evolved from the author's own experience and professional preparation. It may help the reader to know that the selected content represents answers to questions posed in therapeutic recreation service with handicapped children.

REFERENCES

Arnheim, D., Auxter, D., and Crowe, W. (1973). *Principles and methods of adapted physical education.* St. Louis: C.V. Mosby.

Avedon, E. (1974). *Therapeutic recreation service.* Englewood Cliffs, NJ: Prentice-Hall.

Bar-Tal, D. (1975). Individual differences and attribution analysis of achievement-related behavior. Unpublished doctoral dissertation, University of Pittsburgh, Pittsburgh.

Bradtke, L., Kirkpatrick, W., and Rosenblatt, K. (1972). Intensive play: A technique for building effective behaviors in profoundly mentally retarded young children. *Education and Training of the Mentally Retarded, 7,* 8–13.

Braley, W., Konicki, G., and Leedy, C. (1968). *Daily sensorimotor training activities.* Mountain View, CA: Peek.

Burt, J., Meeks, L., and Pottebaum, S. (1980). *Toward a healthy lifestyle.* Belmont, CA: Wadsworth.

Carter, M., Van Andel, G., and Robb, G. (1985). *Therapeutic recreation: A practical approach.* St. Louis: Times Mirror/Mosby.

Council on Exceptional Children and the American Association for Health, Physical Education, and Recreation (CEC and AAHPER). (1966). *Recreation and physical activity for the mentally retarded.* Washington, DC: AAHPER.

Chubb, M., and Chubb, H. (1981). *One third of our time.* New York: Wiley.

Coleman, J., Campbell, E., Hobson, C., McPhartland, J., Mood, A., Weinfeld, F., and York, R. (1966). *Equality of educational opportunity.* U.S. Department of Health, Education, and Welfare.

Cox, G. (1979). Excerpt from a conversation. Dallas, TX.

Dixon, J. (1979). The implications of attribution theory for therapeutic recreation service. *Therapeutic Recreation Journal, 8,* 1, 3–11.

Dixon, J. (1981). *Adapting activities for therapeutic recreation service: Concepts and applications.* San Diego, CA: Campanile Press.

Dixon, J. (1983). Teaching recreation skills to mentally retarded individuals using the whole and part methods. *Journal of Recreation and Leisure, 3,* 1, 5–11.

Dixon, J. (1984). Research on teaching recreation skills to adults labeled mentally retarded. *Society and Leisure, 7,* 1, 259–268.

Dixon, J. (1984). Recognizing orientations for participation in therapeutic recreation service. *Expanding Horizons in Therapeutic Recreation, 12,* 288–307.

Dustin, D., and McAvoy, L. (1984). Toward environmental eolothism. *Environmental Ethics, 6,* 13–18.

Ellis, M. (1971, August). Play and its theories re-examined. *Parks and Recreation,* 51–57.

Ellis, M. (1973). *Why people play.* Englewood Cliffs, NJ: Prentice-Hall.

Frein, J. (1976). Mainstreaming: Origins and implications. *Minnesota Education, 2,* 2.

Glasser, W. (1976). *Positive addiction.* New York: Harper and Row.

Godfrey, B., and Thompson, M. (1966). *Movement pattern checklists.* Columbia, MO: Kelly.

Gold, M. (1976). Task analysis of a complex assembly task for the retarded blind. *Exceptional Children, 43,* 78–84.

Gold, M. (1980). *Try another way training manual.* Champaign, IL: Research Press.

Gold, M., and Pomerantz, D. (1978). Issues in prevocational training. In M. Snell (Ed.), *Teaching the moderately, severely, and profoundly retarded* (pp. 1–15). Columbus, OH: Charles E. Merrill.

Guralnik, D. (Ed.). (1975). *Webster's new world dictionary.* New York: World.

Hackett, L. (1970). *Movement exploration and games for the mentally retarded.* Palo Alto, CA: Peek.

Hastorf, A., Schneider, D., and Polefka, J. (1970). *Person perception.* Reading, MA: Addison-Wesley.

Havighurst, R., and Feigenbaum, K. (1974). Leisure and lifestyle. In J. Murphy (Ed.), *Concepts of leisure* (pp. 117–128). Englewood Cliffs, NJ: Prentice-Hall.

Hayes, G. (1971). Activity analysis: Finger painting for the mentally retarded. *Therapeutic Recreation Journal, 5,* 3, 133–138.

Heider, F. (1944). Social perception and phenomenal causality. *Psychological Review, 51.*

Heider, F. (1958). *The psychology of interpersonal relations.* New York: Wiley.

Illinois Program. (1972). *Systematic instruction for retarded children: Motor performance and recreation instruction.* Springfield, IL: Office of the Superintendent of Public Instruction.

Isaac, S., and Michael, W. (1971). *Handbook in research and evaluation.* San Diego, CA: Robert R. Knapp.

Katz, I. (1967). The socialization of academic achievement in minority group children. In D. Levine (Ed.), *Nebraska Symposium on Motivation, 15.* Lincoln: University of Nebraska Press.

Kelly, J. (1982). *Leisure.* Englewood Cliffs, NJ: Prentice-Hall.

Kraus, R. (1983). *Therapeutic recreation service: Principles and practices* (3rd ed.). Philadelphia: Saunders.

Moran, J., and Kalakian, L. (1977). *Movement experiences for the mentally retarded or emotionally disturbed child* (2nd ed.). Minneapolis: Burgess.

O'Morrow, G. (1980). *Therapeutic recreation* (2nd ed.). Reston, VA: Reston Publishing.

Peterson, C., and Gunn, S. (1984). *Therapeutic recreation program design: Principles and procedures* (2nd ed.). Englewood Cliffs, NJ: Prentice-Hall.

Rosen, M., Clark, G., and Kivitz, M. (1977). *Habilitation of the handicapped.* Baltimore, MD: University Park Press.

Rotter, J. (1966). Generalized expectancies for internal versus external control of reinforcement. *Psychological Monographs, 80,* (1, Whole No. 609).

Schmidt, R. (1975). *Motor skills.* New York: Harper and Row.

Shivers, J., and Fait, H. (1985). *Special recreational services: Therapeutic and adapted.* Philadelphia: Lea and Febiger.

Stein, T., and Sessoms, D. (1977). *Recreation and special populations* (2nd ed.). Boston: Holbrook.

Wehman, P. (1977). *Helping the mentally retarded acquire play skills.* Springfield, IL: Charles C Thomas.

Weiner, B. (Ed.) (1974). *Achievement motivation and attribution theory.* Morristown, NJ: General Learning Press.

Weiner, B., Frieze, I., Kukla, A., Reed, L., Rest, S., and Rosenbaum, R. (1971). *Perceiving the causes of success and failure.* New York: General Learning Press.

Wheeler, R., and Hooley, A. (1976). *Physical education for the handicapped.* Philadelphia: Lea and Febiger.

Wolfensberger, W. (1972). *The principle of normalization in human services.* Toronto, Ont, Canada: National Institute on Mental Retardation.

Chapter 5

ASSESSMENT: A NEED FOR FURTHER ATTENTION

Aubrey H. Fine

There is no known way of reaching
the depths of something without
going through the surface.

D. E. Berlyne

INTRODUCTION

Assessment represents a critical dimension in the overall provision of recreational services for children. Unfortunately, many therapists feel inadequately prepared for their roles in the assessment process. Furthermore, some have a limited understanding of incorporating complete assessment procedures. Consequently, they perceive their work as being unproductive and integrate assessment procedures primarily due to legislative compliance and employers' demands. This chapter is intended to provide a clearer perception of the value of assessment as well as some alternatives to incorporate into the assessment process.

Identifying hidden treasures has always been a rewarding experience. T. S. Elliott reminds us, "We shall not cease from exploration and the end of all our exploring will be to arrive where we started and know the place for the first time." Assessment (for our purposes with children) can be inferred as the process of discovery, which can help one understand clearly the strengths and limitations of a child. In fact, I sometimes view direct assessment as a series of mini-experiments, trying to derive new pieces of data in regards to a specific child.

Many practitioners view assessment as incredibly complicated and mystical. This appears partially due to the lack of familiarity with the possible procedures. However, assessment could be understood as similar to the process of putting a puzzle together. When one applies correct planning and insight, any puzzle is easy to complete. Simply stated, assessment is the gathering of information in regards to a specific client.

There are a variety of procedures available for the inquirer to secure the information desired. Such alternatives are in the form of paper-and-pencil questionnaires and tests, actual performance examinations (e.g. gross motor activities), interviewing, observations, history gathering, as well as the completion of rating scales.

Given assessment is such a large topic and has been somewhat neglected, it seems imperative that this chapter initially provide a global overview. It is the intention of this writer to provide the reader with a sufficient theoretical as well as practical understanding of the usage and application of the data generated by an assessment procedure.

The following outline has been developed to assist the reader in understanding the components within this chapter. I have formulated a series of questions as a method of organizing this outline. Hopefully, these questions will assist the reader in discovering the inherent values of thorough assessment procedures.

1. Assessment: What is it?
2. Why should I invest energies to assess?
3. What kinds of information does an assessment procedure yield?
4. What are some practical suggestions for conducting an assessment?
5. Why do I really need to know anything about test construction and, for that matter, what do I need to know?
6. What are some potential assessment alternatives?

QUESTION 1: ASSESSMENT—WHAT IS IT?

Wallace and Larsen (1978) suggest that assessments allow therapists to make decisions based on the data gathered during an assessment process. They provide a rationale for the inclusion of measurement procedures as an integral aspect of treatment. Some of their points of view are as follows:

(1) **To group children.** At times it is valuable to assess children so they can be placed in programs that fit their strengths and limitations.

(2) **To provide a framework to develop remedial instruction.** Therapists are encouraged to gather information germane to a child or a group so that program development can reflect this information.

(3) **To analyze the capabilities and accomplishments of clients.** Measuring capabilities and accomplishments is the element which many view as being the primary purpose of a comprehensive assessment.

(4) **To measure the outcomes of instruction.** For quality assurance, it is imperative that the impact of implemented programs is analyzed. A major purpose of an integrated and consistent evaluation process is to provide feedback about the program. Consequently, the information derived can assist in modifying or stabilizing the effectiveness of service delivery. Therefore, the assessment process is not a one-time intake procedure but a related process of discovery, conjecture of need, measuring gains and then continually going back to analyze further or in-depth needs.

(5) **To provide material for research.** Although this element may be the least practical, the use of measurement devices are imperative in regards to research. Research impacts the field of treatment by enhancing the present body of knowledge through identifying positive and negative aspects of programs.

Fuchs and Fuchs (1986) suggest that assessment processes are employed to objectively describe children and their instructional environments, to generate hypotheses concerning alternative instructional methods, and to finally appraise, evaluate and inductively develop instructionally sound programs. Furthermore, Wehman and Schlein (1980) noted three additional goals of assessment in therapeutic recreation. They state that an individual's progress on specific skills should be frequently monitored so that staff can do the following:

1. Receive enough feedback to analyze the progress of a child. The more frequently a child's skills are diagnosed, the easier and more proficient the process becomes.
2. Make necessary modifications in the methods or materials being applied as well as ascertaining whether the sequence of instruction is effective or not.
3. Verify that objectives have been obtained.

While all of these aforementioned points are crucial, the primary purpose of the assessment process is to gather information that can be used in planning instructional programs. The data gathered during the process will help the therapist in further understanding a child's specific needs and suggest various instructional strategies and procedures.

Dunn (1984) points out that in regards to therapeutic recreation, assessment should be understood as a systematic procedure for gathering specific information which pertains to the individual. This information then can be integrated for the purpose of making programmatic decisions. Furthermore, Dunn (1984) stresses that the overall process must not only complement the client's needs but the agency's goals as well. For example, she points out that an in-depth analysis may be inappropriate for short-term-based programs. The writer is in agreement with this point of view only to the extent that the professional always considers the feasibility of an in-depth assessment. This is to say, the goals that are formulated for short-term interventions need to realistically project viable alternatives. It would be utterly ridiculous to expect a program to supply all the needed growth for a person when it was extremely short. Furthermore, short-term-based programs are usually ineffective if they are not tied into existing resources available in the community.

The assessment procedure can be viewed sequentially. Salvia and Ysselkyke (1985) conceptualize an assessment model that constitutes five phases. Table I lists the various components.

TABLE I
THE FIVE PHASES OF A SEQUENTIAL ASSIGNMENT

1. Purpose of the assessment
2. Screening
3. Interpretation
4. Application
5. Program modification

The process begins with a referral or a purpose to the assessment. This is then followed by the actual screening or assessment of a child. Within this phase the actual collection of data is generated. However, as it can be easily seen, the four other phases either set the way for the collection or are the methods generated to analyze or apply the information obtained. The three final phases of the model relate to the application of the findings. The third phase represents the stage for the interpretation of the data. This is then followed with the final two stages which pertain to the incorporation of the findings in instructional planning and program modification. Both of these two steps are extremely crucial. Logically, instructional planning should be based on the identified concerns. Furthermore, instructional programs should be continually monitored to assess their overall effectiveness. All of these issues will be elaborated on in an upcoming section in this chapter.

Issues in Assessment Within Therapeutic Recreation

Dunn (1984) suggested several difficulties in the area of assessment within the field of therapeutic recreation. These difficulties will be used as a springboard for further discussion. The four areas are clustered as follows: general lack of assessment devices, inadequacies in test development, application deficits and staff training.

Lack of Assessment Procedures

Dunn (1984) strongly suggests that there is a significant void in assessment instruments solely developed for application in therapeutic recreation settings. She suggests that one alternative is to borrow instruments from other disciplines. The problem with this approach, Dunn points out, is that the findings do not always lead themselves to specific recreational interpretations.

Although this concern may be realistic in measuring generic leisure skills, the rubric of play behavior is dependent on various functional behaviors. These functional behaviors can be efficiently measured by several instruments on the professional market (e.g. gross and fine motor development, social skills, self-concept, self-help, language and cognition). If appropriate tests are applied to sample skills within these specific domains, an enormous amount of information can be secured and incorporated. Realistically, the dilemma may represent a lack of awareness within the field, in taking advantage of the most valid and reliable devices.

Inadequacies of Test Development

Many of the present-day instruments utilized in sampling recreational skills are unrefined and are so agency-specific that they are of limited value in other settings. Furthermore, there is a great difference between test construction and test application. Many practitioners develop tests solely for application and are not specifically concerned with the multitude of test construction problems. Dunn (1984) also suggests that these problems are further complicated because of the lack of an accepted or universal conceptual framework for leisure.

Problems of Utilization

There appears to be widespread abuse of test utilization as well as interpretation. Assessment cannot be looked upon telescopically. There is great diversity in the elements of an assessment. As a consequence, one should not be misled into believing that one instrument can answer all of the formulated questions. There is no simple answer. Information will have to be gathered through a multitude of sources.

Staff Qualifications

Until recently, professional preparation in the area of test and measurement has been significantly limited. However, with the ever-changing demands of the profession, recreational personnel have been required to initiate more comprehensive programs that incorporate an assessment process. Dunn (1984) suggests that there has been some progress made in this area both at the preservice (undergraduate) as well as professional level because of its perceived importance.

It is anticipated that in the future, professionals with a stronger background in the area of measurement will take the major role of supervising or initiating a majority of the measurement duties of their agencies. It is inappropriate to expect minimally trained persons to be responsible for conducting or interpreting and developing comprehensive assessments. The charge of this role should not be considered lightly. It is evident that greater emphasis must be placed in this area in undergraduate and graduate training programs. Attention also will need to be given to providing more comprehensive seminars to professionals in the field. These seminars will need to address practical concerns in addition to being extremely comprehensive.

QUESTION 2: WHY SHOULD I INVEST MY TIME ASSESSING?

The importance of assessment is supported in the philosophical position statement adopted by the National Therapeutic Recreation Society (1982). Within this philosophical statement is the assertion that programs should be developed by assessing the clients' needs and that strategies to monitor and measure clients' progress should be included. The implications of this revised definition will gradually have a significant impact on the field as a whole in addition to the direction in training at institutions of higher learning.

As can be interpreted by the following statement, assessment should be considered as a natural ingredient to program planning. When one does not complete a thorough intake, information in regards to the client's needs is insufficiently addressed. Consequently, the program goals generated eventually suffer and the outcomes attributed to program involvement are questionable at best!

As stated earlier, assessment is something we hear a lot about but remains an area in which some professionals feel inadequate. Some attribute a mystic quality to the field of measurement. However, there is nothing mysterious about it; most of the procedures merely require good judgment and specific training. Nevertheless, numerous assessment procedures really do have significant limitations! In fact, it is not the assessment instruments that lead to a thorough diagnostic impression but rather the professional's ability to glean from the data his/her judgments and interpretations. It is therefore imperative for an assessor to respect the integrity of the instruments applied and recognize that they are only tools by which one can uncover hidden treasures. The ultimate decisions are made by the individual, who synthesizes and interprets the findings and develops realistic expectations.

It is important to acknowledge that even the most reliable assessment instruments are sometimes misused. The art of assessment must not be conceptualized as the ability to administer tests or to observe behavior but, rather, to reveal the findings and apply them. Being able to synthesize and wisely incorporate the information obtained is the benefit of going through this process.

What Information Do You Usually Have At Your Disposal?

There is a wealth of information readily available at the therapist's disposal. I have always found this data helpful in augmenting assessment procedures that are incorporated. Again, let us return to my puzzle analogy. What I know about the design of my puzzle alters my expectations of how I proceed in completing the project. A similar assumption must also take place when analyzing a child's strengths and limitations. Take advantage of the obvious as well as what is already known from earlier situations. So let us briefly look at some of the pre-assessment information that is usually readily available.

(1) What Do You Know About the Client You Want to Assess?

Prior to incorporating formal or informal assessment procedures, efforts should be made to collect as much information about the child under investigation as possible. There are a variety of areas that could be pursued. For example, one should take advantage of collaboration with parents, significant others, and those who have previously worked with the child. All of these sources should be respected and not overlooked. In fact, all of these alternatives should be starting points, possibly in conjunction with the entire assessment procedure.

Numerous available questionnaires can be administered to families in addition to conducting a structured interview as methods to gain insight into the specific needs of a child. Families not only can give examiners a thorough orientation to their child, but they can additionally tell the therapists about their expectations. Parents are frequently the only individuals, aside from a few professionals, who see the child as a whole person. Furthermore, parents are able to observe how their child uses leisure skills for long periods of time in his/her natural environment. Obviously, information from family members should be respected and not overlooked.

Securing information from previous programs that a child was involved in represents another rich avenue for gathering input. Contacting these programs and reviewing pertinent data from schools attended are all excellent sources. Some will argue that it is too demanding to expect a professional to consult with this many resources to only gain a broader awareness of a child. This may not be the alternative of choice for each case under investigation. However, it may be an alternative for some children when more input is necessary.

(2) What are the Behaviors Presently Being Displayed by a Child?

An enormous amount of information can be gathered through the informal use of observation. The astute observer appreciates the fact that through his/her eyes much of the world can be unravelled and understood. Observations represents an alternative method in gathering information. There are several formal and informal observational methods that can be applied. Further attention will be given to this area later within this chapter.

QUESTION 3: WHAT KINDS OF INFORMATION DOES AN ASSESSMENT PROCEDURE YIELD?

The process must provide the professional (for the purposes within the chapter, the use of the term **therapist, examiner,** or **instructor** may be used interchangeably with the term **professional**) with the information necessary for planning and measuring each child's program (Dollar and

Brooks, 1980). Therefore, the included assessment process should: (a) be able to measure a child's current level of functioning so that the group will know where to begin; (b) be global and address all behavioral domains concentrated upon within the program (e.g. motor behaviors, language, social and recreational skills); (c) describe the conditions that are necessary for the facilitator to create the optimal learning environment; and (d) hopefully identify criteria that can later be used as a **measuring stick** for acceptable performance. The critical assumption relates to the position that assessment should be used as a "cornerstone for systematic instruction, uniting testing with instruction" (Dubose, 1979). Furthermore, as suggested earlier, this process must be an ongoing procedure, continually updating the body of knowledge formulated.

Sailor and Haring (1977) have identified four domains that they believe should be assessed from a developmental viewpoint. The four areas that they focused on were self-help, sensory motor, communication and social skills. On the other hand, there are others who suggest developing assessment procedures from an age-appropriate standpoint. Therefore, a couple of other areas that may need attention may pertain to domestic living, community functioning and more specific identification of leisure and recreational skills (Brown et al., 1979).

How can one gather information in some of the other behavioral domains? As was suggested earlier, there are a variety of options that an examiner can apply. The most common alternatives that have been cited can be sampled through criterion-referenced, norm-referenced as well as observational assessment. The following will briefly define each of the procedures for you.

Criterion-Referenced and Norm-Referenced Assessments

The measurement of performance, potential ability, achievement, and progress are crucial elements in the rehabilitation of exceptional children. Presently, an enormous amount of normative data is compiled to allow comparison of an individual's performance to a standard or group score (Wallace and Larsen, 1978). It is important, however, to realize that the primary purpose of a diagnostic workup is to provide professionals with pertinent information appropriately developed for an individual child (Johnson and Martin, 1980).

Typically, criterion-referenced tests use a specific population of persons as the interpretive frame of reference rather than a specific content domain. In this respect, instead of measuring an examinee's perform-ance by comparing the findings with scores obtained by others on the same test (norm referenced), the examinee's performance can be reported in terms of specific skills s/he mastered or has difficulty with (Anastassi, 1976). Glaser (1971) stresses that criterion-referenced measures assess an individual's abilities that provide insight on the degree of competence attained by a child. This information is independent to the performance of others (which is usually secured by norm-referenced procedures). There are numerous researchers who point out the importance of quali-fying what a child can or cannot do rather than just simply comparing the individual's performance to others. Holowinsky (1980), in his review of practices of the past, advocates for techniques that focus on individual growth and mastery.

Popham and Husek (1969) point out that it is sometimes literally impossible to tell a norm-referenced test from a criterion-referenced test simply by looking at them. They point out the advantage of the norm-referenced test is in its adaptability to make comparisons to a standard group. This is an asset when a degree of selectivity is necessary. On the other hand, criterion-referenced measures attempt to ascertain an indi-vidual's abilities with respect to a performance standard. Consequently, with this form of assessment, one would determine what an individual could or could not do. However, criterion-referenced procedures do not lend themselves to making reliable comparisons to others.

It seems only logical that both of these procedures should be utilized. Together, they can generate a reliable source of insight. In the initial intake process, it appears necessary to gather data which compares a child's performance to that of others (normative sample). However, after the initial assessment has been completed, there is very little applicabil-ity in applying standardized tests to make frequent measurements of a child's progress (Proger and Mann, 1973). As a rule, the information gained through normative tests is usually not precise enough for plan-ning specific programs (Wallace and Larsen, 1976). This is where criterion-referenced procedures can play an important role. Criterion-referenced assessments can provide insight about instructional levels and mastery of concepts. Fuchs and Fuchs (1986) strongly suggest that the closer the assessment mirrors the actual learning environment, the more accurate and applicable the assessment data will be. Simon (1969) suggests that the distinction between the two discussed forms of measurement does not relate to the nature of the tests themselves but, rather, to the interpretation and use of the scores from the tests. Perhaps, the most important contribution of the integration of the criterion-referenced assessment in recreation is the probability of determining if a child has mastered the basic concepts explored in the program (Millman, 1970; Proger and Mann, 1973). Through consistent implementation of this procedure, the measurement of the development of skills as a consequence of programming can easily occur (Popham and Hasek, 1969).

As can be seen, there are advantages to utilizing both criterion- and norm-referenced approaches. Table II has been developed to illustrate concisely some of the strengths and limitations of both procedures.

TABLE II

**LIABILITY AND ASSETS FOR NORM-REFERENCED
AND CRITERION-REFERENCED PROCEDURES**

Procedure
Norm referenced.

Assets
Comparing individual's performance to a group.
Adaptability to make comparisons to a standard group.
When a degree of selectivity is necessary.

Liabilities
Not usually effective in frequently measuring a child's performance.
Sometimes not sensitive in measuring slight changes.
Not as effective in providing information about planning specific programs.

Procedure
Criterion referenced.

Assets
Reports data in terms of specific skills which a child has mastered or not.
Measures individual abilities with respect to a performance standard.
More accurate and applicable to programming.
Maximizes the probability of determining if a child has mastered the basic concepts explored
    by a program.

Liabilities
The tests do not lend themselves to making reliable comparisons to others.
There has been significant misuse of this term.
Some of these instruments are not psychometrically well developed.

Like all good things, criterion-referenced procedures can be misused. Johnson and Martin (1980) point out that similar to all new wine, criterion-referenced testing is in a developmental stage. They suggest that there are practices today which negate the value of the criterion-referenced model. A synthesis of their concerns follow.

Some professionals are now classifying many of their observational techniques and checklists as criterion-referenced testing. For example, in the recreation movement, there are in practice many leisure interest finders and behavioral checklists that could be misrepresented. Although, these instruments (e.g. Mirenda Leisure Interest Finder, Comprehensive Evaluation of Recreation Therapy) have their value, they should not be confused with a criterion-referenced approach. Although they note the merits in these approaches, Johnson and Martin (1980) believe it is not appropriate to suddenly begin calling them criterion referenced. They stress that by including such procedures as basic instructor-made checklists, which are not tests at all, the concept of criterion-referenced tests begins to lose its meaning. They also point out that various test constructors are borrowing the term from previously developed norm-referenced tests that may have been weaker psychometrically. This abuse should be considered unjustifiable and very misleading. The unsuspecting test users believe they are in the possession of an appropriate criterion-referenced test. To their dismay, they will eventually recognize that these tests will provide information that is similar to that derived from norm-referenced tests.

Those serving an exceptional child must become educated and aware of how to select and evaluate a useful criterion-referenced instrument. Ignorance due to not taking the time to investigate should not be used as an excuse for misusing an instrument. Attention should be given to how an instrument has been developed as well as its reliability and validity. A section on this topic will be incorporated later in this chapter. However, at this time I would like to discuss another assessment alternative: the area of observational assessment.

Observation: An Aspect of Assessment

The astute observer recognizes that much of the world can be unravelled through his/her eyes. When one is in search of information, one must take advantage of all available avenues. This basic truth applies within the domain of assessment. One alternative is through the use of observation. As Shakespeare once said, "We are creatures that look before and after: the more surprising is that we do not look around a little and see what is passing under our very eyes."

Assessment of overt behaviors can be accomplished in a variety of ways. As Kazdin (1980) points out, behaviors are usually assessed on the basis of separate response occurrences or the amount of time in which the response occurs. Nevertheless, there are a variety of observational techniques which are viable alternatives for the collection of data.

Before discussing formal observational techniques, brief attention will be given to the use of unstructured, non-systematic observation. In non-systematic observations, the observer simply watches an individual and takes note of anything of significance. The most basic type of observational technique is know as **narrative recording** (Cooper, 1981). In essence, the individual simply observes and records all the behaviors elicited by the observee in a specific time frame. Salvia and Ysselyke (1985) point out that non-systematic observations tend to be anecdotal and subjective. When working with a specific child or a group of children, parents and professionals observe an enormous amount of behavior. For example, during a cooking activity, the following questions might pop into one's mind while the activity is going on:

1. Can each of the children complete the task being presented?
2. Is the length of the activity appropriate to maintain the interests of the children?
3. What are the social dynamics of the group?

In reality, all of these questions can be answered by just watching the interaction take place. One major advantage of informal observations is that the information obtained can enhance the productivity of the worker by giving that person some basic insightful information. Moreover, the time and effort expended by the clinician while observing are minimal in comparison to the amount of the information gathered. Nevertheless, the skills necessary to understanding or interpreting one's observations are a prerequisite of an astute observer. One must not only observe the occurrences but, additionally, question their relevance.

There are, however, significant limitations to informal approaches. Most notable is that only a certain amount of information can be gathered, and for that matter it is gathered very unsystematically. There are a variety of alternatives that can be used to systematize one's observations. Within systematic observations, the examiner sets out to observe a pre-specified behavior(s). After specifying the behavior(s) to be observed, the examiner typically counts how often it was displayed and/or the duration or latency of the behavior. The following represents a brief overview of a few alternatives.

Frequency Measure

Obtaining frequency counts simply entails tallying the number of times the behavior occurs in a given time period. This is also known as the response rate. Frequency measures are particularly useful when observable behavior is discrete and takes a relatively constant amount of time to be performed (Kazdin, 1980). Therefore, behaviors such as smiling and talking are difficult to record by counting frequencies, because these behaviors may last varying amounts of time.

When measuring frequency of a behavior, one rule that must be followed is that the behavior should be observed for a constant amount of time, over several observational periods. Moreover, observations should also be made on a multitude of occasions at various time intervals. These time frames should sample the overall period that one works with a person. All of us recognize that children have times during the day when their performance is better than at other times. Therefore, we need to sample various time periods to ensure that our impressions are stable and reliable.

For example, consider a situation in which the observer is concerned with how involved a young boy is in a gardening program. Let us suppose that the boy is shoveling. It may be of interest to the therapist to find out how many times this child actually digs into the ground and shovels during a specified time frame. This may give the examiner some information relating to the boy's usage of time. The frequency measures can be obtained on a continual basis to assess if improvement in the usage has occurred.

Discrete Categorization

Discrete categorization is a very straightforward observational procedure. In many ways it is similar to frequency measures. Discrete categorization is useful only with behaviors that have a clear beginning and ending. Its primary advantage is to classify responses into discrete categories such as correct/incorrect or performed/not performed. It is used primarily to measure whether several behaviors have occurred or not (Kazdin, 1980).

For example, let us focus on a group of six pre-teens cleaning up after preparing a snack for the group. A checklist can be developed to analyze how well the group cleans up after its program. The checklist may include behaviors such as washing the dishes, placing the garbage in the appropriate outlets, putting away the excess food and utensils and many other notable behaviors. Each behavior is then measured as being performed or not. Note that the behaviors incorporated within the checklist may constitute several different steps that relate to a completion of an entire task (Kazdin, 1980).

Interval Recording

The last observational format to be discussed is interval recording. In this approach, the focus is on the amount of time engaged in an activity rather than on specific behaviors per se. When using interval recording, a specified behavior is observed for a specific period of time. This block of time is then divided up into a series of short intervals. Observations are made during each of these intervals to assess whether the behavior has occurred or not. For example, a major goal of working with a child who is extremely impulsive may be to keep the child on task. One method of evaluating the effectiveness of a treatment program is through interval recording. The child can be observed a couple of times per day (once in the morning and once in the afternoon). The total observation period can take place within a 15-minute interval. This 15-minute interval can be further divided into 30-second durations. Consequently, an observer can merely articulate whether the designated behavior was displayed or not within each interval. To assist in the implementation of this procedure, a chart can be designed to keep track of the child's performance. For example, Figure 1 represents an interval recording sheet in which the observer merely circles whether the appropriate behavior was displayed or not within each interval. A plus sign (+) can be designated to indicate observed on-task behavior, while a minus sign (−) can be applied to indicate the child was off task.

FIGURE 1

INTERVAL RECORDING FORMAT

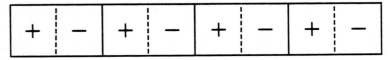

Examiners should circle the plus (+) if the behavior is observed
and circle the minus (−) if the behavior is not observed

A variant of the interval recording approach is duration recording, which involves measuring how long a response was performed. This method is particularly useful for ongoing responses. Programs that attempt to increase or decrease the length of time of a response would profit from utilizing this approach. Again, we can observe the same child in regards to his on-task behavior, but this time address how long s/he was on task.

Before continuing any further, let us review the following information on the various observational paradigms. Table III will be utilized to illustrate the following information.

Basic Steps in Conducting Behavioral Observations

The following discussion of the steps in conducting behavioral observations is based on the work of McLoughlin and Lewis (1986). They suggest five steps within the observational process.

(1) **Describe the Behavior to be Observed.** Prior to conducting an observation, the behavior under investigation needs to be clarified. In other words, one needs to operationally define exactly what will be observed. For example, if one is focusing on disruptive behavior, it is necessary to clearly delineate exactly what one is considering under this heading (e.g. hitting, screaming, answering back).

(2) **Select a Measurement System.** Within this chapter, observational alternatives have been discussed. One of these alternatives should be selected. It has been suggested that with discrete (tangible) behaviors, frequency or duration measures are appropriate, whereas for non-discrete behaviors (such as talking or on-task behaviors), an interval recording is more appropriate.

(3) **Set Up the Data Collection System.** This is a critical step in conducting the observation. Many questions need to be answered before making observations. For example, one must decide who will collect the data, when and where data collection will take place, how long the observations will last, and how the data will be recorded and analyzed. McLoughlin and Lewis (1986) suggest that observations should be scheduled at times and situations where the target behavior is most likely to occur. It is important to select alternate viewing periods so that one can more thoroughly observe the child.

(4) **Select a Data Reporting System.** The data collected should be charted and put on a graph. Graphs are extremely helpful in explaining data and illustrating if change has occurred.

(5) **Carry Out the Observation.** At this point in the process, the therapist is ready to carry out the observation and the analysis of behavior.

TABLE III
LIABILITIES AND ASSETS FOR VARIOUS OBSERVATIONAL PROCEDURES

Procedure
Non-systematic.

Assets
Simple to apply.
The procedure can provide an enormous amount of general insight.

Liability
Only a certain amount of information can be derived.

Procedure
Frequency data.

Asset
Particularly viable for behavior that is discrete and takes a relatively constant amount of time.

Liability
Reported data at times can be misleading. It is imperative that one collect data that is representative of a child's typical day.

Procedure
Discrete categorization.

Assets
Straightforward procedure.
Classifies responses into discrete categories such as correct/incorrect, performed/not performed.
Assists in identifying the various behavioral components within the entire task.

Liability
Useful only with behaviors that have a clear beginning and ending.

Procedure
Interval recording.

Assets
Useful when the focus is on the amount of time engaged within an activity rather than on specific behaviors.
Indicates relative frequency and duration.

Liabilities
Not appropriate for discrete frequency collection.
Requires ongoing observations in conjunction with time monitoring.
May not reflect an accurate representation of the overall frequency of the behavior under scrutiny.

Procedure
Duration recording.

Assets
Effective in measuring ongoing responses.
Often utilized in combination with other techniques.

Liabilities
Not appropriate for discrete frequency collection.
Cannot be used when several behaviors are being monitored.

Once the data is collected, the observer can determine if the behavior under investigation is a genuine problem or not. All too often, people assume that a behavior is a problem when in fact it is not. However, when the behavior is actually observed, they recognize that it is not as significant a problem as they had assumed. However, a word of caution is in order. A significant limitation to the observational approach is that it is informal and thus there are not any norms to go by. Professional judgment or the development of local norms, where appropriate, are necessarily used as standards for comparisons.

Difficulties with Observational Data

Although there are several advantages to using observational procedures to assess the behavior of children, there are several disadvantages. The first difficulty pertains to time (Salva and Ysseldyke, 1985). Incorporating well-designed observational programs into a busy schedule can be difficult, and observers need to be prepared for this investment of time. Another disadvantage is that the very presence of an observer may alter a situation and may make an individual behave differently. If an individual is aware of being observed, the procedure is said to be obtrusive (Kazdin, 1980). However, there have been several studies that have indicated that the presence of an observer has little or no effect on behaviors that are observed (Mercatoris and Craighead, 1974). Nevertheless, the observer should be cautious while observing and should try to stay out of the way.

Finally, a word of caution needs to be incorporated in regard to observer reliability. Observers need to be trained so that they feel at ease with the data generated. Only when observers are appropriately prepared should they be permitted to actually collect data. This entails helping individuals develop the skills to initiate an observational assessment competently. Observers must have a clear understanding of what they are looking for. Furthermore, they need to consistently be able to observe the same phenomenon and record its presence. It is usually helpful if a couple of persons observe the targeted behavior. If they agree that the behavior has been generated, the interjudge reliability is positive. Having high interjudge reliability on what is being observed provides confidence that the observations are accurate. Unreliable data is useless and therefore precautions are necessary. Sometimes unreliable data is generated because of the observer's investment in the outcome. Consequently, what is documented may not be an accurate representation of the behavior under scrutiny.

Observing Play Behavior: What Information Can Be Derived?

Through play, a child can explore and experiment with his or her perceptions of the world. Play can provide an observer with significant insight into a child's life. However, without an awareness of how to interpret such behavior, the impressions would be worthless. An analogy would be similar to getting into a locked room. Without the key, one's entrance may be prohibited.

Thus far, a discussion of various observational paradigms have been presented. A clinician may even desire to tailor an entire play situation for purposes of gathering diagnostic information. Play is rich, revealing many levels of cognition as well as social abilities. Rubin (1983) and Belsky and Most (1981) suggest that research clearly indicates that observation of free play can be a reliable indicator of social, social-cognitive and cognitive competence in children.

Formal understanding of basic child development is imperative for generating accurate conclusions from one's observations. Several interpretations have been formulated as guidelines to follow. Nicholich (1977) as well as many other investigators (Sinclair, 1970; Lowe, 1975) have confirmed Piaget's developmental sequence of play. Table IV lists a developmental sequence of cognitive and social behaviors as they relate to play. Furthermore, there have been others who have even specialized their interpretations so they specifically assess human functions. Nicholich (1977) has described procedures for assessing symbolic play maturity through the analysis of pretend play. The development of symbolic skills as manifested in play can provide a dynamic approach for assessing children's representational abilities and some of the cognitive prerequisites for communicative intentions of linguistic abilities. Westby (1980) succinctly describes the sequence of symbolic play and language stages and provides one method for interpretation: The Symbolic Play Scale. Table V illustrates several of the elements incorporated within the scale. The observer is also provided with an observation form to assist in the documentation of the elicited behavior.

The Play Observation Scale, developed by Rubin and his associates at Waterloo University, is another good example of how play can formally be interpreted. The Play Observation Scale has been used to derive

TABLE IV
DEVELOPMENTAL STAGES OF PLAY

Levels of Social Play (Formulated by Smilansky, 1986)

Autistic play (onlooker play)
Solitary play
Parallel play
Cooperative play
Competitive play

Levels of Cognitive Play

Functional play (sensorimotor stage)
Constructive play (preoperational play)
Dramatic play (preoperational play)
Games with rules (associated with at least concrete abilities)

developmental information on various areas. Several significant benchmarks have been identified with this scale (e.g. from three to five years of age, the frequency of parallel play decreases and group play is strengthened). Reports from various professionals who are acquainted with this instrument have been extremely favorable.

Rebecca Fewell, a respected scholar and educator, has spent an enormous amount of time studying the implications of play, cognitive, communicative, and social development (Fewell and Rich, 1987). Fewell has been instrumental in developing two useful devices that are valuable in assessing the abilities of preschoolers. The Play Assessment Scale (Fewell, 1984) consists of 45 developmentally sequenced items appropriate for children between the ages of two and thirty-six months. In addition, The Learning Through Play Checklist (Fewell and Vadasy, 1983) provides a guide for using a resource manual of play activities for infants and toddlers to the age of three.

As can be easily understood, a clinical interpretation can also be applied as a means of securing insight. To apply these approaches, one would be in need of some background training to develop both the skills of observation and data collection. These skills will also have to be thoroughly combined with a solid theoretical frame of reference on what this information represents.

TABLE V
SYMBOLIC PLAY SCALE

Play (Cognition)	*Language*
Stage I — 12 months	
Child has some awareness that objects exist when he does not see them. Crawls or walks to get things he wants. Will pull string toys. Does not mouth all toys. Uses some common objects appropriately.	No true language. Child may have some performative words, i.e. words that are associated with actions or the total situations, but are not true labels. Child may often vocalize when he wants something.
Stage II — 13 to 17 months	
Child explores toys purposively. Discovers operation of toys through trial and error or hands toys to adults to operate.	Some children develop single words. These words are extremely context dependent, e.g. the child may use the word "car" when he is riding in a car but not when he simply sees a car. Words tend to come and go in the child's vocabulary.
Stage III — 17 to 19 months	
Child knows how to use most common objects. Engages in some autosymbolic play, i.e. child will pretend to go to sleep or pretend to drink from a cup or eat from a spoon.	Beginning of true communication. Child uses single words to refer to agents, objects, rejection, objects disappearing and objects or people recurring.
Stage IV — 19 to 22 months	
Child begins to play with dolls. Will brush a doll's hair, feed a doll a bottle, or cover a doll with a blanket. Child may perform actions on a doll, another child, and adult, and himself.	Child begins to use word combinations. Variety of semantic relations increases and child refers to objects and persons not present.
Stage V — 24 months	
Child plays house — is the mommy, daddy, or baby. REPRESENTS daily experiences. Objects used in play must be realistic and close to usual size. Pretend events are short and isolated. Block play consists of stacking and knocking over. Sand play consists of filling, pouring, and dumping.	Child uses short sentences. Present progressive "ing" markers appear on verbs, and plural and possessive markers may appear on nouns.

TABLE V (Continued)

Play (Cognition)	Language

Stage VI — 2½ years

Child RE–PRESENTS events less frequently experienced or observed — impressive or traumatic events (doctor-nurse-sick child). Child in a school may play teacher. Child still requires realistic props. Roles shift quickly. Events still short and isolated.

Child responds to WH questions in context (who, whose, where, what . . . do). Child asks WH questions by putting the WH word at the beginning of a sentence. Child's responses to Why questions are inappropriate except for well-known routines, e.g., "Why is the doctor here?" . . . "boy's sick." Child asks why particularly in response to negative commands given by adults (e.g. "don't touch that").

Stage VII — 3 years

Continuance of pretend activities of stage V and VI, but now the play has a sequence — events are not isolated, e.g., child mixes cake, bakes it, serves it, washes the dishes; or doctor checks patient, calls the ambulance, takes patient to hospital, patient dies. Sequence EVOLVES . . . NO PLANNED. Child still dependent on realistic props. Associative play appears.

Child now uses past tense and future aspect (gonna) forms, e.g., "I ate the cake," "I'm gonna wash the dishes."

Stage VIII — 3 to 3½ years

Child begins to carry out play activities of previous stages with a dollhouse and Fisher-Price toys (barn, garage, airport). First use of blocks and sandbox for imaginative play. Blocks used primarily as enclosures (fences and houses) for dolls and animals. Play not totally stimulus-bound. Child is able to use one object to represent another.

Descriptive vocabulary expands as child becomes more aware of perceptual attributes. Uses shape, size, texture, color, and spatial relationship terms — not always correctly. Metalinguistic awareness develops . . . child uses language to talk about language. Will give dialogue to toy people.

Stage IX — 3½ to 4 years

Child begins to be able to problem-solve events he has experienced. He hypothesizes "what would happen if." Is becoming less dependent on realistic props.

Child verbalizes intentions and possible future events. May use modals (may, can, might, will, would, could); conjunction (and, but, so, if, because). NOTE: Full competence for these modals and conjunctions does not develop until 10–12 years of age.

TABLE V (Continued)

Play (Cognition)	Language

Stage X—5 years

Play (Cognition)	Language
Child now *plans* a sequence of pretend events. Organizes what he needs—in both objects and other children. Coordinates more than one event occurring at a time. Can be highly imaginative—not dependent on realistic props.	Child begins to use relational terms such as "then, when, first, next, while, before, after." NOTE: Full competence does not develop until 10–12 years of age.

Observation Form

Onlooking	Solitary	Parallel	Associative	Cooperative	
					Game
					Symbolic Spontaneous
					Symbolic Imitative
					Practice

Definition of Play Behaviors for the Observation Form

Practice — The child engages in gross motor activities such as running, riding on bikes or wagons, climbing, throwing balls. Child works puzzles, strings beads, stacks blocks and knocks them down, fills and empties containers, operates cause-effect toys such as music boxes, "busy" boxes, talking toys, etc.

Symbolic Imitative — The child engages in pretend play, but it is initiated and guided by another child or an adult.

Symbolic Spontaneous — The child initiates the pretend activity.

TABLE V (Continued)

Onlooking	—The child observes but does not participate.
Solitary	—The child plays without reference to other children.
Parallel	—The child's play is of a companionable nature with similar materials but with no personal interaction.
Associative	—The children's play is loosely organized around a common activity, shared interests, and materials.
Cooperative	—The play includes different roles, common goals, usually with one or two leaders, and is of relatively long duration and complexity.

The observers using the forms recorded a description of the child's behavior within the appropriate box on the form. If a child engaged in several different behaviors during a recording time, the behaviors were sequentially numbered.

From Assessment in Cognitive and Language Abilities Through Play by Carol E. Westby. In *Language Speech and Hearing Services in the Schools,* 1980, *11*(3), pp. 154–168. © 1980 by permission of the author and the American Speech-Language-Hearing Association.

QUESTION 4: WHAT ARE SOME PRACTICAL SUGGESTIONS FOR CONDUCTING AN ASSESSMENT?

Now that some of the basic material has been presented, it is only logical that emphasis be given to some practical methods for initiating an assessment. McLoughlin and Lewis (1986) and Salvia and Ysselyke (1985) offer suggestions concerning this area of assessment. Their suggestions as well as some personal tips are now discussed.

Interviewing and Incorporating Test Data

As indicated in the beginning of this chapter, it is important to interview parents or significant others to gather information about a child. Too often, professionals do not take full advantage of the family as a source. Unfortunately, an enormous amount of information is therefore lost. The use of family and significant others is especially crucial when children are very young and information acquired through testing may be inaccurate.

If the information gathered is usually loosely put together, all of the facts may be difficult to weed through. The ease of interpretation generally depends upon the degree of structure imposed upon the data collection. It is therefore important for an observer to think through the questions asked in an interview as well as the order in which questions are presented. If the need for further clarification arises, one then can deviate from the original format. By developing a format, the therapist can obtain a great deal of insight. It is also suggested that an interview (when permissible) should proceed all direct assessments. By following this guideline, the clinician can apply the obtained information as input in devising the most accurate assessment process.

The reader may find it helpful to apply a screening device which will assist in gathering pertinent developmental and play history. A good developmental history will provide the examiner with basic intake information as well as pertinent information in regards to the acquisition of developmental milestones. Furthermore, there have been some professionals who have established a play history survey which is amenable to an interview. For example, Takata (1974) developed a play history instrument. The instrument assists the examiner in synthesizing incoming information about the preferred forms of play as well as a child's play skills. From the findings derived in the interview, the clinician can develop a summary about the child's needs and provide some insight on a prescription program.

In reality, assessments in recreation programs are developed for two purposes. One purpose is to identify the needs of a child and to try and develop programs that address those needs. Secondly, continual estimates of the child's progress serve as a method of quality assurance. It is important to know if the programs are effective. If the child has reached the desired goals, new goals must be set and programs should be altered. On the other hand, if the program is ineffective, modifications are imperative. Ongoing measurements should therefore be viewed as necessary and critical to overall program effectiveness.

Formulating Questions in Regards to Assessment Devices

The examiner should formulate several questions when selecting an assessment tool. For example, a basic question is usually, **Which assessment devices should I use?** Too often, people allow the availability or familiarity of assessment tools to dictate their selection. Of course, this procedure is erroneous. The approach, which could be either normative, criterion-referenced or observational, should be selected based on its advantages and disadvantages to the case in question. For example, one needs to know the type of information requested. If the goal is to answer questions about the child's abilities in comparison to others, the only logical selection is a norm-referenced test. However, if the information desired pertains to mastery of a certain task or specific behaviors, criterion-referenced tests, observations, and/or informal checklists may be the most reliable format.

The assessment tasks must be compatible with the skills of the child (McLoughlin and Lewis, 1986). A child should not be required to attempt tasks that are significantly above his/her ability level. Assessment procedures should capitalize on strengths rather than penalize weaknesses (McLoughlin and Lewis, 1986). Additionally, the examiner should also be concerned with how the procedure is presented. For example, is the child required to read, write, listen or look at pictures? What modality is used when the child responds (e.g. verbalizing the answer, writing the answer out, or for that matter darkening-in a box)? Other considerations may include whether the test is administered individually or in a group, and how long the test takes to administer.

Other variables need to be considered. Testing should be discontinued, and the child should be given a break if she/he becomes restless. Furthermore, if the examiner believes that the results obtained are a minimal estimate of a child's ability (due to lack of motivation, distractability, etc.), the examiner should not accept the results obtained. As indicated earlier, the examiner is the master of the process. He/she brings into the examination his/her greatest asset, i.e. clinical judgment. When results obtained do not appear to agree with previous impressions or other test findings, the examiner will have to use his/her judgment to interpret the discrepancy.

The selection of the instrument of choice is also dependent upon the skill level of the examiner. Tools should never be applied by untrained personnel. These individuals will have an enormous amount of difficulty not only administering the test but also scoring and interpreting the results.

Is the Selected Tool Adequate?

One must have confidence in the instruments administered. The test must be soundly constructed and have high reliability and validity. Furthermore, the clinician must also determine whether the selected approach can be efficiently administered and scored.

Understanding and Acknowledging Developmental History and Present Conditions

Prior to conducting a thorough appraisal of a child's skills, it is imperative that the clinician gather information about the individual's past history and current circumstances. An awareness of the child's medical and developmental history may provide clues for understanding present levels of involvement. Past history can reveal intuitive reasoning for activity involvement and skills developed. Salvia and Ysseldyke (1985) stress that it is not enough to only assess a child's current level of functioning; rather, the therapist must become more cognizant of how the past may have influenced and shaped current behaviors. Furthermore, examiners should take notice when children are not performing up to their capacity due to factors such as health, anxiety, or attitudes. If this occurs, the examiner must disregard the results obtained and re-evaluate on another occasion.

Controlling Variables and Providing Encouragement for Efforts

When testing children, attention should be given to eliminating as many extraneous variables as possible. The professional should find a quiet room that has the least number of distractions. There should not be a lot of supplies around, since these may pose as a distraction to the child.

Children should be reinforced frequently for their efforts. This is permitted even in standardized testing. While one cannot tell a child that he/she responded correctly, one should tell a child how happy he/she is because the child is trying hard and/or cooperating. Finally, it is critical to administer tests exactly according to the directions in the manual. Modifying directions or expectations of a standardized test invalidates the findings. This is because the norms formulated have been derived by applying the specified procedure. When this procedure is modified, even slightly, it may make a significant difference in the results.

Interpreting Results

When an individual is assessed, one is basically sampling the performance of that individual at a particular time. These results represent predictions of potential future ability. They represent inferences in which one may place specific levels of confidence.

Probably the most difficult and most important aspect of the measurement process is the explanation of the findings. Additionally, these findings should be translated into practical applications and should play a role in generating program ideas. So, in reality, the therapist must cautiously administer tests s/he understands and that can be useful in generating programming alternatives.

Initially, the data collected from each phase of the assessment process should be individually summarized (interview, developmental history, observations, and actual direct assessment). Within this summary, the major findings should be synthesized. With this structure in mind, it will simplify the next step, which involves incorporating all of the information generated and synthesizing the findings to take some action. The interpretation can be organized around the initial assessment questions formulated (McLoughlin and Lewis, 1986). The outcomes should be described in such a manner that they lend themselves to a simple correlation of why certain programs might be helpful and should be introduced.

The information should be organized categorically to specify mastered and unmastered skills. It is always helpful to have examples of correct and incorrect responses that illustrate a specific problem or strength.

When this has been completed, the examiner can begin to get closure on the results obtained and reach some conclusions. Goals can then be formulated for taking into account the information derived. In many ways, activities are usually selected to remediate the limitations found. Unfortunately, this is not always the best alternative. For some children, activities should initially be developed according to a child's strengths. This will hopefully build the child's level of confidence. As a consequence, the child will be better able to accept working on his/her weaknesses at a later time.

As we have seen, the process of assessment is complicated. A great deal of thought must be integrated if an effective measurement is to take place. The examiner will also have to become experienced in administering the various applicable tests. Experience will help develop more refinement in administration as well as enhance clinical judgment in interpretation.

QUESTION 5: WHY DO I REALLY NEED TO KNOW ANYTHING ABOUT TEST CONSTRUCTION AND, FOR THAT MATTER, WHAT DO I NEED TO KNOW?

Without accurately understanding the essential characteristics of a test, an examiner can inadvertently make many errors in regards to test selection and applicability. For this reason, attention will now be given to those characteristics. The reader is advised that if s/he finds this material somewhat difficult to review, time should be allowed to study some of the primary references incorporated within this section.

Characteristics Essential for Reliable Assessment: Reliability

Reliability is concerned with how much error is involved within the measurement (Wodrich, 1984). Wallace and Larsen (1978) suggest that the term **reliability** is used to refer to the consistency of the findings of a given test. Kerlinger (1973) suggests that acceptable synonyms for reliability are accuracy, predictability, and stability. Reliability is determined through the application of statistical procedures. Correlational techniques are the usual approach to studying reliability. The correlation represents the relationship between two sets of scores acquired from the same test instrument. A perfect positive relationship between the two would be depicted with a coefficient correlation of 1.00. On the other hand, no relationship would be indicated by 0.00. Reliability coefficients somewhere in the 0.80s and 0.90s are generally considered acceptable for tests (Wodrich, 1984).

There are several methods for determining the reliability of a test. One of the most commonly used techniques is **test-retest** reliability, which is also called the "coefficient of stability." To determine this type of reliability, one administers the identical test to the same examinee on two occasions and then correlates the findings. If the test is stable, the findings on both administrations should be similar. Potential sources of error could relate to remembering some of the subtests from the first assessment as well as the possibility of the practice effect. For this reason, it is important to have some delay between the administration of the two tests. The most appropriate time interval between tests will depend upon the type of test and how the results will be applied (Wallace and Larsen, 1978).

Another form of reliability is **alternate forms reliability**, which is also called the "coefficient of equivalence." As its name denotes, an alternate, but equivalent form of the test is administered. Unlike the test-retest format, one should give the two tests in immediate succession when employing alternate forms (usually within a week).

Finally, the most frequently used procedure to determine reliability is the **split-half technique.** Split-half reliability is also known as the "coefficient of internal consistency." To determine this type of reliability, the test is administered to a set of examinees and is then literally split in half so that each examinee has two scores. The scores are then correlated to estimate the instrument's internal consistency. This method is not appropriate for determining the reliability of speeded tests, because a subject's responses may not represent his/her actual abilities (if untimed). The split-half method includes the differences in content sampling between the two halves as error (exactly in the same manner as it is assessed with the alternate forms method).

Factors Affecting the Reliability Coefficient

There are several factors that influence the reliability. For example, the longer the material is of a specific test, the higher the reliability may be. Furthermore, the reliability of a test appears to be dramatically influenced by the sample investigated. The more heterogeneous the set of examinees, the higher the reliability of the test. Finally, very easy or very difficult items generally lead to a reduction in the reliability coefficient.

Standard Error of Measurement

Whenever one assesses another, some error is expected. This error can be estimated by the standard error of measurement which is determined by retesting an individual and comparing the differences between the scores. This error in measurement represents the standard deviation of the scores generated, which is simply a statistical reflection of how disparate the test and retest scores are. The error would be small if the scores of the various administrations are similar, and vice versa. The standard error of measurement also reflects the range that one's true score probably falls within. For example, a person's standard score may be 107 ± 5, meaning that the actual score would probably fall between 102 and 112.

Validity

Whereas reliability refers to the stability of a test, validity represents the extent to which a test is useful. This is considered the most important element in evaluating the effectiveness of a test. If a test is not valid, it is not worthwhile using it. Three types of validity that are considered in most tests are content, criterion-related and construct validity.

Content Validity

Content validity reflects the extent to which a test adequately measures the subject matter under investigation. The test must contain sufficient items so that it is representative of the areas that it purports to have measured (Wallace and Larsen, 1978). Typically, content validity is determined by a thorough analysis and comparison with other relevant tests. Another method of measuring this form of validity is through the agreement of those considered as experts in the field. If the experts agree that the tests sample the subject matter adequately and sensibly, the test will probably have high content validity.

Criterion-Related Validity

Criterion-related validity reflects the degree to which test scores predict performance in relevant real-life activities. One uses a test with criterion-related validity to obtain an impression of the examinee's likely performance on another specific measure (i.e. the criterion). For example, if the purpose of a test such as the Scholastic Aptitude Test (S.A.T.) is to measure success in higher education, what really becomes critical is whether one's score on the S.A.T. predicts actual performance of that specific individual while in college. If a given test predicts success for an individual (and if indeed the individual becomes successful), then the test has criterion-related validity.

There are two types of criterion-related validity. **Predictive validity** is when the criterion measure is sampled some time after the test was administered. The example previously illustrated predictive validity. A high correlation coefficient would indicate that the test is an accurate predictor and that its continued use is worthwhile. **Concurrent validity**, which is the second type of criterion-related validity, is when the criterion measure is administered at the same time or even prior to the test. Therefore, the findings of the measurement either concur with or disagree with criterion. It appears that this form of validity is critical on a practical basis. One may want to give a test to determine if a person is capable of being involved in certain activities. If the findings are accurate representations of what one might expect, the analysis is worthwhile.

Construct Validity

Construct validity reflects the extent to which the test measures a psychological construct, such as a trait or an attribute. For example, if a test is said to assess leisure behavior, it is assumed that there is such a thing as leisure behavior. Furthermore, it is implied that the items on the test incorporate behaviors that are indicative of this trait. Most constructs are relatively abstract and sometimes are defined by a multitude of observable behaviors that are very difficult to measure. Because of this abstractness, there is a need to further refine and clarify our understanding of the trait. It is therefore necessary to determine the construct validity of tests that purport to measure specific attributes or traits. The determination of a test's validity will either confirm or contradict the examiner's belief that the test accurately measures the trait or attribute under investigation. It would be extremely dangerous and erroneous to draw conclusions from an invalid test.

Gronlund (1976) suggests that construct validity is determined by taking the following steps:

1. Identify the constructs (traits and attributes) that are presumed to influence the behaviors under investigation.
2. Develop hypotheses regarding the performance on a test from the theory underlying the construct.
3. Verify the hypotheses by applying various logical and empirical methods.

Construct validity by far is the most difficult type of validity to ascertain (Wallace and Larsen, 1976; Salvia and Ysselyke, 1985). In fact, it is the least reported of all forms of validity. However, it is probably the most important. It is critical that examiners are accurately measuring what they intend to measure. Professionals must not tolerate test constructors who do not report acceptable estimates of construct validity. Without such information, there is not any clear evidence that the test is valid.

Factors Affecting the Acquired Validity Coefficient

There are several factors that influence obtaining an accurate validity coefficient. First, the more homogeneous the sample of examinees, the lower the validity coefficient. Second, the reliability of a test affects its validity. Reliability is a necessary but not a sufficient condition for validity, i.e. a test can be reliable but not valid. However, on the other hand, a test cannot be valid if it is not reliable. This is shown statistically by the fact that the validity coefficient can never be higher than the square root of the reliability coefficient.

Needed Attention to Test Construction, Reliability and Validity

Many examiners do not review test manuals with a critical eye towards issues of reliability and validity, and yet it is the test user's responsibility to thoroughly review the test manual to ascertain the appropriateness of the instrument. Fine (1982) and Dunn (1984) stress that assessment procedures will not accurately provide the information needed unless they are valid and reliable. In many situations, we find professionals using instruments that are ineffectively developed. These same individuals become frustrated later when they do not understand the meaning of the obtained results. It is therefore the responsibility of a test user to meet the qualifications necessary to administer the selected instrument. It is suggested that practitioners take courses in statistics and/or test construction that would be helpful in administering and interpreting test findings. A practical understanding of statistics and the interpretations of the reliability and validity coefficients are essential. With this understanding, professionals can make educated decisions pertaining to the selection and administration of test instruments.

Test Administration Tips

Before discussing various tests, it may be helpful to incorporate some basic tips for test administration. Administering direct testing devices requires both attention to detail and flexibility. Attention to the details of test administration must be accompanied with direct attention to the child under investigation. At times, inexperienced test administrators focus so intensely on the procedures inherent to the test that they at times lose sight of the fact that they need to observe and be involved with the client. The client's cooperation indeed depends on the rapport established between the therapist and the child. Simple courtesies such as comfortable seating and a pleasant working environment are critical. Examiners can use discretion to encourage a child for his/her efforts. It is imperative that words of encouragement are not based on performance but rather on areas related to effort and cooperation. Encouragement solely based on performance would be detrimental to children who were not doing well. In addition, one must be empathetic as well as cheerful. The worst thing a therapist can do in a testing situation is just **test**. I can recall when I started my professional career, when I was assessing I wanted to make sure I executed the procedures to the tee. Unfortunately, that appeared to limit my ability to interact with the child. I wanted the child to merely follow my directions and not detour from any of the procedures. I soon began to realize how this in fact limited my abilities to genuinely assess a child. I now spend alot of time getting to know a child. We may play with some toys, do simple art, talk, tell jokes and even do a few magic tricks, all as aspects of the assessment procedure. I would highly encourage the reader to incorporate some of these traits in his/her assessment techniques.

Salvia and Ysselyke (1985) suggest that the length of testing will vary with the age of a child as well as the disabling condition. As a general rule, a testing session should not exceed more than forty minutes without some form of a break. When children become restless, distracted, or for that matter even disinterested, testing should be interrupted and the child given a break. Furthermore, if the child's performance appears to be a minimal estimate of his/her abilities, the examiner should make note of this and not take into significant account the data that was generated.

Tests must be administered at times when children's attention is optimal. Therefore, we must take into consideration when and where the assessment procedures are implemented. For example, children may not want to cooperate completely when they have been taken out of an activity that they wanted to be at. Schedules must be adjusted at times to account for this concern. Furthermore, the assessment environment must be free of distractions. A room should be found that is quiet, away from others, and not overly arousing with a lot of extraneous stimuli. This will assist the child staying on task.

The examiner should take careful attention to review the test document as well as the manual. Usually within the manual, directions are given on how to deliver the assessment procedures. However, the humanistic characteristics discussed earlier in the section are critical to apply.

Finally, the reader should be cautious about the cost of tests and recognize that s/he will have to review various instruments before purchasing them. The mailboxes of many allied health professionals are replenished weekly with numerous pamphlets from test publishers offering professionals instruments that are supposedly the answer to the testing dilemmas they encounter. I would be suspect to these advertisements and recommend spending the time reviewing the tests and personally making the decisions after being informed. Tests can range in prices from $15–$20 to devices that are several hundred dollars. The clinician should therefore make appropriate selections that will meet his/her general needs, both practically as well as financially. Salvia and Ysselyke (1985) suggest that test users must examine all the pros and cons of utilizing specific test instruments. This may entail evaluating the kinds of behaviors or skills to be tested, the kinds of questions that need to be answered, and the extent to which commercially developed tests ought to be used. As can be seen, while performing assessments, therapists must attend to all details, reason carefully and make realistic decisions based on the client's and the professional's best interests. The following section will provide the reader with some basic information about various test instruments that will help in making appropriate and educated decisions.

QUESTION 6: WHAT ARE THE POTENTIAL ASSESSMENT ALTERNATIVES?

The final section of this chapter will be devoted to reviewing various tests which sample the broad base of behaviors influencing the acquisition of leisure skills. For your convenience, the following will be subdivided into four sections: (A) developmental profiles, (B) motor skills and psychomotor tests, (C) behavior rating scales, and (D) leisure interest and skill instruments. Because of the space constraints, only a limited number of tests could be cited in the document. There are many others that unavoidably had to be left out. The incorporated information is a representation of several viable alternatives.

Part I: Developmental Profiles and Interviews

When working with young children with disabilities or with the severely and profoundly handicapped, the developmental profiles and interviews to be discussed are useful in providing an enormous amount of practical information.

The Developmental Profile II

PURPOSE. The Developmental Profile II (Alpern, Boll and Shearer, 1980) is an inventory of skills designed to assess a child's development from birth through the age of 9-1/2 years. The profile is comprised of 186 items that are designed to assess a child's functional developmental age level. The instrument is administered by interviewing a person well acquainted with the child. Direct observation of the child may be incorporated if necessary (i.e. if the interviewee cannot answer all questions).

DESCRIPTION. The scale is divided into five areas. The five areas yield developmental ages for the child's physical, self-help, social, academic and communication levels. The items within each area are arranged into age levels expressed in terms of years and months. The age levels are presented at six-month intervals from birth to age three-and-a-half and proceeds from there by year intervals until the age of nine years, six months. Most age levels within the profile contain three questions. Items are scored as either being passed or failed, simply by determining whether the child has the skill described in each of the items proposed on the five scales. The scale was set up so that each item passed is credited in terms of a given number of months. The number of months reflecting the items passed is totaled, which represents the child's developmental age in each of the five areas tested.

To summarize one's findings on the profile, the results are then transferred to a profile sheet, graphically displaying the five areas and comparing level of development to the child's chronological age. The results of the profile clearly display if the child has a particular strength or delay in each of the five domains tested. This information can then be translated into instructional goals.

Before administering the instrument, the user should become familiar with the standardization, theoretical rationale, and psychometric properties of the evaluation tool. The author has found this instrument to be a useful method to incorporate into clinical interviews. Furthermore, the Developmental Profile II can be easily applied and used to assess progress via pre- and post-test comparisons.

Learning Accomplishment Profile—Diagnostic Edition (LAP-D)

PURPOSE. The LAP-D is one of the instruments established by the Chapel Hill Training—Outreach Project. The final version of the test consists of a commercially produced and marketed assessment kit published by the Kaplan School Supply Corporation. The instrument has excellent inter-rater reliability.

The test is criterion-referenced and was developed with a solid research base describing normal child development. What is unique about this test is that the findings are easily translated into appropriate instructional goals.

Griffin and Sandford (1975) describe activities that can be applied to remediate potential deficits. The test is composed of five scales and thirteen subscales. The profile was developed utilizing a task analytic approach, whereby tasks are presented in order from simple to progressively more difficult.

As indicated in the test manual, all of the necessary materials needed to facilitate the administration of the test are found in the LAP-D kit. The following are the scales and the subscales under investigation:

Fine motor

Manipulation
Writing

Cognitive

Matching
Counting

Language/Cognition

Naming
Comprehension

Gross Motor

Body Movement
Object Movement

Self-Help

Eating
Dressing
Grooming
Toileting
Self-direction

As can be seen, many of these subtests are critical to recreation participation. Although this scale does not directly measure recreation skills, significant attention is given to the developmental skills which are the foundations of recreation skills.

ADMINISTRATION. The test is designed for infants to children six years of age. However, the test is very practical for older children with developmental disabilities. The examiner begins the LAP–D with items designated for the child's chronological age. However, the test developers suggest that when working with a child with a disability, the starting point should be half of the child's chronological age.

A basal level is determined so that the entire early items of the test do not have to be administered. The **basal** is the item below which it is assumed the child is able to pass all preceding items. When the child passes his/her first three items in a row, the basal has been achieved. If this does not occur immediately, the examiner is required to work backwards until the basal is achieved or the first item on the test is administered. The examiner then continues testing a child (on the specific subscale) until the child fails three items in a five-item span.

This is known as the **ceiling level**. One makes the assumption at this point that the child is not capable of accurately responding to questions past this point. A plus sign (+) is recorded in the test protocol for items passed, while a minus sign (−) is displayed for a failure. Raw scores can be converted to percentages as well as developmental ages. It would be extremely difficult to administer the entire test in one sitting. In fact, one does not have to administer all 13 subscales. One may administer only those subscales that appear to be appropriate for a given child. The test is also extremely amenable to pre post-test evaluation.

The Brigance Diagnostic Inventory of Early Development

PURPOSE. The Brigance is designed for children from ages birth to seven years. In many ways, this test is very similar to the LAP–D. The following are the areas addressed by the diagnostic inventory.

a. Pre-ambulatory motor skills and behaviors
b. Gross motor skills and behaviors
c. Fine motor skills and behaviors
d. Self-help skills
e. Pre-speech
f. Speech and language skills
g. General knowledge and comprehension
h. Readiness
i. Basic reading skills
j. Manuscript writing
k. Basic math

Brigance (1978) lists five functions of the inventory. As an assessment instrument, it (1) determines the developmental level of the child, (2) identifies weaknesses and strengths, and (3) identifies instructional objectives. As an instructional guide, the inventory (4) lists objectives in a functional and measurable manner, and (5) it represents a valuable recordkeeping system in addition to a tool to develop an effective individualized program plan. However, it is suggested that when remediating a child's deficits, the clinician should take care not to promote parroting of the correct response. That is, the child should be taught the real meaning of each desired behavior, rather than just going through the motions in a perfunctory fashion. Finally, the findings attained from the inventory represent a body of knowledge that can be utilized to train parents and other professionals.

ADMINISTRATION. Just like the LAP–D, the Brigance is too comprehensive to be administered as a whole. Therefore, one should consider the reasons for the assessment in order to select the appropriate skill sequence. Furthermore, the assessment should be spaced over a period of time that takes the child's age and attention span into consideration.

In the test manual, Brigance clearly spells out the procedures. Recommendations for more effective use of the inventory are also provided. An example is "Rephrase verbal direction if it helps to check the skills or behaviors being assessed" and "Do not coach, but be prepared to reword the direction if the child has difficulty because of the vocabulary or form of the direction." Brigance also lists questions frequently asked about the inventory and provides a response to each.

As a criterion-referenced test, this inventory is based on observable functions sequenced by task analysis and correlated with child development and curriculum objectives. The skills are based on numerous references which contain published normative data for infants and children who are below the developmental age of seven.

Vulpe Assessment Battery

PURPOSE. The Vulpe Assessment Battery is a comprehensive tool for obtaining and organizing the pertinent information necessary to plan and develop a learning program for a child (Vulpe, 1979). The battery provides a developmental assessment for atypically developing children from birth to the age of six years. It may also be appropriate for older children who are severely disabled.

DESCRIPTION. The battery is divided into eight behavioral domains as well as one environmental domain. The domains include basic senses and functions, gross motor behaviors, fine motor behaviors, language, cognition, behavior, activities of daily living, and basic information about the environment. There are approximately 1,127 items on the test, and the items administered will vary from child to child. For older children, one would have to allow for a couple of assessment sessions, allocating about three hours to complete the entire analysis. The test appears to be more helpful for assessment of the preschool child than the five- and six-year-old. The battery is administered in the same way as many of the other developmental profiles, and the directions for administration are clearly presented in the manual.

COMMENTS. Although the test is very comprehensive, it seems that few statistical evaluations of validity and reliability were conducted. Test items were selected from the developmental literature indicating appropriate age expectations, but field testing was not comprehensive. This appears to be one of the major limitations of the scale. However, this author has found this test interesting and would suggest that professionals working with the developmentally disabled review its contents. Furthermore, just like the other developmental profiles, one uses select parts of the battery for a given assessment. There appears to be a great deal of information gained from this test, and it appears useful in planning and measuring individualized goal-oriented programs.

Part II: Motor Skills and Psychomotor Tests

Measurement of motor skills has become a highly specialized discipline. There are several tests that can be applied. The intent of this section is to globally review a few instruments and discuss in more detail two basic administered scales. It is suggested that those interested in developing skills in this area take classes in motor development or review several texts that present a variety of test instruments.

Purdue Perceptual Motor Survey

One of the earliest examples of a motor skills assessment scale is the Purdue Perceptual Motor Survey. It is not truly a test but rather a survey that allows others to observe a variety of motoric behaviors within a structured situation. The survey diagnoses five types of motor skills: balance and posture, body image and differentiation, perceptual motor match, ocular control and form perception. The manual contains all the necessary information for administering and scoring the instrument.

Bruiniks-Oseretsky Test of Motor Proficiency

A commonly used measure of motor development is the Bruiniks-Oseretsky Test of Motor Proficiency. This test is a norm-referenced, individually administered test for children between 4-1/2 to 14-1/2 years of age. The test is divided into the following three major areas and eight subtests.

Gross Motor Skills
1. Running speed and agility
2. Balance
3. Bilateral coordination
4. Strength

Gross and Fine Motor Skills

5. Upper-limb coordination

Fine Motor Skills

6. Response speed
7. Visual motor control
8. Upper-limb speed and dexterity

This test produces two scores for each subtest. The first is a standard score and the second represents an age equivalent. Furthermore, composite scores are available for gross and fine motor performance as well as a total battery score. The test has a very positive reputation and is extremely well constructed. A representative standardization sample was utilized in field testing, and the inter-rater reliability and the level of content validity of this instrument appear satisfactory.

An overview of additional measures of motor skills that have been widely used are presented below.

Ohio State University Scale of Intra Gross Motor Assessment (OSU–SIGMA)

PURPOSE. The OSU–SIGMA was developed by Michael Loovis and Walter Ersing in 1979. It is a criterion-referenced test that qualitatively measures 11 basic motor skills of children ages two and a half to fourteen. The 11 skills addressed in this instrument are as follows: walking, stair climbing, running, throwing, catching, kicking, jumping, hopping, skipping, striking and ladder climbing.

PROCEDURES. Each skill is assessed on a possible four-level scale, with level one representing the least mature and level four the most mature. The examiner merely observes the child in a natural setting and rates a child on each of the eleven skills. The criteria for evaluating each level has been operationally defined. This test is relatively easy to learn, and, most importantly, it represents a logical starting point to begin evaluating and eventually assisting a child's motor development.

HUGHES BASIC MOTOR ASSESSMENT PURPOSE. The test was developed by Jeanne Hughes in 1979. The test is norm referenced, with norming tables for children ages 6–12. There are ten basic motor skills covered in the Hughes Assessment: static balance, stride jump, tandem walk, hopping, skipping, target, yo-yo, catching, throwing, and dribbling.

PROCEDURES. Each skill is given a score from 0–3, with 0 indicating the child was unable to perform the task or there was a minimum of three observed difficulties, 1 point indicating two observed difficulties while performing the task, 2 points indicating one observed difficulty, and 3 points are awarded if the child did not display any difficulties performing the task. This test is easy to administer and interpret. The total time for administration is about 15 minutes.

As can be seen, the measurement of psychomotor skills can become very involved. It is suggested that a comprehensive workup should include a test of psychomotor skills. The instruments reviewed above should provide a strong foundation.

Part III: Behavioral Checklists

A widely accepted approach to rating children's behavior is through behavioral rating scales. These scales are generally completed by a significant other (e.g. parent, group leader, or teacher) who is very aware of the child's behavior patterns. Most of these scales are checklists that are designed to identify whether the child demonstrates appropriate or negative behaviors. There are many such checklists presently on the professional market. Several checklists that were designed specifically for therapeutic recreation are presented below.

The Comprehensive Evaluation in Recreational Therapy Scale (CERT)

PURPOSE. The CERT was developed by Parker and his associates (1975). The scale was presented and described in the **Therapeutic Recreation Journal** and a separate test manual is not available. However, the procedures for administration are quite clear and easy to follow. The CERT provides a systematic format for observing behavior in a recreation setting. It was originally designed for patients in a short-term psychiatric setting. However, since it's original development, there now is another version developed for persons with physical disabilities. The author believes that the test is appropriate for application with a multitude of special populations.

DESCRIPTION. The CERT is divided into three categories and addresses 25 behaviors related to recreational involvement. The three major domains covered are as follows:

(1) **General.** Attendance, appearance, attitude toward recreation therapy, coordination of gait, posture.

(2) **Individual Performance.** Response to therapist's structure, one to one, decision-making ability, judgment ability, ability to form individual relationships, expression of hostility, performance in organized activities, performance in free activities, attention span, frustration tolerance level, strength and endurance.

(3) **Group Performance.** Memory for group activities, response to group structure, leadership ability in groups, group conversation, display of sexual role in the group, style of group interaction, handles conflicts in group when indirectly involved or directly involved, competition in group, attitude toward group decisions.

PROCEDURES. The 25 behaviors are rated from zero to four, with a high score indicating problem behavior. The author has found this test to be very useful, although it should be kept in mind that the reported inter-rater reliability of the CERT is relatively low. Reliability should increase if operational definitions of the various behaviors are spelled out more clearly. It is suggested that testers spend time together practicing with this scale so that inter-rater reliability is increased.

The Haring and Phillips' Scale (Adapted Version)

PURPOSE. The scale was initially designed to provide educators with an alternative method for assessing children with behavior problems. The scale was published in the book **Educating Emotionally Disturbed Children** and was published by McGraw-Hill in 1962. Fine (1982) adapted this instrument for some of his research in measuring the effects of therapeutic recreation programs for children with spina bifida and learning disabilities. It appears that the scale can also be used for other special populations such as the severely disturbed and other physical disabilities.

The scale assesses numerous social interactional skills that play a role in a recreation therapy program. Areas such as group interaction, responsibility, cooperation, communication, ability to comply to adult and group norms are each rated on a 7-point Likert scale. A low score on this test indicates possible difficulty. It is believed that many practitioners will find this instrument useful in providing good clinical and practical insight. The inter-rater reliability for the entire survey was 0.81.

The author found it critical to train his observers so that they completely understood each of the questions. Table VI illustrates the various questions incorporated within the rating scale.

TABLE VI
THE HARING AND PHILLIP'S SCALE (Adapted Version)

1. Child's ability to stay with group activities and remain integral to them.

Impervious to group.	Hardly knows others are near.	Sees others but is indifferent to them.	Some response to others on occasion.	Takes others into consideration when he wants to.	Usually takes one or many others into regard.	Amenable to and ready to consider others at any time.

2. Child's ability to concentrate on and finish (follow through on) tasks given him.

Extremely flighty.	Flighty most of the time.	May or may not stay with task; not dependable.	Stays with task if supervised some.	Can stay with task on own to some extent.	Stays with tasks very well even against will.	Fine ability to concentrate and stick with requirements.

3. Child's ability to get along with peers.

Fights, or in conflict almost all the time.	In conflict often or most of the time.	Usually has too much conflict for his and others' welfare.	Conflicts coming under some control.	Makes an effort to control discord.	Gets along well nearly all the time; controls self well.	Little or no conflict at all; under good self-control.

4. Child's ability to comply with adult direction.

Defies adult at all turns.	Usually defiant and uncooperative.	Defiant and cooperative in random ways.	Some cooperation under some conditions.	Cooperative if he feels you mean business.	Usually cooperative and dependable.	Seldom or never uncooperative.

5. Child's ability to change to new activity under guidance or direction.

Won't change except under strong pressure.	Usually very reluctant to change; opposes it.	May or may not change; depends on "whim."	Changes with some effort; not willing.	Changes slowly but with some willingness.	Changes reasonably well and willingly in most cases.	Changes and complies well in all or nearly all instances.

6. Child's ability to meet and adjust to new situations.

Can't face or meet them.	Faces them with great difficulty.	Faces them only with specific adult help.	Meets and faces some new situations.	Can face and cope with several new situations.	Usually faces them well and readily.	Relishes new demands and copes readily and well.

TABLE VI (Continued)

7. Child's ability to act fairly and take his turn in appropriate settings.

Always wants to be first; demands it.	Rushes in to be first but can be stopped.	Will take turns if reminded in advance.	Goes first no more often than others.	Goes first only if asked or chosen.	Suggests taking turns; is cooperative and pliable usually.	Very mature; takes normal charge in fairplay terms; very reliable.

8. Child's pleasant and courteous attitude toward others.

Very rude and indifferent; seems to do so with intention.	Usually rude and discourteous.	Rude or not in random, unpredictable ways and at unpredictable times.	Somewhat considerate of others.	Considerate if situation is clear to him.	Usually considerate; a dependable person in this way.	Very considerate, but not artificial or insincere.

9. Child's attitude toward those less capable, younger, or handicapped.

Very rude and indifferent; seems to intend it.	Usually rude and discourteous.	May or may not be rude; is unpredictable.	Considerate of others at times.	Considerate if he is in tune with the circumstances.	Usually considerate and dependable.	Very considerate; highly courteous without falseness.

10. Child's ability to share materials and equipment with others.

Wants all for himself always or nearly always.	Is hard to get him to share.	Shares only if cautioned in advance.	Shares in some ways or at some times.	Usually shares well.	Can be depended on to share in nearly all instances.	Shares and takes responsibility for others readily and always.

11. Child's ability and willingness to help others.

Never helps others.	Helps others only under pressure.	Sometimes helps others.	Helps others if he likes them or what they are doing.	Helps others in many instances.	Usually readily helpful in attitude and action.	An excellent help to others; readily and cheerfully helpful always.

TABLE VI (Continued)

12. Child's care of camp property.

Seems to destroy will-fully and gleefully.	Usually destructive.	Destructive now and then, more by accident and care-lessness.	Fairly care-ful in most ways.	Often care-ful and saving.	Quite care-ful and depend-able.	Excellent carefulness; points out caution to others.

13. Child's ability to face own failures and shortcomings.

A very bad loser; always makes excuses.	Usually a bad loser and excuse maker.	Loses badly now and then; may face it well sometimes.	Usually a fairly good loser.	Faces losses and short-comings on most occa-sions.	A really good loser; faces short-comings well.	Excellent loser but not indif-ferently; seeks cor-rection of weaknesses.

14. Child's willingness to abide by general rules.

Breaks rules right and left.	Generally breaks rules.	Breaks rules and follows them in seemingly random ways.	Abides by rules if held up to him.	Can be depended upon in many ways to follow rules.	Generally follows rules well.	Excellent; very dependable and willing.

15. Child's ability to accept disagreement.

Can't accept disagree-ment ever.	Accepts dis-agreement badly.	May accept it on occasion.	Accepts dis-agreement if well presented.	Can accept it fairly well.	Accepts it well.	Accepts it with open-ness; ready to improve or change.

16. Child's ability to accept constructive criticism.

Fights it bitterly.	Hates it but is passive.	Accepts it or not in inconsistent ways.	Accepts it under some circum-stances.	Accepts it usually.	Takes it in good faith most of the time.	Accepts it readily; asks for it.

17. Child's concern for the welfare of the group as a whole.

Hostile to group and its welfare.	Often op-poses and is hostile to group.	Unpredict-ably hostile and coop-erative.	May accept group wel-fare, objec-tives at times.	Accepts group wel-fare on many occa-sions.	Takes group welfare as important.	Can be depended upon faith-fully to do this.

TABLE VI (Continued)

18. Child's willingness to credit other members of group.

Hostile to credit given others.	Opposes credit to others.	May give credit or not.	Gives credit to others in some ways.	Willing to give credit to others.	Gives others credit most of the time.	Very fair and reliable this way.

19. Demonstrates self-confidence.

Utterly lacking.	Lacks it most of the time.	Shows it now and then; lacks it at random times.	Shows self-confidence in some ways.	Shows self-confidence in most ways.	Comfort-ably confi-dent in most ways.	Very confi-dent with-out bravado in all situa-tions.

20. Child's acceptance of his share of responsibility.

Utterly irrespon-sible.	Very lack-ing in responsi-bility.	Shows it or not in un-predictable ways.	Accepts it in some ways.	Accepts it in many ways.	Very accepting.	A model of acceptance.

21. Child's refraining from violent temper outbrusts.

In a temper all the time it seems.	Frequent temper displays.	Shows tem-per in un-predictable situations.	Controls temper on some occa-sions.	Usually hard to provoke.	Very fine self-control.	Never see temper; solves prob-lems effec-tively.

22. Child's restraint from show-off behavior.

Shows off all the time.	A bit show-off usually.	Shows off and is re-strained in random ways.	Avoids show-off be-havior on some occa-sions.	Usually controls self pretty well.	Shows good control most of the time.	Always under healthy self-control.

23. Child's display of anxiety/apprehension.

Under constant anxiety.	Shows anxiety much of the time.	Is anxious now and then.	No anxiety on some occasions.	Anxious on a few occasions.	Rarely shows anxiety or apprehen-sion.	No anxiety noticed at all.

Burke's Behavior Rating Scales (BBRS)

PURPOSE. The BBRS are designed to identify patterns of pathological behavior problems in some children. The scales consist of a short four-

TABLE VI (Continued)

24. Child's dependency on Counselors for help/attention.

Always seeks help or attention.	Often seeks one or both.	Seeks both in random ways.	Able to get along on own on some occasions.	Gets along on own much of the time.	Very resourceful, usually on own.	Very independent and resourceful.

25. Child's popularity with other children.

Very unpopular.	Unpopular in most respects.	Popular-unpopular in hard-to-tell ways.	Popular with others in limited ways.	Fairly popular with others.	Very popular.	Probably most liked and popular.

26. Child's ascendency in meeting others, contacting others.

Most retiring and shy.	Usually retiring and shy.	Some ascendence in odd ways and times.	Somewhat ascendent at times.	Fairly ascendent and resourceful.	Very ascendent.	Most able and responsible here.

N. Haring and E. Phillips. (1962). *Educating Emotionally Disturbed Children.* Reprinted by permission of the authors and McGraw-Hill.

page booklet containing 110 questions. A respondent who knows the child is asked to rate the child on each question using a prescribed 5-point Likert. One indicates that the respondent has not noticed this behavior at all, while a five indicates that this individual has noticed this behavior to a very large degree.

Factor analyses indicated found that the 110 items cluster into 19 groups. They are: (1) excessive self-blame, (2) excessive anxiety, (3) excessive withdrawal, (4) excessive dependency, (5) poor ego strength, (6) poor physical strength, (7) poor coordination, (8) poor intellectually, (9) poor attention, (10) poor impulse control, (11) poor academics, (12) poor reality contact, (13) poor sense of identity, (14) excessive suffering, (15) poor anger control, (16) excessive sense of persecution, (17) excessive aggressiveness, (18) excessive resistance, and (19) poor social conformity.

PROCEDURE. The BBRS is simple to score. The items are arranged so that boxes in which the scores are entered descend in a column for each of these 19 categories. When one lays a straight edge adjacent to the column of scores, the numbers in a specific column can be added and the total can be transferred to the appropriate location on the profile sheet. When plotting the data on the profile sheet, three levels are indicated.

The first level for clusters with low scores indicates that there is not a significant problem. The second level indicates cause for concern, and the third level indicates very significant problems in the child.

COMMENTS. The BBRS provides parents and professionals with a great wealth of information. It can be used repeatedly over a period of time to assess if changes have occurred in behavior patterns. The scale has undergone significant test development and standardization. Research has yielded acceptable levels of reliability and three types of validity (criterion-related validity, content validity, construct validity).

Experience with the BBRS indicates that it is helpful to get two people who are aware of the child to complete the document. In this way, one can maximize the probability of obtaining an accurate picture of the child. After the checklist is scored, it is helpful to discuss the child's problem with the rater. While discussing these concerns, the raters can elaborate on their perceptions and possibly provide the evaluator with some behavioral examples. Recently, a remediation guide was prepared as an adjunct for the test. The purpose of the handbook is to serve as a guide for clinicians using the BBRS. The handbook provides some innovative assessment techniques and intervention strategies that have worked with many children.

The Devereux Child Behavior Rating Scale (DCB)

PURPOSE AND PROCEDURES. The DCB scale was designed for use with children ages eight to twelve. The scale provides a profile of potential behavior problems. It has been researched extensively and has yielded acceptable reliability coefficients.

The DCB is very similar in purpose to the BBRS. The DCB is intended to be completed by anyone who has had the opportunity to observe the child in a variety of daily situations. This is usually someone who lives with the child. The instructions for making the ratings are clearly defined on the cover sheet of the DCB protocol, and scoring is straightforward and explained clearly in the manual.

Summary of Behavioral Checklists

As can be seen, a wealth of information can be obtained via behavioral checklists. Some of the scales discussed can be completed by the therapist, while others have to be completed by significant others who are familiar with the child's behavior.

There are many behavioral checklists designed for specific special populations. For example, the **TMR Performance Profile for Severely and Moderately Retarded Pupils** was specifically designed to identify a wide variety of daily living skills displayed by children with mental retardation. The results of this checklist are then graphically profiled in six areas (social behavior, self-care, communication, basic knowledge, practical skills and body usage) which enable the rehabilitation staff member to plan for the child's growth in addition to recording change and development. The Client Development Evaluation Report (CDER) has been comprehensively applied in the state of California as a measurement of progress for persons with developmental disabilities. This instrument has been used effectively by many recreational therapists. Finally, two other noteworthy checklists are the Child Behavior Checklist and Child Behavior Profile developed by Doctor Achenbach and his associates and the Inventory of Child Problem Behaviors developed by Doctor Eyberg and her associates at the University of Oregon. The administration of these tests require extensive graduate training.

Part IV: Leisure Interest and Skill Instruments

A variety of instruments have been utilized over the years to measure preferred leisure interests and perceived leisure competence. For this reason, one should be very cautious in selecting tests.

The following is a brief review of a few actively applied instruments.

Leisure Diagnostic Battery (LDB)

PURPOSE. The LDB is the first major assessment tool to thoroughly investigate leisure abilities. No other instrument of this complexity currently exists.

The Leisure Diagnostic Battery (LDB) represents a collection of instruments that were designed to assist in the assessment of disabled and abled-bodied persons.

Witt and Ellis (1987) suggest that the most unique feature of the LDB is its overall theoretical conceptualization. They point out that the battery was based on a more holistic view of leisure with its emphasis on leisure as a state of mind. In essence, the LDB attempts to measure a person's perceived freedom in leisure and factors that are potential barriers.

Witt and Ellis (1982) suggest that the battery has four major purposes:

1. To assess an individual's current leisure functioning level.
2. To determine areas where improvement of current leisure functioning is indicated.
3. To determine via post-assessment the impact of offered services on leisure functioning.
4. To facilitate research on the structure of leisure functioning to enable a better understanding of the value, purpose and outcomes of leisure experiences.

DESCRIPTION. There are several versions of the LDB. Both long and short forms of most of a family of instruments forming the battery have been developed. Both version A's of the long and short form have been applied with individuals nine to eighteen, either handicapped or non-handicapped. The short version consists of 25 items taken from the batteries first five scales.

The LDB is intended to allow an examiner the ability to identify an individual's perception of freedom in leisure as well as to further clarify the causative factors limiting this perceived freedom. Consequently, each of the battery's subtests has a distinct function in securing this data. The scales in Section 1 (A to E) are designed to provide the examiner with an indication of the individual's perception of freedom in leisure. Witt and Ellis (1987) point out that the sum of scores across those scales provides significant information in regards to the individual's level of perceived freedom. Table VII provides a brief description of each of the subtests.

Witt and Ellis (1987) go to great lengths to list the findings of various studies which provide evidence of the reliability and validity of the LDB. Overall, scales A to F and the total perceived freedom in leisure show acceptable psychometric properties. Witt and Ellis (1987) suggest that extreme caution be exercised while using the knowledge test and preference inventory in some setting.

ADMINISTRATION. The instrument is easy to administer and score. All but two of the scales contain about 20 questions. These questions require the examinee to respond in one of the three ways: "sounds like me," "sounds a little like me," or "doesn't sound like me." Each of these responses is given a specific numeric score. The Leisure Preferences Scale and the Knowledge of Leisure Opportunities were designed differently. The preference scale is a 60-item forced-choice questionnaire. The responses to these questions are then clustered into specific categories to ascertain categorical interests. The knowledge subtest is a multiple-

TABLE VII
PURPOSES AND DOMAINS FOR LDB COMPONENTS

Component	Purpose	Domains
Perceived Freedom (sum of scales A–E)	To enable the measurement of perceived freedom in leisure.	A scale is obtained by summing across all items of scales measuring "perceived freedom"
A) Perceived Leisure Competence	To enable the measurement of perceptions of the degree of personal competence in recreation and leisure endeavors.	1. Cognitive competence 2. Social competence 3. Physical competence 4. General competence
B) Perceived Leisure Control	To enable the measurement of degree of internality, or the extent to which the individual controls events and outcomes in his/her leisure experiences.	Each item is designed to reflect the presence or absence of an internal stable attribution tendency.
C) Leisure Needs	To enable the measurement of abilities to satisfy intrinsic needs via recreation & leisure experiences.	1. Relaxation 2. Surplus energy 3. Compensation 4. Catharsis 5. Optimal arousal 6. Gregariousness 7. Status 8. Creative expression 9. Skill development 10. Self image
D) Depth of involvement in leisure	To enable the measurement of extent to which individuals become absorbed, or achieve "flow" during activities.	Each item reflects an element of Csikzentmihalyi's "flow" concept: 1. Centering of attention 2. Merging or action and awareness 3. Loss of self consciousness 4. Perception of control over self and environment 5. Non-contradictory demands for action with immediate feedback
E) Playfulness	To enable the measurement of individual's degree of playfulness.	Based on Lieberman's work with the playfulness concept: 1. Cognitive spontaneity 2. Physicial spontaneity 3. Social spontaneity 4. Manifest joy
F) Barriers to Leisure Experiences	To determine problems that an individual encounters when trying to select, or participate in leisure experiences.	1. Communication 2. Social 3. Decision making 4. Opportunity

TABLE VII (Continued)

Component	Purpose	Domains
		5. Motivation
		6. Ability
		7. Money
		8. Time
G) Leisure Preferences	To determine the individual's patterns of selection among activities. In addition, this scale measures preference for mode or style of involvement.	*Activity Domains* 1. Outdoor/Nature 2. Music/Dance/Drama 3. Sports 4. Arts/Crafts/Hobbies 5. Mental Linguistic
		Style Domains 1. Individual/Group 2. Risk/Non-Risk 3. Active/Passive
H) Knowledge of Leisure Opportunities	To determine the individual's knowledge of specific information concerning leisure opportunities.	1. Cost 2. Who can participate 3. Where 4. When 5. What

From the *Leisure Diagnostic Battery: Users Manual* by Peter Witt and Gary Ellis. Reprinted by permission of the authors.

choice test focusing on general leisure opportunity knowledge. The test can be administered to an individual or group. Scoring the battery is clearly explained in the manual and involves adding all the subtest scores together to obtain an overall total. Scores falling within a given range indicate whether global leisure problems are present or not. It is helpful for the examinee to examine each subtest individually to ascertain whether there are specific problem areas. This examination of subtest scores is critical to a total understanding of the test results.

RESOURCES. A variety of materials come with the LDB, including a user's guide, a user's manual, a manual explaining the instrument's background and structure, and a useful remediation guide. The test can be administered as an entire battery or specific subscales can be selected. The writer has found the descriptive/qualitative information yielded by the test as important and helpful as the quantitative data obtained. This test is highly recommended as a integral part of an assessment battery.

Leisure Activities Blank

PURPOSE. The most widely used leisure interest finder is McKechnie's (1975) Leisure Activities Blank (LAB). The purpose of this test is to explore patterns of leisure interests and to explore the psychological meanings and implications of the reported leisure interests.

PROCEDURES. This test consists of 120 forced-choice questions that gather information about past and expected future interests. The questions are rated on two different dimensions. First, each question is rated on a four-point rating scale for present and past involvement. Second, upon examination of each question, the respondent must indicate future intentions about being involved with selected activities.

The manual clearly articulates guidelines for interpreting various scores. Like the LDB, a major asset to the LAB is its strong psychometric development and field testing. The qualitative results from the test provide added information about leisure-time interests. The test seems much more appropriate for older children and adolescents.

Mirenda Leisure Interest Finder (MLIF)

PURPOSE. Another frequently utilized measure instrument is the Mirenda Leisure Interest Finder (MLIF), developed by Joseph Mirenda. The MLIF is part of a Leisure Counseling Media Kit, which consists of the leisure interest finder, leisure inventory file, and the leisure activity file.

Mirenda and Wilson (1975) describe the finder as a series of 90 questions based on activities in nine areas: games, sports, nature, collection, crafts, art, music, education and culture, volunteer services and organizational services.

PROCEDURES. Following each of the activity statements is a five-point rating scale that indicates the degree of preference for the activity ([1] dislikes very much to [5] likes very much). The responses are then profiled, and questions that are related are clustered (e.g. sports, nature). Each of the nine categories is subdivided, yielding a total of 18 subscales. A profile sheet is used to graphically project the outcomes on each subscale. The most interpretable profiles are those where the questions within a cluster are all rated high or low. For example, all of the questions pertaining to involvement in group sports could be rated with four's and five's. This information would lead the examiner to believe that the child enjoyed active group sports. However, this perfect kind of flat profile does not always occur. There may be a great deal of scatter on various subscale profiles. In this case, although there would not be any general patterns noted, the examiner could determine specific interests.

Other Leisure Interest Finders and Play Scales

There are many other useful leisure interest finders. A few worth noting are the Leisure Interest Inventory (Hubert, 1969), the Constructive Leisure Activity Survey (Edwards, 1978), the Avocational Activities Inventory (Overs, Taylor and Adkins, 1977) and the Self Leisure Interest Profile (McDowell 1973).

There are a couple of play scales and inventories that the reader may find helpful. The Knox Play Scale (1974) may be found useful in the assessing of the psychosocial parameters of children in play situations. The scale has been found to be helpful in identifying various play experiences which may be used in enhancing development. Furthermore, the reader may want to acquaint himself/herself to Hurff's (1974) Play Skills Inventory. The inventory provides a description of play in four general areas (perception, intellect, sensation and motor abilities).

In addition, there are a few techniques established that have been developed specifically for persons with disabilities. The Mundy Recreation Inventory for the Mentally Retarded evaluates leisure skills in the psychomotor and cognitive domains (Mundy, 1981), while Berryman and Lefebvre (1979) developed the Recreation Behavioral Inventory designed for recreation therapists to use with persons with a multitude of disabilities.

Additionally, there have been tests developed that attempt to measure a leisure state of mind. Probably the two best known are the Walshe Temperament Survey, in addition to McDowell's (1979) Leisure Well-Being Inventory. Both of these instruments are easy to administer, but both lack any substantial normative data. The author does not feel that these tests would be useful when assessing young children. However, they could be of some value when dealing with adolescents with at least average intelligence.

Finally, there are a variety of other ways to measure attributes that pertain to leisure interests and well-being. The use of incomplete subjective sentences provides an enormous amount of information. For example, let us examine the following two sentences: "I like . . . "; "When I am at home alone I like to. . . . " While assessing a child's leisure interests, a great deal can be learned from a child's completion of such sentences. It is imperative that the therapist not make any comments to any of the responses until the entire interview is complete. At that time, one can ask a child to elaborate or discuss certain responses. All too often, examiners interrupt a child while s/he is talking. This may cause the child to become self-centered and nervous.

SUMMARY

The process of measurement is a comprehensive and important task. Assessment should not be considered simply for gathering entry data but rather as an integrated aspect in the entire recreational treatment process.

Within this chapter, technical as well as practical suggestions were interwoven together. This was done to provide a basic understanding of how to develop the skills necessary to become a perceptive reviewer. Assessment should not only be considered as paper-and-pencil activities; indeed, we have seen a wide variety of approaches to gathering information about the child. Dowd (1984) elegantly stated that to merely rely upon a paper-and-pencil test is to miss the richness of information to be gained from a candid conversation or an observation. We need to learn how to take advantage of all the information that is around us.

However, I want to caution those who feel that a little information is all that is necessary to get by. This is an inappropriate point of view and is unfair to the child in question. One must understand that integrating assessment procedures into one's battery of skills is just as important as actually leading the selected activities.

We must judge the relative merits of different assessment instruments by first understanding variables such as reliability and validity (Dowd, 1984). For this reason, attention was spent attempting to explain the meanings of these variables. As test users, we need to meet the requirements to deliver an assessment that is safe and accurate. Accuracy also depends on the tester's ability to understand the purposes as well as strengths and limitations of a certain approach.

Assessment procedures need to be clearly linked to the examiner's methods in working with children. One needs to want to gather certain information, with the hope that it will assist in answering the proposed questions. Seneca once noted, "When a man does not know what harbor he is aiming for, no wind is the right wind." An assessment begins with the clinician knowing what information s/he needs to be answered. This is then followed by selecting the best available strategies to treat the prevailing problems. Clinicians' roles can in some ways provide as much excitement as being detectives. Not only will solving the mysteries challenge us, but we (as well as those we serve) will be rewarded by the implications of our findings.

REFERENCES

Alpern, G.D., Boll, T.J., and Shearer, M.S. (1984). *Developmental profile II.* Los Angeles, CA: Western Psychological Services.

Anastasi, A. (1976). *Psychological testing.* New York: MacMillan.

Belsky, J., and Most, R. (1981). From exploration to play: A cross-sectional study of infant free play behavior. *Developmental Psychology, 17,* 630–639.

Berryman, D.L., and Lefebvre, C.B. (1979). *Recreation behavioral inventory.* Unpublished manuscript (available from C.B. Lefebvre, 2225 East McKinney, Denton, Texas 76201).

Brigance, A. (1978). *Brigance diagnostic inventory of early development.* North Billerica, MA: Curriculum.

Brown, L., Branston, M., Nietupski, S., Pumpian, I., Certo, N., and Gruenweld, L. (1979). A strategy for developing chronological age-appropriate and functional curricular content for severely handicapped adolescents and young adults. *Journal of Special Education, 13,* 81–90.

Burk, H. (1985). *Diagnosis and remediation of learning and behavior problems in children using the Burk's rating scales.* Los Angeles: Western Psychological Services.

Cooper, J. O. (1981). *Measuring behavior* (2nd ed.). Columbus, OH: Charles E. Merrill.

DiNola, A., Kaminsky, B., and Sternfeld, A. (1978). *T.M.R. performance profile.* Ridgefield, NJ: Educational Performance Associates, Inc.

Dollar, J., and Brooks, C. (1980). Assessment of severely and profoundly handicapped individuals. *Exceptional Educational Quarterly, 1*(3), 87–101.

Dowd, E.T. (1984). *Leisure counseling: Concepts and applications.* Springfield IL: Charles C Thomas.

Dubose, R. (1978). Identification. In M. Snell (Ed.): *Systematic instruction of the moderately and severely handicapped.* Columbus, Ohio: Charles E. Merrill.

Dunn, J.K. (1974). Assessment. In C.A. Peterson and S.L. Gunn (Eds.), *Therapeutic recreation program design* (pp. 267–320). Englewood Cliffs, NJ: Prentice-Hall.

Edwards, P.B. (1978). *The constructive leisure assessment survey II.* Los Angeles: Constructive Leisure.

Ellis, G.D., Witt, P.A., and Niles, S. (1982). *The leisure diagnostic battery remediation guide.* Texas: Division of Recreation and Leisure Studies.

Fewell, R., and Rich, J. (1987). Play assessment as a procedure for examining cognitive, communication, and social skills in multihandicapped children. *Journal of Psychoeducational Assessment, 2,* 119–137.

Fewell, R. (1984). *Play assessment scale.* Unpublished manuscript. Seattle: University of Washington.

Fewell, R., and Vadasy, P. (1983). *Learning through play.* Hingham, MA: Teaching Resources.

Fine, A. (1982). Modification of the Haring and Phillips' Rating Scale. Cincinnati: University of Cincinnati.

Fine, A. (1982, October). Assessment: Where to begin and what to do with handicapped children. Paper presented at the 1982 National Therapeutic Recreation Society, Annual Meeting in conjunction with the Congress for Recreation and Parks, Louisville, Kentucky.

Fuchs, L.S., and Fuchs, D. (1986). Linking assessment to instructional intervention: An overview. *School psychology review, 15*(3), 318–323.

Garvey, C. (1977). *Play.* Cambridge. Harvard University Press.

Glaser, R. (1971). A criterion-referenced test. In J. Popham (Ed.), *Criterion-referenced measurement.* Englewood Cliffs, NJ: Educational Technology Publications.

Gronlund, N.E. (1976). *Measurement and evaluation in teaching.* New York: MacMillan.

Haeussermann, E. (1958). *Developmental potential of preschool children.* New York: Grune and Stratton.

Haring, N., and Phillips, E. (1962). *Educating emotionally disturbed children.* New York: McGraw-Hill.

Holowinsky, I. (1980). Qualitative assessment of cognitive skills. *Journal of special education, 14,* 153–163.

Hubert, E.E. (1969). *The development of an inventory of leisure interests.* Unpublished doctoral dissertation, University of North Carolina at Chapel Hill.

Hurff, J. (1974). A play skills inventory. In M. Reilly (Ed.), *Play as exploratory learning: Studies of curiosity behavior.* Beverly Hills, Sage.

Johnson, D., and Martin, S. (1980). Criterion referenced testing: New wine in old bottles?. *Academic Therapy, 16,* 167–173.

Kazdin, A. (1980). *Behavior modification in applied settings.* Champaign, IL: Dorsey.

Kerlinger, F.M. (1973). *Foundations of behavioral research.* New York: Holt, Rinehart and Winston.

Knox, S. (1974). A play scale. In M. Reilly (Ed.), *Play as exploratory learning: Studies of Curiosity behavior.* Beverly Hills, Sage.

Lemay, D., Griffin, P., and Sanford, A. (1977). *Examiner's manual: Learning accomplishment profilediagnostic edition.* Chapel Hill, NC: Kaplan.

Lowe, M. (1975). Trends in the development of representational play in infants from one to three years: An observational study. *Journal of Child Psychology and Psychiatry, 16,* 33–47.

Loesch, L.C., and Wheeler, P.T. (1982). *Principles of leisure counseling.* Minneapolis: Educational Media.

McDowell, C.F. (1979). *The leisure well-being inventory.* Oregon: Leisure Lifestyle.

McLoughlin, J., and Lewis, R. (1986). *Assessing special students.* Columbus: Merrill.

McKechnie, G.E. (1974). *The structure of leisure activities.* California: Institute of Personality Assessment and Research.

Mercatoris, M., and Craighead, W.E. (1974). Effects of nonparticipant observation on teacher and pupil classroom behavior. *Journal of Educational Psychology, 66,* 512–519.

Millman, J. (1970). Reporting student progress: A case for criterion-reference marking system. *Phi Delta Kappan, 52,* 226–230.

Mirenda, J.J., and Wilson, G.T. (1975). The Milwaukee leisure counseling model. *Counseling and Values, 20*(1), 42–46.

Mundy, C.J. (1981). *Leisure assessment instruments.* Unpublished manuscript (available from Dr. C.J. Mundy, Department of Human Services and Studies, Florida State University, Talahassee, FL).

National Therapeutic Recreational Society. (1982). Philosophical position statement. In C.A. Peterson and S.L. Gunn (Eds.), *Therapeutic recreation program design* (pp. 321–323). Englewood Cliffs, NJ: Prentice-Hall.

Nicolich, L. (1977). Beyond sensorimotor intelligence: Assessment of symbolic maturity through analysis of pretend play. *Merrill Palmer Quarterly, 23,* 89–99.

Overs, R.P., Taylor, S., and Adkins, C. (1977). *Avocational counseling manual: A complete guide to leisure guidance.* Washington, DC: Hawkins and Associates.

Parker, R.A., Ellison, C.H., Kirby, T.F., and Short, M.J. (1975). The comprehensive evaluation in recreation therapy scale: A tool for patient evaluation. *Therapeutic Recreation Journal,* Vol. 9, 143–152.

Popham, J., and Husek, T. (1969). Implications of criterion-referenced measurement. *Journal of Educational Measurement, 6,* 1–9.

Proger, B., and Mann, L. (1973). Criterion-referenced measurement. The world of gray versus black and white. *Journal of learning disabilities, 6,* 19–29.

Rubin, R. (1985). Play peer interaction, and social development. In C. Brown and A. Gottfried (Eds.), *Play interactions: The role of toys and parental involvement and children's development.* Skillman, NJ: Johnson and Johnson.

Rubin, K. (1982). Non-social play in preschoolers: Necessarily evil? *Child Development, 53,* 651–675.

Rubin, K. (1982). Social skills and social-cognitive correlates of observed isolation behavior in preschoolers. In K. Rubin, and H. Ross (Eds.), *Peer relationship and social skills in childhood.* New York: Springer.

Salvia, J., and Ysselyke, J. (1985). *Assessment in special and remedial education.* Boston: Houghton Mifflin.

Simon, G. (1969). Comments on implications of criterion-referenced measurement. *Journal of Educational Measurement, 6,* 259–26.

Takata, N. (1974). Play as a prescription. In M. Reilly (Ed.), *Play as exploratory learning: Studies of curiosity behavior.* Beverly Hills, Sage.

Vulpe, S. G. (1979). *Vulpe' assessment battery.* Toronto: National Institute on Mental Retardation.

Wallace, G., and Larsen, S. (1978). *Educational assessment of learning problems: Testing for teaching.* Boston: Allyn and Bacon.

Wehman, P., and Schleien, S.J. (1980). Relevant assessment in leisure skill training program. *Therapeutic Recreation Journal, 14*(4), 9–20.

Westby, C. (1980). Assessment of cognitive and language abilities through play. *Language Speech and Hearing Services in Schools, 11* 154–168.

Witt, P., and Ellis, G. (1987). *The leisure diagnostic battery: Users manual.* State Park: Venture.

Witt, P.A., Connolly, P., and Compton, D. (1980). Assessment: A plea for sophistication. *Therapeutic Recreation Journal, 14*(4), 5–8.

Witt, P.A. (1982). *The leisure diagnostic battery user's guide.* Texas: Division of Recreation and Leisure Studies, North Texas State University.

Wodrich, D.L. (1984). *Children's psychological testing: A guide for nonpsychologists.* Baltimore: Brookes.

Chapter 6

BROADENING THE IMPACT OF
SERVICES AND RECREATIONAL THERAPIES

AUBREY H. FINE

*All the world's a stage
And all the men and women merely players.
They have their exits and their entrances
And each man in his time plays many parts.*

WILLIAM SHAKESPEARE

INTRODUCTION

There is still a persistent misconception to contend with in our profession: that recreation is totally synonymous with physical activity and sport. As a consequence, certain stereotypes inevitably developed over the years concerning what one should expect from a recreational professional. These stereotypes, unfortunately, have often restricted what recreational personnel perceived as their domain or expertise. Corbin and Williams (1987) asserted that due to this myopic perspective and outlook, recreation leaders have not adequately explored, or have not even been allowed to pursue, a multitude of potential options in recreation and related fields.

Many energetic new professionals are socialized into these roles, adjusting themselves to the expectations of their peers or to what they perceive to be the scope of their position. While these perceptions are not wrong, they obviously limit our potentials. As a relatively recent profession closely allied with mental health, recreational therapy can impact the lives of many children with disabilities. However, if we equip ourselves only with what has been traditionally accepted, indeed prescribed, as our "domain," we might limit drastically our own scope and effectiveness.

In a traditional sense, the parameters of services provided by a recreational therapist incorporates a comprehensive array of recreational systems, techniques and options. This chapter will focus on broadening the perceptions of what recreational services should consist. It will, additionally, offer suggestions of several alternative recreational modes that will enhance the therapeutic value of the services rendered to exceptional children.

Among the many options, there are several unique methods and activity processes that can be incorporated by a recreational therapist while assisting children. In fact, the intent of this brief exposé is to provide insight into some viable alternatives and to suggest some practical points for implementational purposes with various special populations. Since this chapter by its nature cannot be more than a mere overview, the interested reader should seek additional training in any of the listed alternatives prior to implementing them. Even if some of these procedures may at first glance appear simplistic to apply, lack of training may hinder progress as well as overall effectiveness. As we all are aware, it is unethical to ascribe competence to a specific area of training when experience is limited.

PLAY THERAPY

One of the most frequently perpetuated confusions in the minds of lay persons is between recreational therapy and play therapy. There are, indeed, significant differences between these two. But, for our purposes, both recognize the importance of children's play. That many recreational therapists have not taken advantage of some of the unique benefits of play therapy is, the least to say, unfortunate. They would definitely find some of the approaches useful while interacting with children and helping them work through and master quite complex psychological difficulties within their lives.

Play therapy is an important component of an overall, integrated treatment program. While play which takes place during therapy differs significantly from naturally occurring play, the most distinctive difference being the therapist's (professional or lay) involvement, it only impacts the child's natural willingness for spontaneous play. In spite of this drawback, through play children can be assisted in divulging and possibly resolving any disturbing conflicts and trauma as Schaffer and O'Connor have suggested (1983). Others joined this notion by noting that play techniques and discovery approaches allow children to expose themselves in a non-threatening manner. It must be understood, also, that play therapy must be playful and enjoyable to the child involved. Young people really find it easy to communicate feelings about themselves through play rather than through direct conversation (M. Bijou: personal communication, November 8, 1986). The use of this medium provides the professional with an insight into the child's world; almost any form of child's play can provide a professional with data for understanding, for fantasies, conflicts, anger, and joy can be acted out by children in play situations. It can be used to promote rapport between child and the therapist, for the latter can become more readily accepted in the child's world of feelings and thoughts while engaging in diversional play experiences. A skilled therapist can use this information as insight into the child's mode of feeling (Muro and Dinkmeyer, 1977). F. Amster, the noted psychologist, synthesized succinctly the positive contribution of play therapy in understanding the child:

1. While observing a child playing, one can develop a clearer diagnostic understanding of the child.
2. The medium of play enhances the therapeutic relationship in addition to helping a child verbalize certain conscious-associated feelings.
3. Play can also be used therapeutically to help a child act out unconscious material and, consequently, relieve underlying tensions (Amster, 1943).

Play therapy has a long history encompassing several theoretical orientations. Anna Freud and Melanie Klein were among the first professionals to promote the use of play in psychotherapy with children. Freud incorporated play into her work primarily as a way of developing rapport and making children feel more at ease. Games and toys were used to encourage the child's involvement. Klein, on the other hand, is considered to be the first to incorporate play as a substitute for a child's verbalization (Klein, 1932). This is particularly important for younger children who are less capable of expressing themselves verbally. Due to both Klein's and Freud's theoretical orientations, play therapy took on a strong psychoanalytic framework. Specifically, it was appreciated for its cathartic value, since it appears that a child's own play efforts can indeed be self-healing. A further development was initiated by Levy who established a new approach which he termed **release therapy** (Levy, 1938). This approach was aimed primarily at children who were victims of trauma. It was believed that if a child was given enough support, s/he would be able to recreate a traumatic event and get his/her feelings out in the open.

An eminent play therapist, the humanist Virginia Axline, in the 1940s incorporated key elements of client-centered counseling into her perspective of play such as empathy, understanding, warmth, and acceptance. The child is regarded as the center of attention, and as such, playing is regarded as an opportunity for the child to experience growth under conditions that are unrestrictive and favorable to the child. An array of play opportunities are provided, but the child has the ultimate choice of what to play with. In fact, no directions are given to the child, the child takes the lead, and the facilitator takes a non-directive observational role. Axline explained that by playing out their feelings, children bring their feelings to the surface, face them, learn to control them, or abandon them. Through play, children also realize the power within themselves to be individuals in their own right, to think for themselves, to make their own decisions, to become psychologically more mature, and, by so doing, to realize selfhood. The ultimate goal of Axline's orientation, thus, is to facilitate the child's self-direction and self-growth (Axline, 1947). While not differing in the basic rationale, Crocker Peoples modified some of the principles espoused by Axline by suggesting that the play therapist should become more directive at times and take the lead to ensure that the child engages in productive and meaningful play. This orientation is referred to as **Fair Play Therapy** (Peoples, 1983).

Applications with Special Populations

It should not come as a surprise that various play therapy orientations have been effectively applied with children with special needs. Children with mental or physical disabilities comprise, indeed, a diverse population often in need of individually tailored programs. Each orientation has its strengths and weaknesses, and it is suggested that facilitators be flexible enough so as not to be locked into one perspective, but rather to adopt an eclectic approach. However, some suggestions can be made concerning the use of various perspectives in individual versus group play. Ginnott, for example, strongly advocates the use of group situations as the choice of treatment with young children. Puppets, figurines, small toys, and animals can be used by children for play discovery and self-expression. It has also been suggested that family and animal puppets are more effective in a variety of sessions. They serve as an opportunity to help children examine their behavior in social situations. Like recreation therapy, the intent of group play therapy is to provide children with gratification while interacting with others (Ginnott, 1961; Millman, 1974). A Swedish alternative known as the Sand Box is also a reputable play therapy alternative. Although the procedure was initially established for its diagnostic purposes, it has been found that by utilizing the wet and/or the dry sand with the various figurines, children have been capable of acting out many of their internal feelings. Dora Kalff's book, entitled **Sandplay** (Sigo Press), may be a good reference for a practitioner to learn about the applications of play therapy.

Play Therapy and the Hospitalized Child

When working with children in hospital settings, there are a variety of play therapy techniques that will be of obvious benefit for both the child and the therapist. Dictated by the severity and the type of their illnesses, differing play therapy techniques should be implemented to different groups. Chronically ill children, children with terminal or progressive illnesses, and other children who face lengthy hospitalization (i.e. greater than a week) usually benefit more from individual play with a facilitator than children with shorter hospital stays. The stresses of hospitalization are intensified by the extended hospital stay, and thus a one-on-one play situation can promote rapport and trust between the facilitator and the children (Fine and Siaw, 1987). This is not to say, however, that group play has no benefits for children who are in the hospital for extended stays. In particular, group play is important for the school-aged child, whom Erikson (1963) describes as defining him/herself by comparisons with peers (i.e. the industry versus inferiority normative crisis in Erikson's theory). One of the common denominators, as Golden points out, can be also an opportunity to interact with peers who have undergone similar medical procedures, a valuable means of social comparison with others. But the most important contribution is that group play provides children with a time for social interaction with peers; indeed, developmental research shows that peer interactions are especially important during middle childhood, where social interaction is deemed developmentally critical. In addition, a one-on-one play situation, especially in the case of lengthy hospitalization, not only promotes a rapport and trust between the children and facilitator, but it also helps them to "venture symbolic exploration of anxieties, and the necessity for structuring various specific procedures" (Golden, 1983, p. 222).

In this context, a facilitator can also utilize the group play therapy as a vehicle for observing how children interact with others. Children with chronic illnesses are often socially immature because of what has been called by Boone and Hartman the "benevolent overreaction syndrome." The benevolent overreaction occurs when parents overprotect their child to the point of retarding the child's social development, and thus the ill child does not know how to interact with same-age peers. Many chronically ill children spend a significant amount of time with adults (e.g. their parents and medical personnel) and are inevitably limited in social experiences with peers. In one case, an early adolescent with cancer attended a special camp for children with cancer. This was the child's first separation from his parents and a rare opportunity to spend a significant amount of time with peers. The child had been overprotected by his well-meaning parents and had never learned how to tie his shoes because his mother had always done it for him. The other campers thought this was funny and unfortunately made fun of him. Thus, the facilitator was able to recognize this child's social immaturity by observing him separated from his parents in a peer group situation. Problems such as social immaturity due to the benevolent overreaction can be tackled via various play therapy strategies (Boone and Hartman, 1972).

SPECIALIZED TECHNIQUES IN PLAY THERAPY

Theraplay

One of the unique forms of play therapy, applied with a wide range of exceptional children, is known as Theraplay. The approach was first proposed by Austin Des Lauriers when he discovered its value with children with autism and schizophrenia. The goals of treatment are to help children to become alive. Theraplay, as it was defined by Des Lauriers (1978):

> emphasizes the central factor of high affective impact in all stimulating contacts or communications with the autistic child; this is done through play, games and fun. In this relaxed atmosphere, no special effort is made at teaching the child anything; there are no specific special education methods or tools utilized. What the child learns first is that it is good to be human with another human being: that it is fun to be a member of the human race and that grown up human beings are worth having around to make life pleasant. (P. 317.)

Recently, the internal constructs of Theraplay have been closely aligned to Hayley's cognitive problem-solving therapy in which the responsibility for change belongs to the therapist. S/he is expected to plan a strategy of change to bring about what the patient is attempting to achieve. Within Theraplay, the therapist structures, challenges the child, intrudes and nurtures the relationship. Furthermore, this technique provides an element of fun and the focus of body contact, whether it be vigorous, playful, and or competitive (Hayley, 1972). It is a viable approach for children with emotional, social and developmental problems. These are usually children who usually have little confidence in themselves and trust in their perceived worlds. The term itself, **Theraplay**, describes a process which "is insistently intimate, physical, personal, focused and fun; a form of treatment that replicates the structuring, challenging, intruding and nurturing interest in the mother-infant relationship" (Jenberg, 1979, p. 26).

Theraplay differs from conventional play therapy, in that the therapist is significantly more directive within this approach. Furthermore, within Theraplay, the environment is not stocked with a multitude of toys such as dolls and crayons but rather a room which is almost virtually bare. The major prop for the child to interact with is the play therapist. Ann Jenberg (1979) prepared a list of do's and dont's as guidelines for implementing this approach. The foundation for this list was laid down over years of clinical experiences with hundreds of children. While I have taken the liberty to modify and cluster her thoughts, conforming to my own ideas, the following list basically represents a synthesis of Jenberg's suggested guidelines:

The Do's and Dont's of a Theraplay Therapist

1. The therapist should appear confident and take advantage of his/her leadership skills.
2. S/he should be responsive and empathic in addition to being willing to take charge of all sessions.
3. Assures that eye and physical contact are established.
4. Attempts to project to the child that s/he is a unique and special person.
5. The therapist should be utilized as the primary play object.
6. The focus of the entire session should be upon the child.
7. The activities incorporated should impose limited frustration, challenge and discomfort on the child.
8. The therapist initiates rather than reacts to the child's behavior.

Therefore, sessions are specifically structured so specific issues are clarified and articulated.

Over the years, Theraplay has been applied with several special populations, including the mildly handicapped. For example, Jenberg illustrates vividly the importance of this approach with children with learning disabilities. She feels that Theraplay can assist children in developing their self-esteem as well as building a sense of trust in others. She illustrates clearly some of the remarkable changes she has seen in children over time when they were assisted with this process. Practitioners from a variety of academic disciplines have incorporated aspects of Theraplay within their own repertoires. For instance, Sally Bligh described how she applied activities of Theraplay with 17 children who had a severe language delay. She credited Theraplay with precipitating and facilitating changes, i.e. improvements, with these children.

Before leaving our discussion of Theraplay it seems only logical to highlight some of the possibilities. Table I describes two activities which are potential strategies that a clinician may apply.

TABLE I
TWO POTENTIAL THERAPLAY ACTIVITIES

HAND PRINTS

Materials: Finger paint and finger paint paper.

Procedures: Therapist covers the child's palm and fingers with paint and then presses child's hand firmly to paper. All four hands make interesting paintings and good souvenirs of terminating session.

PILLOW BUMP

Materials: Six pillows (24" × 24")

Procedure: Depending on the size of the child, three to six pillows are stacked on top of the other. Child and therapist stand back to back with the pillows between them. At the count of three both participants rush to claim the largest area of pillow space. Then both stand up, remove a pillow and the contest begins again. This process is continued until all pillows have disappeared.

Mutual Storytelling Techniques

The use of children's stories has always been informative to clinicians. Mutual storytelling takes advantage of children's self-created stories.

One of its founders and a major proponent of this approach, Richard Gardner, saw the efficacy of storytelling in its quality for imparting and transmitting important values. It utilizes a story that is designed to be specifically relevant to a particular time. The stories are specifically elicited by the therapist at each session from the child. This usually ensures the likelihood that the activity will be attended with receptivity and incorporated into the child's emotional being (Gardner, 1986).

The Basic Technique

As previously noted, the clinician elicits a self-initiated story from the child. This event is then followed with a summary story generated by the clinician incorporating some of his/her own perceptions. In Gardner's view, through the therapist's interpretations, a healthier resolution and adaptation can be achieved to the conflicts presented in the child's story. A tape and/or video recorder is recommended to be used, which can enhance significantly the child's motivation to participate. Although these tools might not be regarded as crucial, when they are applied the therapeutic message can be consistently reiterated.

Mutual storytelling usually begins by letting the child know that s/he will be the major star of a make-believe television program (if a video camera is being utilized). The child is then encouraged to make up a story completely from his/her imagination. The facilitator should simultaneously emphasize that it is against the rules to tell stories that really happened either to the child or anyone else s/he knows. This, in turn, usually helps in relaxing and putting the child at ease. The therapist also should discourage the child from revealing a story about things that have been read, heard or seen in movies or television.

After this brief introduction, it is explained to the child that, like all stories, the presentation must have a beginning, middle, and end. When the story is completed, the child is then requested to explain the lesson learned as well as the moral derived. This is followed by the clinician's formulation of a similar story with a discussion about the conclusions drawn from both. If the child is hesitant, which happens often, the clinician can use numerous approaches to encourage a more willing participation. One easy way to accomplish this goal is to suggest that early on the child share a generated story with the clinician. Then s/he is told the clinician will begin the story and the child will eventually be invited to join in. The approach is usually successful in eliciting stories from a majority of children.

Mutual storytelling should be applied only on an individual basis. One of the major reasons is that children may feel uncomfortable with others listening in. It is also imperative that the clinician be actively listening (it is appropriate to spend time jotting down notes) with a dual aim: (1) to foster the child's involvement in the activity and (2) s/he can help formulate better conclusions. The follow-up of requesting a child to elicit the lesson derived from the story is intended to obtain additional details.

Obviously, the therapist is in no position to create a follow-up story unless s/he has an understanding of the original presentation. Again, as suggested earlier, the more training and experience the facilitator acquires, the better position one will be in applying various play therapy techniques. Several excellent resources are available to assist the reader in exploring this technique as well as many derivative activities applying similar procedures (see Gardner, 1971, 1986; Schaffer and Reed, 1986). Furthermore, several other games that encourage dramatized clinical storytelling are the Board of Objects Game (Kritzberg), the Bag of Toys Game (where a child is encouraged to generate a story about an object selected from a bag) and the Feel and Tell Game.

All these activities and techniques are usually appropriate for children ages four to twelve. It seems that children at this age are more candid and less aware that their stories may reveal unconscious feelings. With older children, more age-appropriate strategies can be utilized such as the Talking, Feeling, Doing Game or the commercially available Ungame. Personally, I have used many of these activities when working with behaviorally disturbed and learning disabled children. It will be perhaps instructive to share some of my observations with the reader. Through dramatized storytelling, children can gain a better understanding of their feelings and an ability to be able to deal with them more effectively. Thus, I have developed several similar game-like alternatives which allow children to respond to their internal feelings. Probably the most critical ingredients that I have found to be helpful pertain to the elements of trust and communication. Children will not open up completely if they feel uncomfortable.

One example of a dynamic approach that I have developed is a game that I call Secrets (Fine, 1985). Basically, within the game, all participants make up questions, which must be honestly answered and which is one of the most important rules by the person who draws that specific slip. While the rules are discussed prior to playing the game, the game format is ever changing. Initially, as the child begins playing the game, the questions are very superficial. However, as the therapeutic relationship is established, the questions become more and more deep rooted. What makes Secrets so special? It is the genuine relationship that is formulated with the therapist and the child. Consequently, the approach becomes a catalyst for further interaction and possible discussion.

The Talking, Feeling, Doing Game

This game was also developed by Richard Gardner with the intent of assisting uncooperative children in exploring their feelings. The game includes a **normal appearing** playing board, a set of dice, playing pawns, a spinner, reward chips, and cards that are drawn from the center of the board. It is similar in many ways to most table games. Nevertheless, the core is derived from the directions and questions formulated on each of the cards. Although most children participate due to the competitive nature of the game, children are reinforced for revealing psychodynamically meaningful material for therapeutic utilization (Gardner, 1973). Within this game, according to Gardner, the Talking cards assist the child in making comments that are primarily intellectual in nature, while the Feeling cards focus on emotional issues. Finally, the Doing cards require the child to engage in some sort of play activity or acting. There are 104 cards in each stack and range from very non-threatening to moderately anxiety-provoking questions (Gardner, 1983).

Although the game was devised to interact with resistant children, it has been shown to be useful with defensive children as well. As an additional benefit, this game is very useful and appropriate for groups. The majority of questions are designed to elicit information (talking, feeling or doing) in regards to the fundamental problems of life with which children at some point in their lives may be confronted. In order to acquaint the reader with the essence of this game, Table II illustrates a few sample questions from each of the three domains. The readers should also be informed that there are several other games that have been formulated with a similar purpose in mind (i.e. the Changing Family Game, Assertion Game, Classroom Survival Game).

TABLE II
SAMPLE QUESTIONS FROM THE TALKING, FEELING, DOING GAME

TALKING CARDS
Question: What sport are you worst at?
What things come into your mind when you cannot fall asleep?
Suppose two people you know were talking about you and they did not know you were listening. What do you think you would hear them saying?
Tell about something you did that you are ashamed about.

FEELING CARDS
Question: A boy's friend leaves him to play with someone. How does the boy feel? Why did the friend leave?
Tell about an act of kindness.
What is something you could say that could make a person feel good?

DOING CARDS
Question: What is the most selfish thing you ever did? Make believe you are doing that right now.
You are standing in line to buy something and a child pushes in front of you. Show what you would do.
Make believe you have just met a bully. Show what you would do.

Applications of Other Common Table Games

Among the many games, the table games were found useful as an opportunity for children to deal with aggressive and competitive urges in socially acceptable ways. One of the first recognized pioneers of the therapeutic utilization of games has been E. Loomis. While using checkers in therapy, he recognized the potential application of the game as a vehicle for expression of resistance and unconscious conflict. The game was seen as a safe environment where the child lets lose of his/her defense (Loomis, 1957). Other scholars found that these games might provide opportunities for social learning as well as helping children to communicate, cooperate, learn to respect governing rules and to control anger while in competition. Finally, table games can be applied to help children learn how to deal with power and autonomy. While there are now many games solely developed for purposes of therapy, it has been suggested that several commercially available games are also suitable for prominent therapeutic goals (Schaffer and Reed, 1986).

Sutton-Smith and Roberts, two distinguished play theorists, established three classifications of games that can be purchased in most retail stores. (1) Games applying physical skills, such as Tiddily Winks, Pick

Up Sticks, and Operation, can help children with their eye-hand co-ordination. (2) Games of strategy attempt to enhance cognitive skills which also allow an observer to informally gather insight on a child's problem-solving abilities. Games such as backgammon, checkers, chess, word games, and Connect Four all fit into this category. (3) Finally, there are games of little strategy, which merely involve chance. These games are usually beneficial because they neutralize the adult's superiority in intellect and skill. Games that fit under this category are Chutes and Ladders and several card games, such as War (Sutton-Smith and Roberts, 1971). As for their therapeutic benefit, these games can be further classi-fied into four areas of orientations: (1) communication games (such as the Talking, Feeling and Doing game), (2) problem-solving games, (3) ego-enhancing games, and (4) games that promote socialization. A brief description of these games to acquaint the professional with these classifi-cations is obviously important.

Communication Games

Through games, just like through other play therapy techniques, one can create a non-threatening and permissive atmosphere that encourages self-expression. In working with a variety of children, I have applied several table games for this specific therapeutic benefit in the strong belief that if goals are set and developed prior to application usage and the therapeutic benefits are identified, games can become a dynamic resource for the practitioner. Most communication board games allow children to project certain aspects of themselves. Children over the age of five are usually prepared for this orientation. The most well-known games are the Ungame (Zakick, 1975), Reunion (Zakick and Monior, 1979), Scrabble for Juniors (Gardner, 1975), and the Self-Esteem Game (Creative Health Services, 1983).

The Ungame and Reunion are probably the best known of all listed. Both are non-competitive and encourage the child to explore attitudes, feelings, values and, in general, the self. For example, in Reunion, children might be asked to remember a time when they had their best day. A unique feature of most of these games is that they do not usually have a natural ending. The games are discontinued when the leader and the child decide to stop.

Scrabble for Juniors was adapted by Gardner (the developer of the Talking, Feeling, Doing game). Therapeutically selected words are presented on a game board. The child then goes ahead while taking turns covering the game board with letter chips s/he has drawn. When a word is spelled out, the player must say a little about the term. If the child recounts a personal experience, incorporating the word, s/he receives more points. The person with the most points at the end of the game is the winner. Finally, the Self-Esteem Game is appropriate for children who are about eight to twelve years of age. My experience has found this game enjoyable to play and well received by most children. But, most of all, these games help children learn how to deal with interpersonal setbacks.

Games for Problem Solving

Many of the games that can be purchased for children require some level of problem solving. Indeed, games under this category are intended to encourage children to apply problem-solving skills. One of the observations made by Schaffer and Reid is that games found under this heading usually encourage the process of logical thinking. It appears that many children with behavior problems do not take their time in thinking through problems. They tend to react quickly and do not appear to absorb the consequences of their actions. This is also true of children who make poor choices socially as well as academically. They assist children in focusing more on the logic which they need to apply. Children and the leader may act as role models to each other displaying appropriate problem-solving mechanisms. I have found games of this nature to be effective with children with learning disabilities and emotional disturbances. These games can promote abilities to use reliable critical thinking strategies. Games such as checkers and backgammon are two prominent examples. After the game has been completed, it is suggested that attention be given to what has occurred which, in turn, may ascertain if a transfer of learning has occurred (Schaffer and Reed, 1986).

Ego-Enhancing Games

Under the rubric of ego-enhancing games, there is a host of activities that focus on a multitude of personality traits, including perceived competence, impulse control, frustration tolerance, and concentration. Many games such as Sorry, Connect Four, Monopoly, and Risk can relate to goals achieved under this category. Bruno Bettelheim, the noted psychologist, suggests that within the game of Monopoly several emotional feelings can come into account, such as the feelings of helplessness, the need to feel powerful, and aggressiveness (Bettelheim, 1972).

There are several other games that have proved useful in helping children with attention deficit disorders to improve their self-control. For instance, the manifested purpose of the game Beat the Clock is for the child to outlast the clock, so that s/he is actively engaged in the activity while the buzzer goes off. A practitioner who is interested in finding additional games of this nature may consult Margie Golick, who has prepared a book entitled **Deal Me In** which lists a number of card games and their therapeutic application (Golick, 1973).

Socialization Games

In ancient Greece, Plato recommended that in working with children, it is advantageous to allow children to learn while playing. Socialization games are used in this context by helping children, dependent on their chronological and mental ages, to practice various social behaviors such as group cooperation and sharing. Several table games and group activities (New Games, Cooperative Games) can be selected to influence or alter a certain behavior. Active games such as blanketball, knots and the log roll can all be exercised to encourage cooperation and the mere joy of participation.

The contributions of game play to recreational therapy are obvious and, as we have seen through the preceding pages, recreators, teachers, and parents can naturally take advantage of the underlying benefits of game play. This is an area that has not been exhausted, and the contributions to pediatric therapy are endless.

Summary of the Value of Play Therapy

The applications of play therapy are far-reaching. The procedures have been applied with many special populations, including the physically disabled, emotionally disturbed, mentally retarded, and learning disabled. The procedures incorporated are applied to help children conceptualize their internal conflicts and feelings. In many ways the advantage of this procedure is the knowledge of what to watch for while playing with children, in addition to knowing how to enhance the therapeutic play opportunities for children.

ART THERAPY

There are some who would say that play is the art of childhood and art is a natural form of play. Gerson, a professor of recreation, suggests that at times we reserve the name play for those activities which are pursued with the conscious intent of realizing pleasure. This is likewise true in art. In this regard, there is also complete agreement between both of these two activities.

Recreation therapists are not psychotherapists, and complex, deep-seated interpretations of art are generally beyond the level of training of most practitioners. However, it is appropriate to listen to children and synthesize what they say about their art, for they can provide revealing clues about the children themselves, their feelings and their personalities. Dinkmeyer and Caldwell state that through artwork the child may be able to project meanings only dimly revealed in his/her verbal expression (Dinkmeyer and Caldwell, 1970, p. 366).

Art therapy is the use of art for personal expression of feelings rather than primarily for the creation of aesthetically pleasing products. It has been employed as a significant self-expressive therapeutic approach with people of all ages, but through art a child can reveal hidden concerns more willingly and easily than may be possible through verbal communication (Liebmann, 1986). We must be aware that art therapy is a huge umbrella concept, encompassing the use of art expression for many purposes with several distinctive philosophical approaches. The three major theoretical orientations are: (1) the psychoanalytic orientation, where art is used in conjunction with psychotherapy and takes into account many of its principles; (2) the creativity approach, which sees art as inherently therapeutic and is applied to allow the child to display and explore his/her talents; and (3) the humanistic orientation, in which art is used as a means of establishing one's identity.

Indeed, art as a form of communication can also facilitate communication even when children are not able or willing to interact with others. While many of them do not engage in art activity for its cathartic value, there are times when children are worried, and art can allow them the opportunity to express their feelings. It can be used to help children feel better about themselves by promoting feelings of success, and the completion of the project can bring much joy to a child.

The use of art therapy was refined in the 1940s through the pioneering efforts of Margaret Naumberg, who relied heavily on her psychoanalytic orientation in encouraging her clients to associate freely through drawings (Wadeson, 1980). Edith Kramer, on the other hand, placed emphasis on an alternative direction; more toward a humanistic approach. Her work with children emphasized the healing properties of the creative process. In this scheme of things, art therapy obviously differs greatly from psychotherapy, for the therapist and/or teacher does not engage in interpretations but rather encourages an artistic experience. According to Kramer, then, art therapy presents the individual with satisfaction and pleasure which can be generated through creative production (Kramer, 1971; Fleshman and Fryrear, 1981). Several artistic methods are incorporated into this orientation. Some examples of procedures include the following:

1. **Automatic Drawing.** This technique is also known as the scribble technique. It is here that the individual is allowed to free draw. In free drawing, the client is encouraged to express him/herself using any form of art media.
2. **Color Exploration.** The child may produce a piece of artwork using his/her least and most preferred colors. The child is then asked to discuss how the colors interact. Furthermore, this approach can be refined to also incorporate exercises where a child can draw pictures expressing feelings. Each of the feelings are captured by incorporating a specific color. Again, as the example previously elicited, the final product is then discussed.
3. **Drawing Completion.** The child is presented with a few lines or shapes. S/he is then requested to make a picture using all of the elements. Denny (1972) suggests various techniques that can be applied to increase the child's self-awareness. For example, the child may be requested to paint and discuss the phrases "I feel" or "I am." They could also be asked to draw three figures which would include the ideal self, the real self, and the way others perceive them. Another example is the Squiggle Game (Winnicott, 1971), which is particularly useful as an icebreaker and as a means for identifying hidden concerns that a child may have. In this game, the facilitator draws a small figure (e.g. a curve, straight line, or other ambiguous figure) and the child is asked to create a picture out of the figure. This task is enjoyed by most children, it encourages creativity, provides a stimulus for conversation, and may uncover hidden concerns.

Adaptations of equipment for art activities may be necessary for children with some form of limitations. These limitations are obviously wide-ranged, from a child confined to bed, to those with physical or other disabilities. Wilson, for example, described a badly burned child who chose to finger paint the only way she could: with her feet. In addition, she devised a variety of methods, in effect overcoming her handicap, such as the use of "prism glasses, vertical lapboards with clips to hold drawing paper, horizontal mirrors suspended amidst traction and long tongs to allow for reaching" (Wilson, 1964, p. 218).

Art therapy has also been utilized with children with a variety of developmental and emotional problems and chronic illnesses. One of the advantages of art activities is that they are usually best initiated in groups, because it appears that children inspire one another. There are many types of supplies that can be applied or utilized in art, and a therapist must be aware of what materials need to be selected with well thought purpose and with the child's needs in mind (Robbins and Sibley, 1976).

BIBLIOTHERAPY

Bibliotherapy is a natural and effective intervention technique for helping children in a therapeutic setting. After all, most children enjoy reading or having some read to them. It is an approach that is being increasingly utilized by recreational personnel, child life specialists, nursing staff and psychologists. Through careful selection of material relevant to a given child, the facilitator helps the child to understand and accept him/herself. The reading materials serve as a springboard for discussion of sensitive issues while at the same time giving the child an opportunity to explore these issues in an indirect and more comfortable manner.

One of the latent benefits of this method is that there are many messages that can be transmitted from literature without the child even knowing. Bibliotherapy allows an issue to be exposed to a child in the least threatening manner. It also provides an opportunity for youngsters to identify with characters having problems similar to theirs. Moreover, this approach promotes an awareness that no man is an island and that problems are universal (Malkiewicz, 1970). Many stories have non-human main characters, such as animals or objects (e.g. bears, trains, balloons). These non-human characters are most valuable in their capacity to serve as a model without regard for gender or age. Melamed and Siegel, and others as well, suggest that a seven-year-old male main character may serve as an acceptable and effective model for children of both sexes and different age groups (Melamed and Siegel, 1975). The following represents some guidelines for applying bibliotherapy. These suggestions represent my thoughts and experiences as well as the insights of many authors:

1. Make sure you know the reading level of the child or group as well as the content of literature used. Although this suggestion may seem simplistic and certainly a step that should be routinely employed, it is ironic that this position is often overlooked, especially the review of the text. I feel it part of a professional obligation to preview the material my students will be given. The most significant reason for following this procedure pertains to the content of the material integrated. One must completely understand the plot of the book if it will be applied appropriately with children. There are times when books appear on the surface to be well suited for the targeted child; however, after considering the material at a more in-depth level, the professional may sense that the story is inappropriate for the given situation. Other factors that should be taken into consideration prior to the selection of a book can be divided into two categories: child factors and book factors.

Child Factors	**Book Factors**
• Child's age	• Type of book
• Sex	• Plot
• Why bibliotherapy is being applied	• Difficulty level
• Reading abilities	• Appropriateness for child
• Reading preferences	

2. A child can participate in the selection of stories. Presentation of choices of relevant books allows the child to feel some control. Whenever a book is suggested to a child, the child should always have some input on the final selection. I have found it helpful to have a few books to choose from. In this way, the child feels some autonomy and control over the situation. Sometimes, a child may not be willing to read a book on a sensitive subject. If this is the case, there is no justification to push the child at that time. If you

meet with resistance after several prompts on your part, it is wise to wait awhile and make suggestions at a later time.

3. The selection of short material is especially critical for young children. Zaccaria and other scholars highly recommend using brief articles, poems, short stories and, for that matter, even chapters from a story. Brief passages allow the child to get to the heart of the point, thus allowing the child to focus his/her attention on the area of concern and then to talk about it immediately. After the reading is completed, the leader should then facilitate a conversation. Questions should be open-ended and should initially only center on the story. As the child becomes more comfortable, s/he may begin to self-disclose. There are a variety of ways to encourage self-disclosure after reading a passage. I have found it quite helpful to center the locus of attention on the principal characters in the story. If the child is comfortable, s/he will alter the focus and discuss him/herself. With younger children, as a child ages, a more direct approach is feasible. Realistic stories about non-fictional situations should be presented sensitively and directly. In addition, I have found it helpful to draw feelings generated from the theme of the story. All of these techniques seem to allow a child the security to begin opening up and sharing feelings.

When stories are selected to encourage a child, it is likely that children will be more willing to share their thoughts and generalize conclusions. The writer has found such situations to be the most rewarding. All children, including children with disabilities, typically enjoy discussing stories with happy endings. Furthermore, there are many stories that are inspirational. The conclusions drawn can enhance a child's perceived competence and additionally may make the child more willing to try and change (Zaccaria, Moses, and Hollowell, 1978).

Some scholars, such as Rubin (1978) and Peller (1962) noted that young children can be significantly affected by stories because they nurture their dreams. They also found that animal characters are especially useful in helping young children to explore their feelings. Animal characters are useful because the elements of sex, age, and race are not involved.

Although there are several advantages to selecting books for therapeutic purposes, there are disadvantages. For example, there are many books that children enjoy but which make adults very uncomfortable (e.g. books on sexuality, divorce).

4. Bibliotherapy should be combined with other recreational therapy procedures, since it can be incorporated easily by a recreational therapist in programs that serve a wide range of children. That is to say, bibliotherapy must be integrated and utilized in conjunction with other techniques such as drama, art or other activities that might help the child act out, enact or express (i.e. through art) what the moral is suggesting.

5. A facilitator who does not possess adequate experience should utilize already available published literature. Bibliographies of stories focusing on specific affective areas are available (e.g. Fosson and de Quan, 1984). With increased experience and effectiveness, however, many facilitators have found it useful and easier to develop their own stories that are individually tailored to a specific child's situation (e.g. Fosson and deQuan, 1984).

The previously cited texts should be used as a starting point for selecting children's books. However, it is not a substitute for personal reviews of books. The therapist should still take the time to review specific texts to make sure they are appropriate for a given situation. A comprehensive and useful resource book is **The Bookfinder,** published by the American Guidance Services. In addition, several of the major texts on bibliotherapy include a comprehensive listing of appropriate outlets (see Zaccaria et al., 1978; Rubin, 1978).

As we demonstrated here, bibliotherapy can be applied as a unique and very effective strategy with children. Depending on the specific disabling conditions, bibliotherapy can be utilized to supplement and enrich the ongoing activity programming in a wide variety of ways. For instance, the specific utilization of bibliocounseling for chronically ill children who are hospitalized is only one of the many promising and viable areas that might incorporate this technique into the repertoire of therapeutic techniques (Fine and Siaw, 1987).

There are at least two other ways this approach can be applied. First, if a child is residing in a hospital or another institutional setting, the parents can record stories on audiocassette or even videocassette so that the stories can be played by the child in their absence. A second variation of bibliotherapy involves having the child record stories. This is best illustrated by the following case example: Bobby, a nine-year-old boy with spina bifida, was hospitalized for an extended period of time. While in treatment, Bobby's perceived competence, which was low to begin with, decreased. This sense of helplessness appeared to be directly related to the loss of control he felt in the hospital environment that was structured for him by others. As we already noted, this **benevolent overreaction** syndrome often occurs in chronically ill children (Boone and Harman, 1972). The hospital's recreational specialist tried numerous therapeutic play strategies to boost Bobby's morale. Stories about kids like himself who overcame barriers and became successful were well received and seemed to have a positive influence on Bobby. He came to the realization that he was capable of many things, which propelled him to begin to take more responsibility for his actions. Bibliotherapy, however, assisted this child in other, somewhat non-traditional ways as well. The therapist asked Bobby to read simple stories for a visually impaired child. The therapist practiced the stories with him and then Bobby tape-recorded the stories for a visually impaired child. With the knowledge of having made a useful contribution, Bobby's perceived competence increased significantly.

PET THERAPY

Mental health professionals and social scientists have come to the conclusion, in recent years, that the ownership of a pet has positive correlation with improved health. Scholars from several disciplines reported notable advantages and benefits derived from establishing a pet-facilitated therapy (PFT) program, with effects often seen immediately. Clinical studies showed, for example, that pet therapy facilitates a shorter recovery time from illness. It has also been found that people who are responsible for taking care of an animal usually appear to take better care of themselves in all areas of daily living (Beck, 1985; Corson and Corson, 1981; Leitner and Leitner, 1986; Smith, 1982).

Pet-facilitated therapy has been recently recognized for its numerous direct benefits to children, as well. The most noticeable among them related to children who tend to be withdrawn and uncooperative but become more involved and alert with animals. Among the many examples of how PFT can be applied with exceptional children, animals have been credited with eliciting speech from people who had not been verbal (Beck, 1985). I have found it easy to incorporate PFT as a component within a recreational therapy program, although its utilization, goals and objectives must depend inevitably on the specific disabling condition. Over the years, for instance, I have developed activities using pets with children with learning disabilities, spina bifida and severe mental retardation. In my work with the severely handicapped, the training of guinea pigs so that the children could pet and feed them proved especially useful. With the proper training, these animals can learn to be gentle and interactive with the children. Furthermore, they are very easy to train. With the basic knowledge of shaping and reinforcement, the animals can acquire behavioral routines appropriate with this special population. The children, on the other hand, needed to be taught how to be gentle with the animals, and they were delighted to hold and pet the animals.

In other programs that I have coordinated, the incorporation of the animals as the group's mascot was effective. The children were responsible for taking care of all of the animal's needs. The group members had to collaborate with one another to decide who would take care of the animal as well as to accept the responsibility of making sure that the particular animal was fed and her cage was clean. In fact, an entire home management program was implemented in which each of the children had the opportunity to take the guinea pig home for a week. With the commitment and cooperation of the parents, this aspect of the overall recreational therapy program was successful in helping the children learn to take more responsibility.

PFT has also been used on a different level. Children who have cerebral palsy learned horseback riding, which is a highly rewarding activity in itself. Some believe that therapeutic horseback riding gained its formal public recognition when Liz Hartel of Denmark won an Olympic medal. Ms. Hartel was stricken with polio, but she overcame her disability and won a silver medal in the 1952 Olympics. Since that time, in 1969, the North American Riding for the Handicapped Association, Incorporated (NARHA) was established. The organization was established for many purposes. In general, the organization was initiated to investigate the effects of riding on persons with disabilities, as well as providing proper training and examination of instructors for possible organization certification. As many members of the NARHA suggest, persons with disabilities can learn to ride and control a large animal, develop spatial awareness and enhance their perceived competence.

They truly can learn to sit tall in the saddle as a consequence of their training and involvement.

Beyond the obvious joy that is inherent in this type of activity, the child-animal interaction, and, especially, mastering a situation, appears to increase the children's self-confidence and self-esteem markedly.

An interesting case study dealing with human-animal interaction and the benefits that a child can gain from it, and which otherwise would have been unattainable, has been described by Conderet. As a worker with preschool-aged normal and disturbed children, he became fascinated by the impact of a dove on a child with autism. Previously, this child had only shown interest with inanimate objects such as blocks and was never heard to verbalize or permit any physical contact. On the day that the dove was brought to her class, the animal flew right in front of the child. For the first time, the girl appeared to smile, and she began tracking the flight path in addition to mimicking the bird's flight and uttering a new word. Consequently, the dove was used therapeutically with her. A dramatic change occurred in subsequent sessions. The girl even became affectionate with the animal and was seen kissing her. A pre- and post-videotape has been produced, documenting the significance of this case. Dolphins have also been used to elicit communication from children with autism. However, using dolphins appears to be extravagant, and the same benefits can be obtained using less expensive and more readily available animals.

In conclusion, there is an overriding incentive on the part of the therapist to incorporate PFT into therapeutic recreation programs. Its use can range from the simplistic programs to significantly comprehensive ones. Either way, the use of animals in treatment deserves consideration.

HORTICULTURAL THERAPY

Horticulture, which is the art and science of growing plants, flowers, or food, is a promising intervention technique that can be easily incorporated into a therapeutic recreation program. In his well-respected book, **Horticulture for the Disabled and Disadvantaged,** Olszowy (1978) discussed numerous benefits of horticultural therapy to one's intellectual, emotional, and physical development. Intellectually, one can learn about plants, about plant anatomy, or about different classes of plants. Emotionally, children can attach themselves to the plant as well as to the activity. They learn to be patient in taking care of their crops, develop a greater sense of control over the environment and their own actions, and in group situations they learn to interact with a team. Physically, horticultural activities promote physical exercise, manual dexterity, and, if an outdoor activity, the opportunity for children to be in the fresh air for a short time.

According to Relf (1981) and evidence supporting his claim, horticulture is now widely accepted as an effective therapeutic tool. He points out the role that horticultural therapy plays in interaction, action and reaction. Interaction is directly related to how people interact in settings that utilize horticulture. Action relates to how persons interact with plants, and, finally, Reaction pertains to the outcomes of this orientation. There are several critical elements within each of these areas. The most significant among the three is the Action category. It is within this facet of the process that the child will interact with plants and become more responsible.

The two main disadvantages of horticultural therapy are its dependence on the weather and the limited knowledge of many therapists about plants. Both of these factors, however, can be easily rectified with minimal effort. Even a short course or book should provide the therapist with enough knowledge to embark on horticultural therapy. There are numerous indoor horticultural activities that will allow children to engage in planting activities on a year-round basis, and there are numerous resource books that provide activity ideas in addition to a more thorough presentation of horticulture therapy (e.g. Brooks and Oppenheim, 1973; Olszowy, 1978; Watson, 1960).

Throughout the country there are several programs focusing on the application of horticultural therapy. Several of these programs have developed comprehensive activity manuals that describe hundreds of horticultural activities. **Project Grow** is one such program that has received national attention for its impact in serving children. The root of **Project Grow** is a hydroponics greenhouse. In this garden facility in northern California, children are responsible for cultivating and harvesting vegetable crops. They plant, feed, and pollinate the young crops. Additionally, they are responsible for picking, packing and sorting the mature vegetables. **Project Grow** was established to mainstream children who are moderately mentally retarded with students who were in regular education. What is unique about the project is the curriculum manual developed by its staff. The manual contains 14 essential skill areas based on a horticulture skill checklist. Approximately 150 activities have been developed that exercise the 14 skill areas. The material can be used for all grade levels and for children with various disabling conditions. The curriculum is multi-faceted and deals with cognitive, affective, and vocational development. A resource handbook has also been established. The handbook contains the basic information necessary for a teacher to construct a greenhouse, which can be adapted to many settings and up-to-date reference materials. **Gardening as Therapy for the Summer Season** by Coxon and Tarrant (1979) is the second in a series of manuals designed to assist in developing a horticultural therapy program. The manual represents the input of several members of the University of British Columbia Botanical Garden staff. Twelve unique activities are described.

In order to illustrate the advantages of horticultural therapy, I can provide a personal experience. Within a therapeutic recreation program that I was involved with, a staff member helped a group of children make terrariums that they could eventually keep. One of the children showed particular interest in her terrarium, and, because of the interest sparked by this activity, the group leader decided to implement one of Coxon and Terrant's summer activities. The group leader was able to secure the use of a small garden, and the children planted a "quick-to-grow" garden consisting of lettuce, tomatoes, green peppers and shallots. The commitment required of each of the children the designation of different responsibilities and their rotation among the children, and, finally, the pleasure of eating the vegetables at the end of the summer party were immeasurable benefits of this horticultural therapy program.

SUMMARY

The umbrella of play-facilitated approaches incorporates a wide array of techniques and applications; among the most eminent of them are play therapy, bibliotherapy, PFT, horticultural and art therapy, and each has been briefly introduced in this chapter. Play theorists have postulated that play is many things to many people; it serves many purposes. It can provide an observer with an opportunity to watch children alone or in a group setting while giving the child a sense of control and promoting creativity and responsibility. Various developmental areas in childhood, including intellectual, emotional, and physical development, are positively influenced by play. Through play, children develop ways to cope with their anxieties and stress, and they learn to work out their feelings and to vent frustrations. Most of all, children can gain a sense of satisfaction and joy as a consequence of their involvement in play. The implementation of various play therapy paradigms and intervention techniques within the repertoire of a therapeutic recreation professional expands the individual's abilities to apply viable strategies for promoting feelings of security and a sense of comfort in all children. While the usage of some of these techniques is strongly encouraged, it is also imperative that practitioners examine their level of competence in the techniques under scrutiny within this chapter. Conceivably, many may see it valuable to continue their training and develop the necessary skills to accurately apply some of the therapeutic play strategies in their own settings. In the long run, the initial investment should definitely pay off. We must admit that these interventive play strategies have generally not been investigated by most of our practitioners. Yet, the time seems ripe for a change. Thus, it is our duty, as a new generation of recreational professionals, to now begin expanding our horizons and truly taking advantage of all the advances and available alternatives that are offered to us for the betterment of human life and existence.

REFERENCES

Amster, F. (1943). Differential uses of play in treatment of young children. *American Journal of Orthopsychiatry, 13,* 62–68.

Axline, V. (1947). *Play therapy.* New York: Ballantine.

Beck, A. (1985). The therapeutic use of animals. *Veterinary Clinics of North America: Small Animal Practice, 15*(2), 365–375.

Bettelheim, B. (1972). Play and education. *School review, 81,* 1–13.

Bligh, S. (1977). *Theraplay: Opening the door for withdrawn and autistic children.* Paper presented to Illinois Speech and Hearing Association, Chicago, IL.

Bligh, S. (1977). Theraplay: Facilitating communication in language-delayed children. In J. Andrews and M. Burns (Eds.), *Selected papers in language and phonology, 2: Language remediation.* Evanston, Ill.: Institute for Continuing Education.

Boone, D.R., and Hartman, B.H. (1972). The benevolent-over-reaction. *Clinical pediatrics, 11,* 268–271.

Brooks, H., and Oppenheim, C. (1973). Horticulture as a therapeutic aid. *Monograph Institute of Rehabilitation Medicine, New York University Medical Center 49.*

Cianciolo, P. (1965). Children's literature can affect coping behavior, *Personnel and Guidance Journal, 43,* 897–903.

Corbin, P., and Williams, E. (1987). *Recreation: Programming and leadership.* Englewood Cliffs, NJ: Prentice-Hall.

Corson, S., and Corson, E. (1981). Companion animals as bonding catalysts in geriatric institutions. In B. Fogle (Ed.), *Interrelations between people and pets.* Springfield, IL: Charles C Thomas.

Coxon and Tarrant. (1979). *Gardening as therapy for the summer season.* Vancouver, B.C.: University of British Columbia Botanical Gardens.

Creative Health Services. (1983). *The self esteem game.* South Bend, IN.

Denny, J. (1975). Techniques for individual and group art therapy. In E. Ulman and P. Dachinger (Eds.), *Art therapy in theory and practice.* New York: Schocker.

Des Lauriers, A. (1962). *The experience of reality in childhood schizophrenia.* New York: International Universities Press.

Des Lauriers, A. (1967). The schizophrenic child. *Archives of General Psychiatry, 16,* 194–201.

Dinkmeyer, D., and Caldwell, E. (1970). *Developmental counseling and guidance.* New York: McGraw-Hill.

Erikson, E.H. (1963). *Childhood and society* (2nd ed.). New York: Norton.

Fine, A., and Siaw, S. (1987). *Therapeutic play for children with chronic illness in hospitals.* Manuscript submitted for publication.

Fine, A. (1985, May). *Secrets.* (Available from Aubrey H. Fine, Cal Poly University, 3801 W. Temple Ave., Pomona, California.)

Fleshman, B., and Fryrear, J. (1981). *The arts in therapy.* Chicago: Nelson-Hall.

Fosson, A., and deQuan, M.M. (1984). Reassuring and talking with hospitalized children. *Children's health care, 13,* 37–44.

Gardner, R. (1971). *Therapeutic communication with children: The mutual storytelling technique.* New York: Aronson.

Gardner, R. (1973). *The talking, feeling, and doing game.* Cresskill, NJ: Creative Therapeutics.

Gardner, R. (1975). *Psychotherapeutic approaches to the resistant child.* New York: Aronson.

Gardner, R. (1975). In *Psychotherapeutic approaches to the resistant child.* New York: Aronson.

Gardner, R. (1983). The talking, feeling, and doing game. In C. Schafer and K. O'Connor (Eds.), *Handbook of play therapy,* 259–273. New York: Wiley.

Gardner, R. (1986). *The psychotherapeutic therapeutics of Richard Gardner.* Creeskill, NJ: Creative Therapeutics.

Ginnott, H. (1961). *Group psychotherapy with children.* New York: McGraw-Hill.

Golden, D. (1983). Play therapy for hospitalized children. In C. Schafer and K. O'Conner (Eds.), *Handbook of play therapy,* pp. 213–234. New York: Wiley.

Golick, M. (1973). *Deal me in! The use of playing cards in learning and teaching.* New York: Norton.

Guerney, L. (1983). Client-centered (nondirective) play therapy. In C. Schafer and K. O'Connor (Eds.), *Handbook of play therapy,* 21–64. New York: Wiley.

Guerney, L. (1983). Play therapy with learning disabled children. In C. Schafer and K. O'Connor (Eds.), *Handbook of play therapy,* 419–435. New York: Wiley.

Haley, J. (1973). *Uncommon therapy: The psychiatric techniques of Milton H. Erickson, M.D.* New York: Norton.

Haley, J. (1976). *Problem-solving therapy: New strategies for effective family therapy.* San Francisco: Jossey-Bass.

Jenberg, A. (1979). *Theraplay: A new treatment using structured play for problem children and their families.* San Francisco: Jossey-Bass.

Kantrowitz, V. (1967). Bibliotherapy with retarded readers. *Journal of Reading, 11,* 205–212.

Klein, M. (1932). *The psycho-analysis of children.* London: Hogarth.

Kramer, E. (1971). *Art as therapy with children.* New York: Schocken.

Leitner, M., and Leitner, S. (1985). *Leisure in later life.* New York: Haworth.

Levy, D. (1939). Release therapy. *American Journal of Orthopsychiatry, 9,* 713–736.

Liebmann, M. (1986). *Art therapy for groups.* Cambridge, MA: Brookline.

Loomis, E. (1957). The use of checkers in handling certain resistances in child therapy and child analysis. *Journal of the American Psychoanalytical Association, 5,* 130–135.

Malkiewicz, J. (1970). Stories can be springboards. *Instructor, 79,* 133–134.

Melamed, B.G., and Siegel, L. (1975). Reduction of anxiety in children facing hospitalization and surgery by use of filmed modeling. *Journal of Consulting and Clinical Psychology, 43,* 511–521.

Mendell, A. (1983). Play therapy with children of divorced parents. In C. Schafer and K. O'Connor (Eds.), *Handbook of play therapy,* 320–354. New York: Wiley.

Millman, H. (1970). Minimal brain dysfunction in children. Evaluation and treatment. *Journal of Learning Disabilities, 3,* 89–99.

Muro, J., and Dinkmeyer, D. (1977). *Counseling in the elementary and middle schools.* Dubuque, Iowa: Wm. C. Brown.

Nickerson, E. (1983). Art as a play therapeutic medium. In C. Schafer and K. O'Connor (Eds.), *Handbook of play therapy,* 234–250. New York: Wiley.

Olszowy, D. (1978). *Horticulture for the disabled and disadvantaged.* Springfield, IL: Charles C Thomas.

Peller, L. (1962). Daydreams and children's favorite books. In J. Posenblith and W. Allensmith (Eds.), *The causes of behavior.* Boston: Allyn & Bacon.

Peoples, C. (1983). Fair play therapy. In C. Schaffer and K. O'Connor (Eds.), *Handbook of play therapy,* 76–89. New York: Wiley.

Relf, D. (1981). Dynamics of horticultural therapy. *Rehabilitation Literature, 42*(5–6), 147–149.

Robbins, A., and Sibley, L. (1976). *Creative art therapy.* New York: Brunner/Mazel.

Rubin, R. (1978). *Using bibliotherapy: A guide to theory and practice.* Phoenix, AZ: Oryx.

Schafer, C., and O'Connor, K. (1983). *Handbook of play therapy.* New York: Wiley.

Schafer, C., and Reed, S. (1986). *Game play.* New York: Wiley.

Smith, E. (1982). Dolphins to elicit communication responses from autistic children. In Katcher, A., and Beck, A. (Eds.), *New perspectives on our lives with companion animals,* 460–466. Philadelphia: University of Pennsylvania Press.

Sutton-Smith, B. (1971). Play, games, and controls. In J.P. Scott (Ed.), *Social control.* Chicago: University of Chicago Press.

Sutton-Smith, B., and Roberts, J. (1971). The cross-cultural and psychological study of games. *International Review of Sport Sociology, 6,* 79–87.

Wadeson, H. (1980). *Art psychotherapy.* New York: John Wiley and Sons.

Watson, D., and Burlingame, A. (1960). *Therapy through horticulture.* New York: Macmillan.

Whipple, G. (1969). Practical problems of school book selection for disadvantaged pupils. In J. Figurel (Ed.), *Reading and realism.* Delaware: International Reading Association.

Wilson, J. (1964). *The mind.* New York: Life Science Library Series, Time.

Winnicott, D.W. (1971). *Therapeutic consultations in child psychiatry.* New York: Basic Books.

Zaccaria, J., Moses, H., and Hollowell, J. (1978). *Bibliotherapy in rehabilitation, educational, and mental health settings: Theory, research, and practice.* Champaign, IL: Stipes.

Zakich, R. (1975). *the ungame.* Anaheim, CA: Ungame.

Zakich, R., and Monroe, S. (1979). *Reunion.* Placentia, CA: Ungame.

Chapter 7

PARENTS—THEIR PERCEPTIONS AND INPUT: THE IMPORTANCE OF COLLABORATION

Aubrey H. Fine

Speak to us of Children. And he said . . .
Though they are with you yet they belong not to you . . .
You are the bows from which your children as living arrows
are set forth. . . .
Let your bending in the archer's hand be for gladness;
For even as He love the arrow that flies, so He loves also
the bow that is stable.

Kahlil Gibran

One of the areas that is imperative to incorporate in this book is the value and the importance of collaborating and working closely with parents. I had the opportunity to be guided into this field by concerned and active parents who were committed to ensuring a better life for their child. After years of working with several families, I realized that they represented **the key** to a successful program. Since that time I have been motivated to teach those who serve any child so they could recognize and understand the value of parents' participation.

This chapter will present several issues that relate to parent participation and will discuss other important areas as they relate to providing services to the child and parents.

1. Parenting a child with a disability. What impact does the child have on the family?
2. Why is parental involvement important?
3. What is the rationale for enhancing parent-professional relationships?
4. How can parents and professionals relate to best serve the child?
5. What are parents searching for when asking recreational services for their child?

6. How is the least restrictive placement for the child explained to the parents?
7. How does one develop a parent component?
8. Why is recreation in the home important?

PARENTING A CHILD WITH A DISABILITY

All parents hope for the birth of a normal happy child. When parents are confronted with the birth of a child with a disability, some will have relatively no difficulty with acceptance. For others, the task will be an arduous, perhaps impossible task. On the one hand, they want to love and care for the child, but on the other hand, they reject the young infant. The parents may feel dejected, confused, and insecure. These internalized feelings can persist because the problem can be envisioned as long term. The adaptation to one's child is truly an individual phenomenon. Parental adjustment is depressed or enhanced by the sum total of the physical and the emotional resources that surface in coping with the situation.

The family must represent a loving, caring and nurturing environment. Giving and receiving is an integral part of the family relationship. **The Giving Tree** by Shel Silverstein is a delightful story about the quality of giving. The story revolves around the warm relationship between a little boy and a befriended tree. As a child, he always visited the tree, ate her apples, and slept under her branches. The boy and the tree had a wonderful relationship, and the tree loved the boy. As with any relationship, changes do occur over the years. The tree was devoted to her friend, and the tree kept giving and giving until all that was left of her was a stump. The story offers an interpretation of the gift of giving and the serene acceptance of another's capacity to love in return (Silverstein, 1964).

Parents have an enormous responsibility in raising children, and when a child has special needs, there are even more responsibilities. Raising a disabled child can be challenging and difficult. The physical, social, and psychological aspects of having a child with special needs in the family can be a draining experience. However, there is also the opportunity of extraordinary reward and extreme joy.

Many families have indicated that home life is greatly changed by the presence of a disabled individual. Much of the research that has been conducted in the past perpetuates the assumption that the family with a disabled individual often exhibits attitudes that have been greatly and negatively shaped by the presence of that member (Spaulding, 1986).

Sheridan (1965) stated in **The Handicapped Child and His Home** that in the background of every individual handicapped child, there is always a handicapped family.

How does a family provide that support to the child with disabilities? An important and difficult step is coming to terms with the actual disorder: a difficult process not only for parents but the siblings as well. Adults and children have to deal with feelings of guilt, fear, anger and loneliness. There are many other reactions that parents can develop because of having a child with a disability within the family. Many of these reactions depend on the severity of the disability as well as when it occurred in the child's life (e.g. spina bifida which is a birth defect or if a child becomes disabled due to an accident). Other variables that influence the acceptance of a child pertains to the parents' understanding of the actual disorder as well as their knowledge of the range of support and treatment facilities available to the family. When learning how to care for the disabled child, it is the rare parent who knows exactly where to go or how to obtain help for their child.

Over the years, parents will usually begin to look beyond the disability and recognize a child with many of the same characteristics as any other child. An important milestone for parents is being able to see through the child's disability and recognize the abilities that do exist. This will also help family members cope with the subtle and not so subtle outcomes of prejudice and discrimination against the child with a disability.

Influence on Siblings

Parents have to be conscious of their responsibilities to all of their children. Unfortunately, some mothers and fathers try to become **super parents** to compensate for their disabled child.

The presence of a disabled sibling changes the living experiences of every member in the family. Families with a disabled member usually offer normal siblings unusual opportunities for growth as well as unusual problems. Nya Fine explains: "I was eleven years old when my sister became ill and went into the hospital. I also remember a sister coming home who was quite different. My father tried to explain to me why and what condition this disease, leukodystrophy, had on my sister. His explanations were clear, but the words were hard to comprehend. She will not be able to walk, talk or take care of herself anymore. I found myself feeling confused and very angry. How could this be? She was just fine the other day. Was it because I did something bad and God punished her? She is just a baby. Why her? Why not me? Feelings of fear, guilt, anxiety, and anger filled me. How was I going to cope with this situation?"

Meyer, Vadasy, and Fewell (1985) discuss the various feelings and experiences many siblings may encounter. They suggest that some of these feelings are hard to talk about with peers. Some of the children may benefit from a sibling support group. They note that the feelings of jealousy, a sense of neglect, worry, and embarrassment are some of the feelings that these children encounter.

Sometimes, siblings feel ignored by their parents. It may appear that their parents do not notice them unless they do something to get into trouble. Parents usually spend more time with the special sibling, which in turn may promote jealousy. Siblings also feel guilty experiencing the feelings of embarrassment towards their disabled sibling. Children need to realize that it is alright to feel indifferent and that these feelings do not mean that one does not love their brother or sister. These feelings may suggest that the child may need a little space to grow and learn. Furthermore, these feelings may also be indicative of the need for the child to learn a little bit more about their sibling and how they can accept them as an integral part of the family.

Normal siblings may be burdened with excessively high parental aspirations to compensate for parental frustrations due to having a disabled child. Furthermore, some children may be given excessive responsibility for taking care of the disabled child (Seligman, 1983). Consequently, it is imperative for parents to fully understand the ramifications of having a child with a disability. Within this realm of understanding, parents need to be cognizant of some of the pressures placed on their non-disabled child.

The literature suggests that there are some positive aspects about having a disabled sibling. A number of studies point out that some siblings seem to be more tolerant and more aware of the consequences of prejudice. They also seem to be more sensitive to the needs of others. The strongest single factor affecting the normal sibling's acceptance seems to be how parents react to the child, especially the mother (Seligman, 1983). Unfortunately, there is evidence that some siblings are hardened by the experience. Scholars suggest these children may display bitter resentment to the family's situation, guilt about the rage, and anger they feel towards the parents and the sibling who is disabled, and the everlasting fear that they themselves might be defective (Seligman, 1983).

Communication and education are two ingredients to remedy potential problems. Communication among the entire family unit will help to keep the members of the family in touch with each other's feelings. When new situations arise, they possibly will be more willing to discuss and confront these situations. In addition, education should focus on strategies to enhance the family dynamics as well as how to live effectively with a child with a disability. Professionals as well as parents need to recognize how important siblings can be while interacting informally with their brother or sister. The following suggestions are for encouraging interaction among siblings.

1. Establish realistic expectations. (Remember that the sibling is not there to entertain the child. In the beginning, set a time limit on the activity so that the activity can end in a happy manner.)
2. Select activities and toys that lead to interaction. (Do not select an activity in which you know your child has no interest. Select a few activities so that if the first activity is not working, another activity can be selected).
3. Praise siblings for interaction. (Sometimes it is easier for parents to pick out the negative actions instead of the positive. Reinforce all of the positive behaviors and acknowledge their efforts.)
4. Directly teach interaction. (Parents need to set an example and teach their children how to interact with the child. For example, John loved his disabled brother, but he knew how concerned his mother was about his brother. He was terrified that while he was with his brother, he would get hurt or sick. This was a terrifying feeling. It makes an enormous difference when a child has confidence in what he is doing.) (Power and Ogle, 1985).

THE IMPORTANCE OF PARENT INVOLVEMENT

Most parents of children with disabilities, like parents in general, come to know, respect, and love their children. While others may view a child as **handicapped** or **different**, these parents come to see within their child and recognize his/her individual strengths and limitations. Parents represent a rich and available resource not to merely advocate for their children but to help others understand who they are. Parents have seen their child conquer challenges, as well as fail, and have a wealth of information about their child. In regards to recreation, what parents want most of all for their child is for the child to be part of a group, to be wanted, and appreciated by others. One mother describes the feelings of isolation her son experiences. Groce (1985) tells her readers about the stares her son endures, as well as the superficial greetings he receives from many who pass him in the halls of school. What her son wants and needs is to be one of the crowd, for someone to know who he is.

Parents of a disabled child are often so anxious for their child to be rehabilitated that some often have unrealistic expectations for improvement from all of the services a child is involved in, including recreation programs (Kronick, 1973). Determining what types of programs disabled children would benefit most from in addition to when and where the programs should take place are typical questions that concern parents. Furthermore, these are questions that need to be addressed by the recreation therapists.

The insightful recreation therapist recognizes the important role that parents play in the total rehabilitation process of their child. Heward, Dardig, and Rossett (1979) point out that parents need the support of professionals so that they can access relevant and understandable information about their child. Through collaborations, parents equip themselves with strategies for dealing with the everyday concerns of bringing up their disabled child and establishing long-term goals. Likewise, professionals need and benefit from the support and wisdom of parents.

The following examples illustrate the influences that parents can have on their child's rehabilitation. The first example portrays how important it is to work with parents. The situation that occurred fourteen years ago involved a seven-year-old named Barry who had a very poor self-concept. Barry was clumsy, had very poorly developed fine motor skills and, as a result, was very self-conscious about his abilities. He was involved in a social recreational program developed for children with learning disabilities. The staff was frustrated because they could not motivate Barry to participate in any of the art projects. After months of encouragement, Barry felt secure enough to complete a project. Although his project would not have been considered a masterpiece by many, he was proud of his work and that was all that really counted. When his father came to pick them up, Barry was seen exuberantly running out to show his father his completed work. To Barry's dismay, as well as to all those who observed, his father merely glanced at the piece of paper and said, "What is this garbage?" and then proceeded to crumple the paper and throw it on the ground. Barry was shattered emotionally and it would be a long time before he felt confident enough to try another art project.

With this awakening experience, it was discovered that designing programs which encourage parental involvement and commitment are of vital importance. These programs do vary in the demands placed on both parents and professionals. They range from simply making sure that appropriate channels are developed for open communication, to programs that have parent participation as a major component. Various programs will be elaborated later in this chapter.

Now let us examine a situation where parents facilitate positive outcomes for their child. For a year, Steven was enrolled in an individually prescribed recreation therapy program. Steve was diagnosed as autistic and displayed some of the severe ritualistic behaviors that are characteristic of autism (e.g. self-stimulation and rocking). He was also extremely manipulative and appeared to need a very structured program.

Steve's parents asked the recreation therapist for assistance to help Steve develop a few of recreational skills. His mother was very concerned that Steve had limited leisure abilities, which was evident each day after school when he had free time. This frustrated his mother, since Steven was difficult to manage and needed constant supervision. Because of Steven's age, the therapist felt that the primary emphasis of his training should be on developing functional play skills. A great deal of time was spent with his family to understand Steve's life-style and to determine what would be the most likely activities he could perform. After a period of collaboration, activities and goals were established.

Two students were trained as group leaders for Steve. They met twice a week for two hours. Since a child like Steven needed constant and consistent programming, progress would have been limited if the family did not work in close collaboration with the student therapists. Due to the parent-therapist interaction, Steve's parents worked on the same goals at home and kept the student therapists posted on Steven's progress. Furthermore, due to the complexity of the interventions applied in Steven's case, it was necessary for his parents to educate anyone serving their son about the program. This was done to ensure consistency in all interations with Steven.

Over the next several months, progress with Steven was phenomenal. However, this was not totally due to professional involvement. Open communication was established between the therapists and Steve's parents.

The role of his parents as adjunct therapists was clearly established. In this example, both parents seemed willing to be involved and contributed immensely to the ultimate success of the program.

THE RATIONALE FOR ENHANCING PARENT-PROFESSIONAL RELATIONSHIPS

Heward et al. (1979) provides a rationale for enhancing the parent-professional relationship. Foremost, parents can provide the professional community with a clearer understanding of the needs of their child as well as what they expect from the program. Several of the interviewing techniques as well as the developmental profiles discussed in Chapter 5 are viable avenues for gathering information from parents. Parents should be encouraged to be honest with professionals and to tell them as much as possible about their child. Unfortunately, parents are sometimes not given an opportunity to disclose all pertinent information. This is usually due to time constraints or staff limitations within a therapeutic recreation program. Professionals oftentimes neglect questioning the parents' intentions for enrolling a child in any given program. The rationale for enrolling a child and clarification of expectations need to be discussed.

When collaboration occurs, parents can represent a rich resource base. If parents know specifically what the professional is focusing on and are assisted in establishing a routine, children can practice similar play skills at home. The repetition would allow the newly established skills to become a more natural aspect of a child's play repertoire. For some children especially the severely disabled, limited structured recreation opportunities will not dramatically develop skills. They typically will be enhanced only if additional time is devoted outside the group to practice the skills. This is also true for children who are less disabled. It is imperative for the child to try out the new skills so that the child will eventually incorporate them into their daily life patterns. A major weakness in leisure skill instruction appears to be the lack of insight of professionals in training self-initiated play behaviors. It really does not matter in the long run if a child performs an activity only in the presence of an adult. For the behavior to have any long-lasting effect, it must occur spontaneously without the constant supervision of an adult.

It is noteworthy that the lack of self-initiated play behaviors is one of parents' most severe criticisms of recreation therapy programs. While they acknowledge that their child is enjoying the program, they cannot understand why the child does not use these trained skills at home.

Some of this pertains to perceived competence, while a portion can also be attributed to opportunity. Both of these variables will be discussed in detail in Chapter 8. However, by collaborating with parents, one can ensure that lack of opportunity and consultation are not considered as the source of the problem.

FIGURE 1

THE IMPORTANCE OF COLLABORATION
WHILE SERVING A CHILD

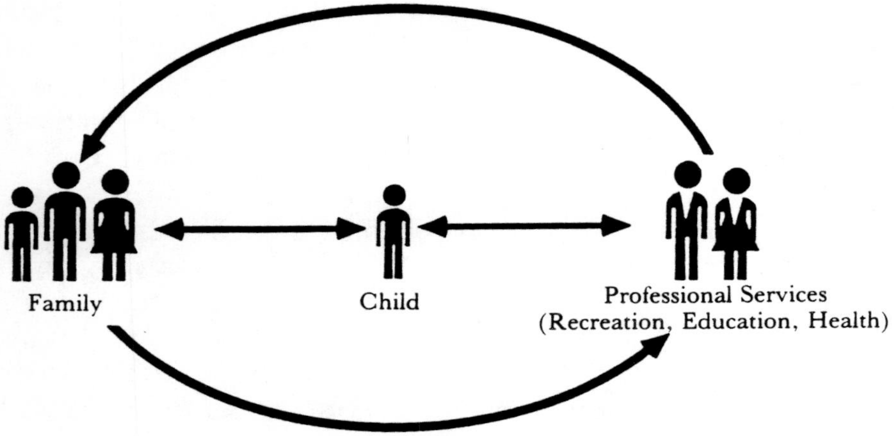

Family   Child   Professional Services
                                        (Recreation, Education, Health)

Figure 1 portrays the collaborative relationship between parents and the professional community. The figure projects all sources commonly working with each other to strengthen the opportunity for a child's growth and learning. The cooperation between parents and professionals promotes greater consistency in a child's most important living environment. Emphasis in how school personnel can be helpful in this process is presented in Chapter 8. Note that unless a system that enhances the natural extension of skills taught in therapy is developed, there will always be a void in the provision process.

Parents cannot only encourage the practice of skills being taught, but they can also act as an informant to update the professional on their child's progress. Furthermore, parents should be approached to discuss their perceptions of programmatic goals. They may have extremely relevant ideas that may not have been incorporated into their child's program. Additionally, if parents are not consciously made aware of what a program entails, they may inadvertently discourage the acquisition and development of skills being generated. Therefore, uniformity of expectations must occur.

A situation occurred where program goals were not uniformly understood by a young boy's parents and his therapists. Within the leisure education and self-help aspects of the program, he began to develop an interest in cooking simple meals. However, this conflicted with his parents' expectations of him. When he attempted to employ his newly acquired skills at home, his family was not supportive. They were uncomfortable with the idea of their son utilizing the electric range and oven. After consultation with the therapists, the parents were willing to adapt their expectations and allow their son to cook at home.

Working with families provides increased opportunities for learning, and it also expands the likelihood for greater services to the child. Another factor that promotes quality interaction with parents pertains to consistency in methods of management. All too often there is a discrepancy between the approaches utilized in the home versus in outside programs. Expectations should be clarified to encourage more uniformity and consistency in approaches.

In 1975, Ed Sontag, then chief of the Division of Personnel Preparation for the Bureau of Education for the Handicapped, expressed his commitment to the parent-professional relationship. He stated that educational research indicated that when parents are involved in the educational process, their children are more likely to achieve on a higher level. When parents are involved, they tend to be more committed as well as cognizant of a program's goals.

Unfortunately, some professionals find it difficult to accept the position of working closely with parents. They believe in the myth that it is easier to facilitate programs for children if parents are kept out of the picture. Although parents have a right to be informed and involved in their child's treatment, the parents' involvement is often discouraged and considered meddlesome. For too long, this was the orientation chosen by most professionals. Kratoville (1973) suggests that parents hate to be stigmatized as meddlers, but sometimes their only alternative is to meddle.

Furthermore, parents must become more familiar with the resources that an agency can provide. Parents are often unfamiliar with or have misunderstandings about the field of therapeutic recreation. The need to define and clarify therapeutic recreation's role in rehabilitation is quite evident. Due to this lack of understanding, parents may have inaccurate expectations about what therapeutic recreation can offer. Many lay persons perceived the field as either exclusively recreation for the handicapped or to the opposite extreme: therapy. A parent who is expecting therapy when the purposes of the program are totally recreational can lead to frustration and misunderstanding. Nevertheless, this predicament has partially been resolved with the formation of the new philosophic definition adopted by the National Therapeutic Recreation Society. According to this new definition, the purpose of therapeutic recreation is the facilitation of the development of an optimal leisure life-style for individuals with a variety of disabling conditions. Three areas of professional services are incorporated in therapeutic recreation: (1) therapy, (2) leisure, and (3) recreation participation. While these three processes have unique contributions in relation to the clients' needs, conceptually (according to the definition) they are formulated employing similar processes. However, there is a lack of uniformity among professionals. There are simply too many programs that claim that they provide recreation therapy but provide services that are developed and executed poorly. Additionally, these programs are not based on the results of each participant's assessed needs but, rather, on a general program that attempts to cater to a multitude of different children. This issue is not to frustrate the reader but to inspire the individual to make an impact on the future. Professional leaders of today and those neophytes who are emerging as leaders must function as the change agents of the profession. These individuals need to assume responsibility for establishing and maintaining the profession's credibility and serve as advocates for helping others understand.

The program goals must be explained to parents. It is acceptable to tell parents that the sole purpose of the program is for fun (if that is the major goal). In fact, that is frequently what motivates the child to attend. The impact of therapeutic recreation originates with the participation in activities to promote changes that are desired. False expectations precipitate poor experiences that only frustrate families, which then questions the professional's credibility. Professionals, therefore, need to take the responsibility of clarifying to parents the type of entry information that would be helpful. It is crucial that all of those involved establish the ground rules at the beginning of the collaborative working relationship.

WHAT PARENTS SHOULD BE AWARE OF WHEN SEEKING RECREATIONAL SERVICES

The parents' first concern usually pertains to where a recreation program is offered. Some communities do not have the luxury of having a host of alternatives and the choices are, therefore, quite simple. However, when there are several alternatives to consider, parents should take their time to select the best option. Alternatives can range from fun recreation clubs to programs that emphasize therapeutic values. All of these alternatives provide children with some of the skills necessary for integrated functioning.

Integrated Versus Segregated Settings

A major dilemma that parents encounter concerns the decision of placing their child in either an integrated or segregated program. Should the child be placed with children who have a similar disability or not? Kronick (1973) suggests that some children at different stages of their life may initially function better in a segregated setting. However, how does one determine whether a child would profit more from a segregated or an integrated program? One way to consider this dilemma is to perceive readiness on a continuum. Placements range from the most restrictive sheltered programs to venues that are totally integrated. The least restrictive alternative for children should be considered as the environment that allows children the freedom to perform in activities in the most normalized fashion. Certainly, not all persons with disabilities need to be in segregated programs and, for that matter, programs sponsored by recreation therapists.

Placement into an integrated program for a child who is not ready or for a program that is not prepared could prove to be disastrous. Parents whose children have minor disabilities must consider their options prior to making their decision. Key variables that should be considered are summarized below.

The most critical issue to focus upon is the discrepancy between the child's chronological age and present functional level. This discrepancy is also interrelated with a child's social and behavioral skills. If the child is developmentally immature and has difficulty interacting with the same-age peers, then integration is not the selection. Although integration may be the ultimate goal, it should not be sacrificed for an unsuccessful adventure. With the appropriate preparation, a child may eventually develop the skills to join in. Unfortunately, too many bad experiences are caused by bringing a child into an integrated program before he or she is ready. This experience will reduce a child's perceived competence and eventually diminish the motivation to try to be with others. David Elkind's book, **The Hurried Child** (1982), defines the abuse of hurrying "as the pressure on children to make social accommodations at the expense of personal assimilations." At times, we tend to push children because of our need.

An easy way to judge a child's readiness for integration is to observe and assess the child's neighborhood play and the extent of friendships with non-disabled peers (Kronick, 1973). While observing the child, parents focus on the child's willingness to follow directions, the child's attention span, the child's ability to comprehend and participate in age-appropriate activities. Age-appropriate behavior in these three areas serves as criteria for whether a child is ready for an integrated program.

A Continuum for Least Restrictive Placement

Figure 2 projects a theoretical understanding of how parents and professionals should perceive the child's movement from a segregated one into a more integrated environment. The lines between each of the phases are permeable which represents mobility between the phases. When a child reaches a prescribed level of ability, the child should then be promoted to the next stage. A neglected area of many programs is the lack of provisions built in which ensure that a child will be promoted when ready.

Phase One of the placement model is the most restrictive. It is within this program that we find a low staff-child ratio and children who are severely disabled. This is usually the first group experience encountered by the child. Furthermore, due to the severity of the disability, the duration of each program period is quite short. The second phase (**Phase Two**) of the program would still be considered quite restrictive, but the children in this phase would have the ability to be involved in longer programs with a higher staff-child ratio.

Programs falling into either of these categories occur in a centralized or decentralized environment. Centralized programs are placed in environments exclusively developed for the special population. On the other hand, decentralized programs take place in an integrated environment.

FIGURE 2

THEORETICAL REPRESENTATION OF VARIOUS STAGES
OF THE LEAST RESTRICTIVE ENVIRONMENT

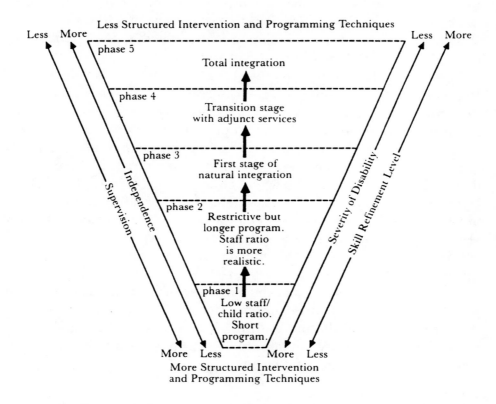

All programs should be scheduled in a decentralized environments whenever possible. This facilitates the sharing of community resources as well as promoting normalization.

Phase Three represents the initial aspect of the integration process. The majority of children who are moderately disabled should begin their recreational involvement in programs that adhere to this orientation which has a built-in integration component. Activities are specifically designed to provide support and enhance the child's readiness abilities for total integration. Attention should be given to the child's strengths and limitations with activities designed to enhance physical and mental well-being. In the past, much of the focus centered on working on limitations. This has been a major thrust in the field of special education as well as many of the remedial therapies. However, academics are now arguing that it may be inappropriate to focus the locus of attention solely on the children's developing deficiencies. Rather, they advocate emphasis should be focused initially on developing the children's strengths. Proponents to this orientation suggest that the child become more confident in activities that accentuate the child's skills. Consequently, when attention is returned to the remediation of deficiencies, the child is prepared emotionally to handle this.

The proposed continuum reduces the opportunity for possible failure. In the third phase, opportunities for interaction with non-disabled children compliment the child's specialized recreation program. These interventions help prepare the child for optimal integration. Depending on the condition that disables the child and the program, it may be helpful to pair a child with a peer who does not have a disability. This should definitely occur in situations where children who are severely disabled lack the opportunity for this experience. The buddy system may promote increased interaction between all of the children involved. Stein (1983) suggests that the buddy system is equally valuable to able-bodied children, because they may become more sensitive to and accepting of a person with disabilities.

Within the integrated program, activities such as simulations or role playing can be incorporated to encourage children to be aware of the disabled person. Furthermore, through these directed experiences the professional community can impact the children's sensitivity and understanding of exceptional population.

Cross-Age Tutoring

Cross-age tutoring, which is the process where children are effectively used as tutors for peers, has been found to provide unique and uplifting experiences to a wide variety of children, including the disabled student. Over the past decade, there have been a number of studies investigating the impact of peer tutoring and its relationship to the enhancement of self-concept and social achievement (e.g. Krouse, Gerber, and Kauffman, 1981). It appears that the tutor derives psychological benefit from functioning in a helping role (West and Ray, 1977). It is often the tutor who appears to make the greatest improvement, as well as profit the most from the experience.

Keat (1976) suggests that the tutor derives a good feeling from helping others, because helping makes one feel useful. When people feel that they are needed, they develop positive feelings about themselves. Moreover, the tutee may reinforce the tutor by recognizing the tutor's efforts. Fitts (1971) noted the importance of an individual in one's own rehabilitation and, thus, stresses the tutee's involvement in achieving actualization and realization of potential. If properly implemented with appropriate safeguards built in (i.e. appropriate training and supervision for the peer tutors), cross-age tutoring can lead to experiences which are of great value to all of the individuals involved. The two examples that follow illustrate the benefits of cross-age tutoring.

Over a six-year period, I was responsible for developing and implementing a therapeutic recreation program for children (ages eight to twelve) with learning disabilities. Many of these children were in the level three program and appeared to be almost ready for total integration, but they seemed to lack self-esteem and confidence. An asset to the program was the counselor-in-training component in which the children took on the role of cross-age tutors. The children appeared to enjoy their positions and were willing to accept the extra responsibilities. Furthermore, the participants were trained with the necessary skills to become successful in their roles.

The children experienced great pride in their work. In fact, many parents commented that they had not seen their child so happy. The program appeared to contribute to the well-being of the children. This is not to say that there were not times when the children and their supervisors became frustrated. However, a great deal of support was built into the training to promote success. Time was still designated for the children to have their own recreational periods. Taking away this added incentive would have been devastating. In fact, due to their involvement, the children became closer and developed a strong sense of community. As a consequence, they would get together as a group outside the program.

A second example involves a normalization program that was established for pre-teens with myelomeningocele (a form of spina bifida). The majority of the children were involved in an integrated school setting. However, they found their exclusive group of peers with myelomeningocele very enjoyable, and for some children, these group members were their only friends. They frequently tried to set up special events to get together informally. Vicariously, over the years the participants acted as role models for one another. When they saw others reach a **milestone** that they had at one time perceived to be impossible, they appeared to become motivated to achieve higher goals.

The most unique and long-term effect of this program was the peer-tutoring aspect. During the three years, seven children participated in this dimension of the program. Many of the findings portrayed previously in the first example were replicated in this program. The most significant impact of the program occurred in the summer of 1986, which was four years after the program had been discontinued due to lack of financial support. However, the participants kept up their network of contacts and met informally over the years, which attests to the fact that the program was an important part of the adolescents' lives. Consequently, with great efforts the graduates of the program took it upon themselves to solicit financial support and reinitiate the project under their own leadership. They were proud of their accomplishments, and through their persistency they provided an opportunity for younger children with myelomeningocele to reap comparable benefits.

These two programs also included participants' families and incorporated a parent component. It is believed that parents, if willing, should have the opportunity to be involved in their child's program. An adjunct program should be provided on an intermittent basis where the parents meet to discuss their concerns about their child. The parent groups can also focus on educational topics, such as how to encourage independence in one's child, gaining a better understanding of community resources, how to enhance a child's level of perceived competence, and so forth. Furthermore, these parent sessions can represent an opportunity for the therapists to assemble with the parents while discussing the parents' important roles. A discussion of how a parent component can be incorporated into a recreation program will be discussed in more detail in the latter part of this chapter.

Phase Four is probably one of the most critical in the continuum. When a child is ready for a minimally supervised program that is completely integrated, steps need to be formulated to assure the effective transition. All too often, children are discharged from one program and are not registered in another. The problem is sometimes compounded by the unfamiliarity of the staff of other programs who are at times inadequately prepared to serve the child.

This fourth stage, if properly implemented, will ensure success and continuity. It is suggested that the therapeutic recreation agency contact other community programs in an attempt to develop cooperative transitional relationships. These agencies will become an integral part of the process. With proper in-service training, these agencies will be prepared to accept their future roles with these children. In the transition period the child will be served by two agencies. Although this may appear to be difficult and unrealistic, this is the most optimal and effective method.

The child will receive the necessary support from his/her previous staff, which will usually guarantee a follow-up.

A child who reaches the final point on the continuum (independent functioning within an integrated program) will be ready for the **Fifth Phase**. A child at this point is ready to be involved in an integrated program without any adjunct services. Following this logical progression, one can ensure quality and the appropriate placement for a child.

Parents are also concerned about a variety of operational concerns that may impact the child and family such as the time of day when the program will be conducted and how often. Prior to setting up a program, parents should be consulted so they know what to expect. The professional staff should also let the family know how often they will be in contact so that parents will become more aware of their child's progress.

Developing a Parent Component

The incorporation of a parent component within the overall recreation program is highly recommended. This component should be considered an integral part of the overall services provided. Recreational services become an asset to families by providing a resource. It can also broaden the typical role and function of a recreational therapist to include that of a community educator. Due to budgeting limitations, some agencies will find it impossible to develop a parent component. Moreover, lack of parental support and apathy may also stand in the way. Nevertheless, a parent program is vital, because it can become the vehicle that promotes communication between professionals and lay persons. In addition it acts as a built-in support mechanism.

The format for such a program can vary. Scheduling events depends on the families who are willing to participate. Group leaders should begin slowly by providing a monthly meeting. At these meetings, an overview of the group's general progress can be reported as well as what parents can do at home to enhance the program's impact. In addition, several topics could be presented in a lecture-discussion format. There are usually many members of the community who are willing to serve as guest facilitators. Topics can range from discussions of child-rearing practices to preparing for the future (adolescence, education, employment, etc.). It is imperative that parents are involved in selecting the topics that are important to them. These meetings can also equip the families with recreational skills that they could utilize in their homes. Parents can be introduced and familiarized with a multitude of resources (e.g. ideas for games, art projects, drama activities, and music) that would enhance their child's productivity. Through this extra effort the professionals would be indirectly assisting the child by building upon the parents' competency levels. Furthermore, parents would have an opportunity to learn and employ therapeutic recreation principles in the home.

RECREATION WITHIN THE HOME

All of God's critter have a place in the choir.
Some sing low, some sing higher,
Some sing out loud on the telephone wires,
And some just clap their hands....

MANTLE (1985)

Children need to learn to identify as family members by actively joining the everyday routine in family responsibilities and actively sharing in the family recreation (Ferris, 1980). The home is the first school and recreation center; the parent is the first teacher and recreation leader. What goes on in the family is the foundation of learning. It includes guidance in play and recreation which, in turn, provides opportunities for growth (Brightbill and Mobley, 1977). Families who engage in enjoyable and rewarding activities together will enhance family interaction and maintain the involvement of the child in community functions. A child who knows how to play and has acquired leisure skills will be able to utilize his/her leisure time. Thus, the child will be less dependent on his/her parents and siblings for leisure activities. At times, families find themselves occupying every second of their child's time. This proves to be a great injustice to the child as well as to the family.

Parents are encouraged to look at the child and try to remove the obstacles that prevent family activities (Goodman, Grotsky, and Mann, 1979). Parents should take chances and try new activities. Some activities will spark interests and others may not. These activities can represent a special sharing time between child, parents and siblings. Sometimes, parents are so concerned about providing for the child's physical well-being that they neglect to join the child for fun. When parents and children enjoy a game or other activities, hostility is reduced and harmony can be enhanced. Play allows the child to see the child within the parent, not the authoritarian. The experiences allow the family to view the disabled child in another light. They may begin to recognize some of the child's assets and realize the disabled child's contribution to the family as a whole. The family can encourage social interaction and effectively teach interaction skills to other children. This becomes quality time which enhances all family members.

Some families incorporate a **family meeting** which is a special period of time set aside each week where the family comes together to talk and have fun. It may be quite a chore to get all family members together, but the end result is well worth the effort. Families can begin to see how enjoyable it is to be together. It is a must for all families. Dinkmeyer and McKay (1982) and Popkin (1987) are two excellent resources for the reader to learn how to initiate and organize these meetings.

Family recreation may differ depending on the level of functioning of the child. It may not be easy to involve the child, but it should not be impossible, either. If one looks for reasons why not to do things, one will find a million excuses for not attempting to do it. Parents need to look at the opportunities that are available. Most children like to have company, and being able to be part of the action is a wonderful learning experience. There are benefits to be gained both from participation and watching an activity. Nya Fine provides a personal point of view of her sister, who had a profound disability. "My sister enjoyed the company of people. My mother would have my sister in the room while she was performing homemaking tasks. If she was cooking, she would involve my sister in that activity. It may have been only to assist in the stirring, but what occurred? There was the contact, the experience of feeling the texture, smelling, and, best yet, the tasting. We quickly learned what she did like and what she did not. She did not have speech, but Lisa would definitely let the family know when things were not right."

It is important for families that have existing leisure interests to involve the child with the disability in those activities as much as possible. It is imperative to be realistic in the selection and the degree of participation. Parents are encouraged to look at the activity and see how the child can participate. What skills are required? What can be adapted? For example, within a family which enjoys camping, several aspects of the activity can be modified for almost any child's participation (e.g. assisting in setting up the tent, hiking and cooking).

Resources for Family Recreation

Let's Play to Grow which was created by the Joseph P. Kennedy, Jr. Foundation is a program of play, recreation, and shared experiences for the disabled child and his/her families. The program provides a chance for the child and the family to play, learn, and grow from the interaction. Families are assisted in adapting activities so that everyone can enjoy the fun. This program was initiated by parents or people interested in establishing a program like this.

Nothing is so important to the disabled and their families as information in all areas of daily living, including recreation. A wonderful resource in the community is the local library. The library should provide materials concerning resources and services for the disabled. If the community library does not have the information readily available, they usually are able to help the individual locate the required information elsewhere. Information pertaining to recreation activities may include some of the following areas: wheelchair sports, camping, horseback riding, arts for the disabled, outdoor recreation activities, transportation and organizations that are related.

Finally, no explanation of recreation within the home is complete without a brief overview of the value of neighborhood peers. Probably one of the biggest complaints against segregated educational programs is that children do not develop positive relationships with children who live in their surrounding area. It is therefore imperative that professionals become more aware of this dilemma when serving a child. Hopefully, they will attempt to incorporate within their programming an emphasis on developing the skills which will enhance friendship making. Of course, most parents will welcome this added element of instruction.

The neighborhood has always been an important avenue for the opportunity of social interaction and the acquisition of many developmental and survival skills. Some of the benefits that can be gained are:

1. The child acts as a role model for the child with a disability.
2. The disabled child will be exposed to age-appropriate behavior.
3. The opportunity for socialization.
4. The acquisition of various skills.
5. The opportunity for friendship.
6. The non-disabled child develops an awareness of the similarities between all children.

7. Neighborhood children can be of great assistance to the disabled child in adapting activities for participation. Furthermore, they represent a natural opportunity for the child to practice the skills he/she has learned both from the home and the recreation program.

SUMMARY

Parental involvement within the overall therapeutic recreation process is strongly recommended. Its benefits will be quickly evident and will far outweigh the initial hardships of developing such a program. Recreational personnel need to engage in a campaign to re-educate the community about how they can actively have an impact on a child and his/her family. When families recognize the quality program that has been established and how the parental component is an integral element, it is likely they will be more receptive to participate. In addition, parents must be encouraged to initiate positive family recreation. These experiences should be helpful in enhancing the family bond as well as promoting a more positive living environment.

Endnote

Appreciation is given to Nya Fine for her assistance in preparing this chapter. Specifically, Nya contributed information in the sections related to parenting a child with a disability as well as recreation within the home.

REFERENCES

Brightbill, C., and Mobley, T. (1977). *Educating for leisure-centered living.* New York: Wiley.

Dinkmeyer, D., and McKay, G. (1982). *Systematic training for effective parenting.* Circle Pines: American Guidance Service.

Featherstone, H. (1980). *A difference in the family: Life with a disabled child.* New York: Basic Books.

Fitts, W. (1971). *The self concept and self actualization.* Nashville: Counselor Recording and Tests.

Groce, N. (1985). *Everyone here spoke sign language.* Cambridge MA: Harvard University Press.

Heward, W., Dardig, J., and Rossett, A. (1979). *Working with parents of handicapped children.* Columbus: Charles E. Merrill.

Keat, D. (1976). Training as multimodel treatment for peers. *Elementary School Guidance and Counseling, 11,* 7–13.

Kratoville, B. (1973). Telling it like it is. In D. Kronick (Ed.), *A word or two about learning disabilities.* San Rafael: Academic Therapy.

Kronick, D. (1973). *A word or two about learning disabilities.* San Rafael: Academic Therapy.

Krouse, J., Gerber, M., and Kauffman, J. (1981). Peer tutoring: Procedures, promises and unresolved issues. *Exceptional Education Quarterly, 1,* 107–115.

Meyer, D., Vadasy, P., and Fewell, R. (1985). *Living with a brother or sister with special needs.* Seattle: University of Washington Press.

Powell, T., and Ogle, P. (1985). *Brothers and sisters: A special part of exceptional families.* Baltimore: Paul Brooks.

Popkin, M. (1987). *Active parenting: Teaching cooperation, courage and responsibility.* San Francisco: Harper and Row.

Seligman, M. (1983). *The family with a handicapped child.* New York: Grune and Stratton.

Silverstein, S. (1964). *The giving tree.* New York: Harper and Row.

Spaulding, B., and Morgan, S. (1986). Spina bifida children and their parents: A population prone to family dysfunction. *Journal of Pediatric Psychology, 11,* 359–373.

Stein, T. (1983). Recreation and persons with physical disabilities. In T. Stein and H. Sessoms (Eds.), *Recreation and special populations.* Boston: Allyn and Bacon.

Turnbull, A., and Turnbull, R. (1986). *Families, professional and exceptionality — A special partnership.* Columbus: Charles E. Merrill.

Wehman, P. (1979). *Recreational programming for the developmentally disabled persons.* Baltimore: University Park Press.

West, J., and Ray, P. (1977). The helper therapy principle in relationships to self-concept in the commuter peer counselors. *Journal of College Student Personnel, 18,* 301–305.

Zetlin, A. (1986). Mentally retarded adults and their siblings. *American Journal of Mental Deficiency, 91,* 217–225.

Chapter 8

THE GOAL OF LEISURE WITHIN THE SCHOOLS

AUBREY H. FINE

All our dreams can come true
if we have the courage to pursue them.

WALT DISNEY

It has long been said that children are our most valuable resource. Today's youngsters will shape tomorrow's society. However, we are not presently harvesting our young people to meet the challenge of the future. The problem lies in the fact that while our patterns of work and leisure are changing, attitudes are not. Thus, archaic values become the legacy that is passed on to future generations. If filling gaps of free time is difficult under the present value system, it will necessarily become much harder in the future. It becomes imperative to teach children about the importance of leisure. Furthermore, we need to help children understand the relationship between work and play so they can gain an appreciation of both dimensions.

The nation's schools have been given the responsibility of educating children . . . more specifically, to educate them for work. Indeed, children have been indoctrined to believe that success in school is necessarily tied to success at work. These same children will someday face the reality of fewer jobs and shorter working hours, and they will not be prepared for such a situation. Since the school system has been charged with educating our children, it appears that they need to recognize that there is more to preparation than just academic learning! Brightbill and Mobley (1977) stress that the ultimate test of our education system will pertain to its effectiveness in assisting students so they will have a well-balanced emotional and intellectual life that includes leisure participation.

Education within our schools must place far more emphasis on all aspects of preparation towards life rather than just education for work. Furthermore, education should prepare all of us for complete living

255

(Brightbill and Mobley, 1977). The task of teachers should not be to cram knowledge into young minds but, rather, to cultivate potential and the thirst for the pursuit of knowledge.

There are many aspects of education, ranging from liberal, historical, scientific, physical, religious to vocational. All aspects of the education process are helpful in developing the complete person. Each element of learning is critical in building the well-rounded person. However, to this date, there is little evidence to suggest we are efficiently prepared (through education) to apply leisure in socially viable ways (Brightbill and Mobley, 1977).

When focusing specifically on exceptional children, there are several variables that must be incorporated. We believe that it is imperative to accept the position that leisure skill training should be incorporated within the special educational services. Bender, Brannan and Verhoven (1984) concur with the point of view that there is increased acceptance by educators that relevant education must extend beyond the contrived environment of the classroom. Many disabled persons are faced, when compared with others, with a disproportionately large amount of leisure time.

If children do not acquire the skills necessary to utilize leisure time, then the problem will be compounded as they become teenagers and then adults. One neglected area in the life of a teenager with a disability is recreation and socialization (Ayrault, 1974). My co-author (Nya) had the opportunity to work with two children with Down's syndrome at an early age. She had the unique privilege of watching these children grow up. As young children, there were many adults and older children who gave them a lot of attention. Many people played with them because they thought they were cute. However, as they aged, their child-like behaviors were not appreciated by many. As some would say, the sad part about the kitten is that one day it becomes a cat. Unfortunately, although the interactions began to cease, this did not eliminate the need for interaction and social recreational experiences.

This chapter is designed to orient the reader to the value of leisure instruction within the schools and how it can be incorporated. Barriers, both psychological and physical, will also be incorporated to give a global presentation of what may influence a child's leisure involvement. Furthermore, attention will be given discussing the variables of leisure guidance (counseling and education) and how we must help the field of education recognize the importance of leisure time.

THE GOAL OF LEISURE INSTRUCTION IN EDUCATION

The goal of leisure instruction, based on Gerson's leisure-educated adult, for exceptional children is to expose the student to a whole reservoir of different activities that are adaptable and pertinent to different situations and environments. The students should be encouraged to include some activity daily, to have at their disposal activities that can be conducted either alone or with others, and activities that involve active participation as well as being a spectator.

Each person in partnership with the student (parents, teachers, therapists) should respect the rights of a student to reject a particular activity and to respect the rights of others to indulge in activities they may not enjoy.

Through this process, the student should learn activities that will continue throughout a lifetime. When proper leisure guidance occurs, the inherent feelings of identity and self-worth carry over to the educational process and facilitate learning. Scholars stress that play and leisure involvement are an important part of the maturation process. In fact, some believe that the play act is a function of the ego, an attempt to bring into synchronization the bodily and social processes.

Leisure Instruction for the Severely Disabled

We recognize that there are curriculum differences between objectives formulated for the severely handicapped in comparison to students who happen to be more mildly disabled. Nevertheless, the importance of recreational skill acquisition is important for all.

In programs for the severely handicapped, less emphasis is typically placed on traditional academic skills and more attention is given to activities of daily living and functional development. Falvey (1986) has suggested that traditional curricula for students with severe handicaps have often included activities within the leisure domain. Recreation incorporates a set of activities that most non-disabled people engage in. Consequently, providing children who happen to be disabled with the opportunities to develop a repertoire of skills is a normalizing experience.

However, it is equally as critical to recognize that individuals who are higher functioning would also benefit from training in areas that will assist in their adaptive living. Independent living (or the least restrictive alternative) and quality of life should be a prime concern in the total education of all children (Fine, Welch-Burke, Fondario, 1985). Developing self-satisfying recreational pursuits assists all children in avoiding dead time. In other words, recreation involvement can fill in free time and help an individual feel productive (Falvey, 1986).

Furthermore, it is important to recognize that all people have an enormous amount of time outside their obligations (work, school, etc.). Professionals must accept the responsibility of providing guidance so children can develop inventories of skills that will be utilized in their avocational pursuits. This appears to be of utmost concern. Too many exceptional children and adults do not utilize their free time effectively (Fine, 1982). Fine has noted that many children appear to lack the awareness, skills, and the internal drive to secure their desires. Many become passive recipients to whatever they are subjected. Unfortunately, for some, their homes become their asylums or jails, and their guardians their jailers. A couple of examples can illustrate this point of view.

I have worked with many parents who have felt trapped and frustrated. These parents were discouraged because they could not understand why their child did not appear willing to try and get involved in outside play pursuits. Although some of their children have developed partial skills and desired friendships, they appeared to lack the confidence and or the drive to self-initiate the activity. This same dilemma appears to be evident in many sheltered activities for young adults who happen to be mentally retarded. Parents are overheard saying how dejected they were to observe their child sitting home idly, when activities were not planned for them. What has developed for many of these individuals is they tend to only get involved in activities when others structure the outcome. Although their involvement was enjoyable, we have not taught our children to make the necessary choices to self-select their leisure interests. As can be seen, the professional community should not only be investing energies in merely teaching or providing recreational programs but how and where individuals can utilize them. Within our schools, educators must spend time sensitizing individuals to the ultimate amount of resources that can be utilized.

RECREATION THERAPY WITHIN THE SCHOOLS

As previously stated, schools should have a great impact on encouraging recreational skill acquisition. Throughout the book, we have strongly advocated the development of leisure skills and the therapeutic application of recreational activities. The same premise holds true within the schools. Activities can be applied for their therapeutic benefits. Recreation can be considered as an intriguing, ubiquitous, and a developmentally significant phenomenon. Gottfried (1986) underlines this concept by indicating that play contributes to and reflects many aspects of psychological development. It should not be surprising that play should be taken advantage of for its inherent practical implications. It is an accepted fact that curricula in early childhood education has a strong emphasis on learning through play. This rationale needs to be considered within the elementary and secondary educational pursuits of children, including those persons who happen to be disabled.

Collaboration must occur between the community recreational therapist and the educational system. Previously, not enough co-active adventures have been initiated. It is imperative that those in leadership roles within special education are provided with the insight on how and why recreation should be incorporated within the schools. This should then be followed with an analysis on how this alternative of instruction will be funded, instructed, and incorporated. Although we would strongly advocate that recreational therapists be hired by the school districts to perform these duties, we believe that this will not occur in the immediate future. Consequently, energies need to be focused on helping educators develop the necessary skills to incorporate the application of recreation within the classrooms, or at least to hire recreation personnel as consultants. Realistically, community-based therapeutic recreators could have a significant role in this process. They could cooperate with schools to assist in educating for leisure (as well as how to apply recreational therapy principles in the classroom). Creative cost-sharing procedures could be developed at the local levels to assist in the funding of these programs.

RECREATION PROGRAMS FOR THE SEVERELY HANDICAPPED

As indicated earlier, for children who are severely handicapped, recreational provisions should be incorporated for critical skill development. These activities, whenever possible, should be incorporated with the mainstream population. We have met many parents who are very frustrated with their child's segregated education program. Of primary concern is the lack of friendships the children have developed with neighborhood peers. This lack of peer interaction causes many of the children to become social outcasts. Recreational opportunities can be viewed as an avenue to promote friendships between children. If we were capable of providing leisure education within the schools, we would be helping children cope with the realities of excess time. Too many of our children today are dependent on external resources for their entertainment. In a recent report, Chance and Fischman (1987) surveyed children's involvement in the noted top ten activities listed for specific developmental age groups. On the whole, watching television was listed as the recreational activity in which the most time was spent (even more than informal play). Unfortunately, we have created television addicts. Qualitatively, it is only appropriate to suggest other recreational alternatives be taught to children so they do not get hooked on T.V. as their major source of avocation.

Guidelines for Instruction

When incorporating recreational programs for children who are disabled, many elements come into play. As discussed consistently within the text, one must assure the activities selected are age appropriate. As such, assurances must be taken that not only are the activities appropriate, but that all the materials utilized within the play environments are also conducive for the specific developmental age (i.e. one would not want to see young adults in a preschool environment). The programs selected should be wide based and provide the skills necessary for a child to engage in activities either by him/herself, in small group settings, as well as with groups of others.

Activities should also be selected that are both active and passive. Too often (as was indicated earlier), children are not exposed to the diverse possibilities. Consequently, if children know only how to recreate in the presence of others, they are not constructively prepared to deal with time on their own. This becomes the dilemma that many children face. They cope well when they are pampered by others. However, when left on their own, they are defenseless. Instruction, therefore, should not necessarily take only a developmental perspective but also incorporate selected activities that are accessible, realistic and potentially viable. Falvey (1986) suggests singling out skills that are environmentally sound (can be conducted in a number of places) and, hopefully, activities that the child and his/her family enjoy. Falvey (1986) states, "Considering activities preferred and valued by the student's family increases the likelihood that the activity will be available to her during nonschool hours" (p. 105).

BARRIERS TO RECREATIONAL INVOLVEMENT

Psychological Barriers

While in London, England, I had the most extraordinary experience. I had a chance to see a play about a legendary train race in which the fastest trains from around the globe competed in this most prestigious event. There is Electra (the most technically advanced), Diesel (strong and powerful) and even Rusty the Steam Engine. When the rest of the competitors heard of Rusty's registration, they all were amused. They laughed and encouraged Rusty to reconsider. Rusty, however, informed them of his full intention to participate. He believed he was going to be successful because the Starlight Express was going to help him.

Within this imaginary world of trains, the Starlight Express is like a fairy train-mother. If you call to her loud enough, she may grant you your wishes. Rusty, over the entire year, had called upon Starlight to give him strength to compete. Unfortunately, he did not have confidence in his own abilities and was basing his probability for success on the help of others.

Rusty entered the first heat against many competitors, hoping that Starlight Express would grant him his wishes. Inauspiciously, several of the other competitors responded very angrily to his participation and indicated their displeasure with him. Others found his enrollment amusing and just laughed. They told him how outdated he was and how he did not have a chance against the more advanced trains. However, he tried to not let their kidding bother him. He lined up with the rest of the pack and the race began.

Nevertheless, Rusty could not live up to his pre-race enthusiasm. He could not compete with the internal strength that he needed to win. As a consequence, Rusty had a miserable experience. Immediately after he crossed the finish line, he was greeted by his disenchanted Dad. Rusty explained to his father that he was outdated and, without Starlight's assistance, he could not win. His Dad seemed a little puzzled by this remark and told his son he would show him that steam was still good.

The next morning, his Dad entered the final preliminary race. To the surprise of everybody, he was a good competitor and won. However, since he did not **train** for the event, he physically was not prepared for the abuse his body had accepted. As a result, he did not feel that he could get ready for the final, which would be held on the next day. He asked his son to take his place. Rusty reluctantly accepted, but doubted his ability to succeed. This angered his Dad, who immediately snapped and told his son that the Starlight Express was really a figment of his imagination, a folklore. He went on to explain to his son that it was critical that he thought well enough about himself to succeed. He also attempted to instill within Rusty the courage he needed to be a competitor, an individual who was driven. Rusty respectfully listened to his father, and although he respected his input, he still had self-doubt about his skills.

That evening, in a dream, he heard the voice of the Starlight Express. She told him many things, but one statement seemed to have the greatest impact. I quote:

> . . . Only you have the power within you. Just believe in yourself, the sea will part before you. Stop the rain, turn the tide. If only you use the power within you, you needn't beg the world to turn around and help you. If you draw on what you have within you somewhere deep inside. . . . You are the starlight.

That next morning Rusty competed and won; a perfect ending for a fairy tale.

The synopsis you have just read is from the play, entitled **Starlight Express,** produced by Andrew Lloyd Weber. The play is now being presented in both London and Broadway. As I became enthralled with the production, I began to see beyond all of the interesting props. In fact, all I saw were children, similar to those who I had served who perceived themselves as being inadequate. These were the outcasts of our society, who unfortunately did not value themselves for their assets. As a consequence of their disabilities, society has made some of them feel different and incompetent. This is one of the most devastating tragedies that can influence a person. A famous quote by Goethe captures the significance of this outcome: "The greatest evil that can befall man is that he should come to think evil of himself."

Learned Helplessness

One of the most intriguing and important concepts developed in the field of social psychology is the syndrome of learned helplessness. This syndrome was classified by Seligman (1975) and his associates. Helplessness results when a person expects that the important events in his/her life are independent or his/her own responding. In essence, when the things that matter to a person are felt to be (or truly are) beyond that person's control, then she/he becomes a victim of learned helplessness.

It is easy to recognize how children with disabilities develop this sense of incompetence, which afterwards causes them to live more sheltered lives and become passive recipients of whatever their environment provides. Many scholars have suggested that individuals who have low estimates of their own ability to influence the outcomes of their perform-ance are likely to perform incompetently.

Such feelings may or precipitate further problems, especially in response to daily failure experiences. Table I illustrates some of the potential hardships that children may encounter when they experience personal failure. What learned helplessness may indirectly cause is an increased probability of avoiding situations where there is a high possibility of failure. Children eventually attribute their failures to what they perceive as their own inadequacies.

TABLE I
IMPLICATIONS OF LEARNED HELPLESSNESS AND PERCEIVED COMPETENCE

Able to cope	Unable to cope
Adapt ↓	Adapt ↓
Adjust ↓	Adjust ↓
Produces Maturity ↓	Produces persistent anger ↓
Increased probability of achievement behavior ↓	Development of severe frustration ↓
Augmented pride and enhancement of self-esteem ↓	Higher probability of failure
Higher probability of success	

Acknowledgment is given to Doctor C. Papazian for allowing the author to adapt his unpublished model to include in this manuscript.

The first studies by Seligman were conducted with dogs. The animals were given unavoidable shock. The end result was that the animals became passive recipients of the aversive stimulation. They did not even try to avoid the shock, because they did not feel they had the power. In essence, the animals learned they had no control! This pilot research has generated significant insight into understanding individuals who feel they are inadequate. Individuals with any degree of learned helplessness lower their expectations for future success and attempt avoidance. This avoidance is initiated to offset future encounters with failure. In essence, it is clear that failure at a task eventually induces deficits in subsequent encounters. The sense of helplessness develops from an awareness of an inability to succeed in spite of trying and expecting to succeed.

It's probable that individuals take the most pride in those accomplishments that they attribute to be within their own abilities and efforts. Gottfried (1986) suggests that children play to experience control over their environment. Bandura (1978) found that most children were successful when they measured their behavior against personal standards of what constitutes a worthy performance. One of the key issues in developing a sense of helplessness pertains to the degree of locus of control.

Locus of Control

The theory of locus of control was developed by social learning theorists. Locus of control can be understood as a child's perception of who or what is responsible for one's success or failure in a particular area. Internal versus external locus of control pertains to the degree to which an individual feels that his/her outcomes are contingent upon his/her actions. Children who are oriented towards internal locus of control are those who perceive themselves as primarily responsible for their successes and failures. These are children who feel they are in control of their reinforcements. The opposite is true for children who feel their outcomes to be independent of their responses. This is classified as external locus of control. According to Weiner (1985), locus of control refers to a belief that a response will or will not influence the acquisition of a reinforcement. Locus of control, in essence, is a problem-solving expectancy that addresses whether behaviors are perceived as instrumental in obtaining the desired behavioral goal. Deci and Ryan (1985) state that locus of control refers to whether outcomes are believed to be contingent on one's behavior. They contrast this theory with locus of causality by suggesting that the locus of causality is concerned with why a person behaves as she or he does.

Weiner (1972) applies different terminology to explain causality. Attribution theorists investigate persons' perceptions of causes. Usually, the allocation of responsibility influences subsequent behaviors. In his recent writings, Weiner (1985) suggests that causes are identified on the basis of several factors, including such variables as specific informational cues (i.e. history of past successes or failures, patterns of performance), causal preferences, reinforcement history, and feedback from others. For example, a person who attributes playing a game to his/her performing inadequately will be a person who will probably not be motivated to play in future similar activities. Many who have investigated this process recognize the positive correlation between learning and performance. Dixon (1979) prepared an excellent document synthesizing the implications of this theory and participation in recreational therapy. The major impetus of the paper suggested that a better understanding of attribution theory (and the other theories noted within this section) would assist professionals in developing more efficient intervention techniques.

The literature suggests a positive correlation between internal locus of control and achievement in most areas. Those who believe that they are in control of their outcomes have a greater chance of being successful. Specifically in regards to the disabled population, there have been many researchers who have suggested that persons with disabilities have a higher expectancy of failure than those who are able-bodied. Studies by MacMillian (1969) and MacMillian and Knopf (1971) have tested situations where children were prevented from completing several tasks. Ironically, most of these children blamed themselves for not completing the tasks. Results of many studies suggest that many children who are disabled are external only in relation to success ("It was a fluke," or "They let me do well because they felt sorry for me"). Unfortunately, these same children consistently accept responsibility for failure but not for success. Many are likely to ascribe their success to whims of luck (Gibson, 1980). Weisz (1982) points out that in regards to mental retardation, the child's life may be something of a macrocosm of helplessness, in that it involves repeated exposure to failure. In many cases, persons with disabilities appear unlikely to accuse controllable factors for insufficient effort. Instead, they appear to see their failure as resulting from the stable uncontrollable factor of low ability. Finally, it is important to note how labels, such as learning disabilities, physical disabilities, mental retardation, and special education, affect the functioning of an individual. There is some evidence that such labels may encourage many to expect failure or below-standard achievement. The label may also lower expectations for the child's potential.

Locus of Causality Orientation

Deci (1980) was the first to introduce the concept of causality orientation. He applied the terminology developed in the word of Heider (1958) and DejCharms (1968) and developed three orientations. This work was eventually updated by Deci and Ryan (1985) to incorporate three areas of causality: autonomy, control and impersonal orientation.

Central to the autonomy orientation is the degree of choice that individual has made. Deci and Ryan (1985) state the autonomy orientation involves the tendency to select or interpret initiating and regulatory events as informational and to be associated with intrinsically motivated behaviors and extrinsically motivated behaviors. On the other hand, the control orientation focuses its attention on what controls. One's functioning is primarily based on controls in the environment or internal characteristics. The central element of this orientation is the struggle of being the controller or controlled. Behaviorally, most children and adults seek controlling situations. Furthermore, most individuals seek to conceptualize and understand predisposing controlling factors.

Finally, the impersonal orientation is based on areas where an individual feels incompetent to deal with the challenges of life. To its worst degree, a person may experience a severe degree of learned helplessness.

Being a Risk Taker

An individual's feelings of incompetence and sufficient effort to improve may impede the child's acquisition of developing appropriate functional skills. It appears that many children who feel incompetent lack being risk takers. This seems to occur because society has indirectly taught them that they are inadequate and, for that matter, helpless.

It is apparent that the most successful and independent people are those who are willing to take chances and be risk takers. They are usually people who experience positive responses to their curiosity and are gamblers because the outcomes seem to be worthwhile.

Canfield (1987) suggests that the only way to grow is to take risks and get involved. People have to value themselves as well as see themselves as worthwhile. In essence, a major element to securing and developing a positive self-esteem is the willingness of the individual to take chances. One way of viewing success in risk-taking people is to recognize that most "risk takers make a habit out of doing uncomfortable things losers will not do" (J. Canfield, personal communication, May 23, 1987).

People who are risk takers gamble by trying to produce a unique outcome to their behaviors. In most cases, people complain about the outcomes in their life. However, we need to realize that we are capable of changes, if we so desire.

Canfield (1986) suggests that we spend too much time on what we have rather than what we do or contribute. He identifies three elements:

1. BE (Context)
2. DO (Process)
3. HAVE (Content)

He suggests that risk takers spend less time addressing the content of their behaviors but invest energies on their context (who you are rather than what you have).

Risk taking represents the feasibility of experiencing failure as well as adverse feelings. However, if one is not willing to embark on new adventures, he/she may never optimally grow. This appears to be a major obstacle facing many children we serve. They are not willing to take chances, because their fear of failure hinders their efforts. In fact, it reduces their drive to seek knowledge. I feel very strongly that all children, disabled and non-disabled, thirst for knowledge, except some may need some assistance to get to the fountain. What we need to do is to help children want to reach out and risk growing up. For example, a young man was being instructed on how to serve in tennis. At one point during the lesson, the instructor told his student to move his racquet back higher when he was to serve. The student immediately snapped and told his teacher he thought he had the racquet high enough. His teacher responded by asking, "How high is high enough?" This is a question we could formulate for most life experiences. We as individuals need to aspire to be the best we can while always appreciating the fact of who we are at a specific time.

There are many variables that influence a person on taking a chance to learn and experience. Figure 1, which was inspired with a conversation with Jack Canfield, graphically represents the basic influence of wanting to take chances (Fine, 1987).

For example, let us use a liking scenario. It appears only logical that an experienced hiker would regulate his/her water intake. Part of the decision would be based upon availability. Consequently, a hiker who

FIGURE 1

The Difficulty
of being a
Risk Taker

The
Empty   vs.   The
Glass   Full
                         Glass

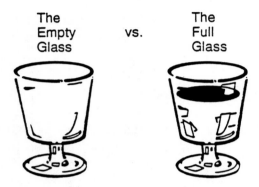

had a larger reservoir of water would drink more liberally on the excursion. The figure basically describes this position. Risk takers tend to be people who have a larger reservoir of successful experiences. They are individuals who are willing to take chances, because they can afford failure (i.e. more water to drink). Those who repeatedly experience failure appear to become passive and conservative in taking chances (their glasses are empty in regards to obtaining success).

The following poem portrays the dilemma that we have tried to formulate in this section. The dilemma represents an overshadowing problem that many children with disabilities face: the willingness to take risks.

RISKS

To laugh is — to risk appearing the fool.
To weep is — to risk appearing sentimental.
To reach out for another is — to risk involvement.
To expose feelings is — to risk exposing your true self.
To place your ideas, your dreams before the crowd is — to risk their loss.
To love is — to risk not being loved in return.
To live is — to risk dying.
To hope is — to risk despair.
To try is — to risk failure.
But risks must be taken, because the greatest hazard in life is to risk

nothing. The person who risks nothing, does nothing, has nothing, and is nothing. He may avoid suffering and sorrow, but he simply cannot learn, feel, change, grow, love — live. Chained by his certitudes, he is a slave, he had forfeited freedom. Only a person who risks is free. (Author unknown)

Implications

In regards to leisure education, we need to help children recognize their competencies so they will be willing to take a chance. Merely exposing children to activities and encouraging their involvement will not be enough to stimulate self-initiation. Children must feel a sense of competency if they are willing to risk failure. Parents and teachers must help children develop a more realistic acceptance of abilities and develop a more positive internal locus of control. This can initially be accomplished by selecting activities that will allow for success. When programming, one should take advantage of children's abilities and develop activities that highlight their strengths rather than their limitations. This will eventually give these children the internal confidence to take risks while engaging in activities which they are less adequate at. We should also teach and motivate children to have greater control over self-generated effort, so they can begin to believe that their own effort influences their ability to perform in other contexts.

Whenever possible and the conditions are appropriate, we should attempt to encourage intrinsic motivation as the primary driving force. Research reported by Deci and Ryan (1985) suggests that when the conditions are right, student's learning, particularly conceptual learning and creative thinking, are more dramatically increased when facilitated by intrinsic motivation rather than being fostered by extrinsically rewarded learning. Holt (1964), an outspoken critic of education and how we fail children, condemns the usage of extrinsic rewards to encourage growth. He states: "We destroy the love of learning in children by encouraging and compelling them to work for petty and contemptible rewards; gold stars, or papers marked 100 on the walls . . ." (p. 168). These perceptions are also espoused by other noted educators such as Montessori (1967) and Neil (1960). Montessori suggested that rewards are not necessary and are at times even harmful. The writer would concur with her position but points out that with some children, one may have to initially incorporate the application of reinforcers. As discussed in Appendix II on behavior management, it is critical to select the appropriate strategies that are least restrictive in nature. The ultimate goal for any child is to have them **self-actualize**, a term suggesting internal controls. However, we realize that this will never be possible with all children.

We also should be focusing some of our energies to help children overcome their dysfunctional reaction to failure. We should help children interpret failure as feedback, an indication that more information is needed. We also must assist individuals on focusing attention on effort rather than blaming it on personal ability.

Seligman (1975) suggests that behavioral immunization ought to be started in childhood, so children can develop feelings of personal control. The child can learn to establish realistic personal goals and expectations. This should not be misunderstood as placing ceilings on attributions. Rather, the effort is made to help children realistically understand their strengths and limitations. Not all people will be able to climb to the tops of mountains, but attempts are just as important. Bob Weiland, a disabled athlete, has recently been the subject of an enormous amount of press for completing the New York and Los Angeles Marathons by walking the entire race on his hands. At a recent lecture at the California State Polytechnic University, he stated, "Success is never based on where you start, but where you finish." We must help individuals aspire but be careful and not support the cultivation of unrealistic goals. Although the example of Rusty is beautiful, not all people will win the race. It is, however, equally important to appreciate the endeavors. We have to help children recognize their efforts and improvements. Too often we focus on the final accomplishment. By doing so, we ignore all of the ingredients and efforts put into the process. We have to give children reasonable control over their lives and help them experience success. Finally, many children do not know how to react to their failure. Consequently, we should take the time and model to individuals how to react realistically to failure. By taking advantage of modeling, we will begin to assist children to use feedback as information. We should teach children to take advantage and observe those who accept their failures logically. These individuals may become helpful in demonstrating that inadequacies are not always generated because of personal incompetency.

It is imperative to understand that if needed energies are not placed on changing attributions, involvement in independent leisure pursuits will probably not occur. We have to help children see their adequacies, so they will be willing to take chances. Providing recreational experiences within any environment must focus on this issue. Without changing attributions, I definitely do not feel that significant long-lasting effects will be generated. Dixon (1979) and Niles, Ellis, and Witt (1981) suggest some other alternatives that can be utilized in recreation programming to decrease perceived incompetence. The author encourages the readers to review these documents to learn about some other prominent points of view. Furthermore, Weiner (1986) devotes part of a chapter dealing with a review of various procedures that can be utilized to influence dysfunctional attributions. In the document, several primary research studies are identified with the solutions obtained. The reader should find this chapter rich with theoretical information which is combined with useful practical suggestions.

Other Related Environmental Barriers to Leisure Acquisition

There are a variety of other obstacles that naturally influence leisure involvement. Many of the elements pertain to ecological constraints such as accessibility to recreational environments (transportation, proximity of activities, environmental accessibility), financial support, and leisure awareness.

Environmental Barriers

Is there really a conceivable barrier-free environment? What constitutes an accessible environment for one population could possibly make the surroundings inaccessible for another. For example, the modifications made to areas allowing people in wheelchairs free mobility may be oppositional to the needs of persons who utilize walkers or who are visually impaired. Most often, persons with disabilities are forced to take it upon themselves to find resources that allow them full access. However, as we can all appreciate, many venues have not been developed with the disabled community in mind. In most cases, access to the disabled person is given as an afterthought. Psychologically, inaccessible environments send the disabled community an unconscious message to stay out.

Adults with disabilities (especially physical disorders) usually have to develop what is called **environmental cognition**. Since many have experienced segregation due to inaccessibility, they have learned to develop internal maps to help them think through the gaps. Also, unlike most citizens, many persons with disabilities develop lists of resources of areas within their neighborhood that allow them free access. However, the outcome can represent a significant hardship when a surrounding area does not have enough resources providing optimal leisure involvement.

Although buildings are more accessible today to wheelchair users, playgrounds are just beginning to be modified. Parks are designed primarily with only able-bodied children in mind. The equipment is usually surrounded with landscape, which prohibits mobility in a wheelchair. Stairs are usually the only means to gain access to the top of the slide. Simple modifications can be incorporated to alleviate these existing problems.

Natural barriers also place significant hardships on the leisure pursuits of persons with disabilities. Forest trails, beaches, and campsites are often too narrow or have rough terrain. As can be easily seen, although progress is being made, change is slow. Consequently, many children with disabilities will still be impeded by the environment for many years to come. In fact, in the mid-1970s, the Architectural and Transportation Barriers Compliance Board determined that one of the major problems facing the disabled community in regards to recreation was the inaccessability of facilities and transportation (Vellman, 1979). Furthermore, Vellman (1979) reports that one of the reasons we are not seeing the outcomes of progress reached as early as we would like is the failure on behalf of politicians to commit themselves fully to follow through and legislate the change.

Transportation and Financial Restrictions

Transportation to the various sites as well as financial restrictions can also cause barriers to leisure involvement, especially in families with limited funds. Due to some of the special needs a person with a disability may have, families may encounter a greater expense in bringing up their disabled child. Recreation provisions usually are not considered as a priority. As a consequence, if there are not many moderately priced activities (or the child or parents are not aware of these), children may not be enrolled in or taken to a wide range of experiences. Furthermore, some of the accessible or perhaps specialized activities may be a greater distance to the child's home. Therefore, transportation becomes a factor.

Family and Peer Support

All children need to have the opportunity to interact positively with others. Some children with disabilities lead restrictive lives. A major void appears to be in the area of social contemporaries. Furthermore, if a child is in a special school, away from his/her neighborhood, he/she may lack the opportunities to develop local friendships. This lack of exposure may be devastating. Efforts must be initiated to ensure that provisions are established that the child receives sufficient social stimulation. As was discussed earlier in the chapter, the parents' attitude about the child, and their willingness to strive forward, are very important ingredients to encourage independent leisure involvement. Families who are supportive are usually more instrumental in rearing a more independent child.

THE CONTROVERSY OF LEISURE INSTRUCTION

Several terms are often confused by school personnel, parents, and others that delay the integration of leisure guidance within the school. This confusion is especially apparent in dealing with the child with disabilities.

The term **leisure-facilitated instruction** represents a systematic teaching process that will culminate in the students becoming aware of the role of leisure in their life and how leisure contributes to their ability to adapt to their environment. A knowledge of leisure allows a daily, liberal inclusion of leisure into the life-style of the leisure-educated person.

Within the field of therapeutic recreation, there exists a problem in defining the scope of leisure education and leisure counseling. In fact, this controversy appears to have stagnated the growth of this area and has caused some undue stress.

McDowell (1976) reviewed the existing literature and identified three areas that he assumed were under the rubric entitled **leisure counseling**. The first category he classified as **leisure counseling as a leisure resource guidance service**. It is within this category that one assists an individual in matching proposed interests with possible alternatives. McDowell (1976) points out that within this component, no efforts are made to treat the elements that cause unproductive usage of free time. For example, this form of leisure guidance would be helpful if an individual moved to a new geographic area. Potentially, under this domain, a person would be assisted in identifying prospective interests without any attention given to possible underlying barriers.

Leisure counseling as a therapeutic remedial service pertains to an individual's lack of skills relating to leisure involvement. This lack of skills could be due to absence of knowledge or limitations in performing desired leisure activities. Finally, **leisure counseling as a life-style developmental-educational service** focuses on the barriers individually developed that discourage leisure involvement. The problems faced by a workaholic would be best treated by this orientation.

The Leisure Education Component

On the other hand, Mundy and Odum (1979) defined leisure education as a total developmental process through which individuals create an understanding of self, leisure and the relationship of leisure to their own life-styles and the fabric of society. Friedrich Froebel understood that in small children, play was life itself. Joseph Lee, like Maria Montesorri, believed play to be a serious educational tool and a part of nature's law of growth. He pointed out that play is purposeful and rooted in a person's desire to produce results. Play at its best is the challenge to creative skills, ingenuity and enthusiastic application to a task and to accomplishment.

Mundy and Odum (1979) identified five integral components in an inclusive leisure education program. Therapeutically, emphasis on these areas depends on the population served and the individual needs. The five components are listed in Table II.

Applications of Leisure Education Components and Exceptional Children

Mundy and Odum's leisure education process has numerous universal benefits. Although I agree with the elements incorporated, I feel that when working with children who have many limitations and barriers to face, the process of changing their involvement is not a simple procedure of education. Too often, we tend to focus on superficial areas which influence the acquisition of leisure behaviors. As a consequence, our efforts ineffectively influence the prevailing problems.

Secondly, there are some individuals who have difficulty selecting areas of emphasis when developing programs. The two easiest areas to introduce in a curriculum are those that focus on leisure awareness and leisure skill development. I do suggest that these two components are initially focused upon in any leisure education program. Social skills should be an emphasis in any educational pursuit; therefore, aspects of this dimension should always be incorporated.

The areas of self-awareness and decision making appear to be the

TABLE II
LEISURE EDUCATION COMPONENTS

Leisure Awareness. Emphasis within this area is given to assisting the individual in taking information one has about leisure and relating the findings to his/her life situation. It is within this component where an individual is assisted in learning about the vast amount of opportunities available to him/her.

Self-Awareness. Within this component, emphasis is given on encouraging individual understanding, and relating how leisure participation fits a need in one's life.

Decision Making. Within this component, attention is given to developing appropriate problem-solving skills. These skills are promoted to assist in exploring and selecting potential leisure opportunities.

Social Interaction. Within this area, focus is given to the development of appropriate social skills. Well-chosen social behaviors are correlated positively with productive leisure experiences. Consequently, direct and indirect instruction of this area are incorporated within the gestalt of leisure education.

Leisure Skills. Within this final aspect of the continuum, attention is given to assist an individual in identifying and developing the skills necessary to engage in leisure activities. An analysis is conducted assuring compatibility with one's awareness of self and leisure.

hardest to develop within children, especially elementary school age. In addition, I strongly suggest waiting to focus on these areas until the child is over the age of nine or ten. Furthermore, when one is working with children who have cognitive impairments, these programmatic domains will be more difficult to focus upon. Even children with mild disabilities (i.e. learning disabilities) may have difficulty focusing specifically on this area. There may have to be other alternatives incorporated to assist children in developing the necessary prerequisite skills. For example, there are social problem-solving programs (i.e. Shure and Spivak, 1976) that attempt to assist children in developing social competence. There are also self-instructional training programs (i.e. Bash and Camp, 1985) that attempt to teach children appropriate strategies to mediate their behavior. Some of these approaches would be valuable additions in providing leisure guidance.

The Dilemma

Over the past two decades several have argued about the true nature of leisure consultation (Reynolds and O'Morrow, 1985). A great deal of time has been invested debating the process as well as the terminology applied (leisure counseling or leisure education). Tinsley (1984) suggests that recreators, as a whole, are ill equipped and prepared to deal with the total ramifications of poorly developed leisure behaviors. He cautions that many recreators appear to superficially address leisure problems and attempt to merely treat the apparent, overt leisure dysfunction. All of us can appreciate the complexity of developing leisure behaviors. There are many psychological, financial, environmental as well as health factors that come into play that influence our possible involvement in leisure time. Tinsley (1984) cautions that recreators (in general) might be inadequately prepared to deal with these overwhelming problems. He also strongly argues that one should not call him/herself a counselor if he/she has limited training in counseling. I concur with this point of view and strongly advocate performing within the guidelines of our training.

Furthermore, Edwards (1981), a strong critic of recreators, states:

> [R]ecreators are neither philosophically, socially, or professionally attuned to the requirements of counseling. They must use psychology in their work with others, of course. But they use it to spur others to action rather than self-examination. They are basically action people while counselors are basically contemplative people who emphasize self-awareness (p. 42).

Consequently, there has been a move by some in higher education to develop a specialty area within the field of parks and recreation. Within this area of special concentration, those who are interested can take the added training and academic courses to develop the skills to perform effectively and reliably. Furthermore, there are some professionals such as Hayes (1977) and Fine (1985) who strongly argue that recreators should not feel they are the only professionals competent in treating leisure-developed problems. Therefore, consultation must be done with other disciplines such as psychology, counseling, and education to develop course work within this area.

Fine (1986) has argued that professionally we have expelled too much energy on semantics. We need to become more clear on the scope of our teachings. What matters is that we are capable of articulating what we are competent in performing, and that we are well versed in various strategies. For this reason, I have classified both of these two interventions under the rubric of **leisure guidance**. At times, it may be necessary to utilize verbal facilitation strategies (counseling) to assist an individual in understanding barriers to leisure involvement. On the other hand, we also may want to incorporate some instruction (education) to enhance an understanding as well as the application of activity involvement. These can be initiated in small groups or individually. Furthermore, one can provide services prior to a problem's initiation (prevention) or when it has already been manifested. It should be evident, as indicated in these writings, that it would be preferable for leisure guidance to be initiated prior to the onset of any problems. The literature strongly points out that it is likely that some persons with disabilities will encounter leisure barriers. If these barriers are not removed, it is very probable that some of the individuals will experience significant problems. For this reason, the position for preventive maintenance is highly suggested.

Guidelines for Implementing Leisure Guidance Within the Schools

The inclusion of the leisure guidance within the schools should be carefully administered. The following represents a brief outline of the various elements that need to be focused upon to successfully develop a viable instruction plan.

The recreational therapist or leisure educator should be a member of the school guidance team and provide input through the aforementioned process. The leisure guidance facilitator will provide:

1. An identification of the handicap as it relates to leisure guidance. An evaluation must be conducted, articulating both the child's strengths and limitations. Additionally, a realistic account must be incorporated addressing the accessibility to leisure pursuits.
2. An overview of the student's current level of performance in basic areas that influence recreational participation. Furthermore, an analysis should be incorporated of realistic opportunities where leisure skills can be naturally enhanced within the academic environment.
3. The development of realistic student goals based on current level of performance. The genesis of goals must be defined, with appropriate attention given to a clear plan of action.
4. Instructional objectives should be prepared based on the broader goals. In addition, an evaluation plan must be expatiated so an identification of what is to occur will be established.
5. Attention must be given to the availability of community resources outside of the school setting. Collaboration must be initiated with the family and community recreators to assure realistic application.

Furthermore, an inventory of potential recreational sites and resources should be established to assure appropriate follow-up.

7. The role and function of the primary recreation programmer will have to be examined. Furthermore, a realistic overview of how other educators will apply leisure instruction within the class will also have to be reviewed. At times, the instruction by the leisure guidance specialist will be exclusive. Nevertheless, my initial reaction and perception is that leisure guidance and recreational programming should become an integral component of the educational process. For this reason, I do not feel it should be given special individual attention. If leisure is to be given equal consideration, then it should be just that: a critical domain in the educational training of our students.

SUMMARY

Within this chapter, an overview has been presented addressing some of the variables of incorporating leisure instruction in the education of our children. Perhaps, the change in the proposed new focus pertains to the awareness of educators that they are charged with the responsibility of educating the whole child. Too often, many confuse the purpose of education as being merely preparation for employment. While this may be partially true, the education process is initiated to prepare our young (disabled and able-bodied) for the realities of their life (both at the present time or in the future). This also definitely includes leisure time. We are seeing too many children becoming dependent on others (including television) to provide them with the appropriate sources to secure pleasure. It is unfortunate that many children with disabilities fail to achieve optimal leisure involvement. Some may blame some of the many variables discussed earlier in the chapter. I, too, would concur partially to this assumption. However, I also see the problem being generated by apathy and lack of willingness to accept responsibility. For too long, we have been misled that academy preparation does not incorporate the social domain. We are now becoming more conscious of the fact that this lack of attention can no longer be tolerated. As concerned parents, students and professionals serving children with disabilities, we must become advocates and help inform the educational community in regards to the importance of the leisure domain and the need for educational attention in this area. With appropriate consultation between the fields of recreational therapy and education, we may be able to diminish this present void in our children's education. Consequently, we can help enhance the likelihood of more productive leisure involvement for our youth with disabilities.

Endnote

The author is indebted to the input provided for this chapter by Doctor Gus Gerson, Professor, California State Polytechnic University. Specifically, Doctor Gerson was very helpful with editorial comments. He also prepared some of the information included within the section entitled leisure guidance in the schools.

REFERENCES

Ayrault, E.W. (1974). *Helping the handicapped teenager mature.* New York: Association Press.

Bandura, A. (1977). *Social learning theory.* Englewoods Cliffs, NJ: Prentice-Hall.

Bender, M., Brannan, S., and Verhoven, P. (1984) *Leisure education for the handicapped.* San Diego: College Hill.

Brightbill, C., and Mobley, T. (1977). *Educating for leisure-centered living.* New York: Wiley.

Camp, B., and Bash, M. (1985). *The think aloud.* Champaign: Research Press.

Canfield, J. (1986). *Self-esteem in the classroom.* Pacific Palisades: Self-Esteem Seminars.

Carlson, B., and Ginglend, D. (1968). *Recreation for retarded teenagers and young adults.* New York: Abingdon.

Chance, P., and Fischman, J. (1987). The magic of childhood. *Psychology Today, May,* 48–58.

Deci, E.L. (1980). *The psychology of self-determination.* Lexington, MA: D.C. Heath (Lexington Books).

Deci, L., and Ryan, R.M. (1985). *Intrinsic motivation and self-determination in human behavior.* New York: Plenum.

DejCharms, R. (1968). *Personal causation: The internal affective determinants of behavior.* New York: Academic Press.

Dixon, J. (1979). The implications of attribution theory for therapeutic recreation service. *Therapeutic Recreation Journal, 8,* 3–11.

Edwards, P.B. (1981). Leisure counseling: Recreators, keep out. *Parks and Recreation Magazine, 16*(1), 106.

Falvey, M. (1986). *Community based curriculum, instructional strategies for students with severe handicaps.* Baltimore: Brooks.

Fine, A. (1982). Therapeutic recreation: An aspect of rehabilitation for exceptional children. *The lively arts,* 4.

Fine, A. (1985, April). *Leisure counseling: Implications for individuals with learning disabilities.* Paper presented at the 63rd annual convention of the council for Exceptional Children, Anaheim, California.

Fine, A., Welch-Burke, C., and Fondario, L.J. (1985). A developmental model for the integration of leisure programming in the education in individuals with mental retardation. *Mental Retardation, 23*(6), 289–296.

Fine, A. (1986, March). *Children and leisure: Leisure guidancecounseling in the schools.* Paper presented at the 38th Annual California and Pacific Southwest Recreation and Parks Conference, Fresno, California.

Gibson, B.J. (1980). *An attributional analysis of performance outcomes and the alleviation of learned helplessness on motor performance tasks: A comparative study of educable mentally retarded and nonretarded boys.* Unpublished doctoral dissertation, University of Alberta, Calgary.

Gottfried, A (1986). *Introduction.* In A. Gottfried and C. Brown (Eds.), *Play interactions: The contribution of play materials and parental involvement to children's development.* Cambridge: Lexington.

Hayes, G.A. (1977). Professional preparation and leisure counseling. *Leisure Today, April,* 14.

Heider, F. (1958). *The psychology of interpersonal relations.* New York: Wiley.

Holt, J. (1964). *How children fail.* New York: Doll.

Howard, W., Dardig, J., and Rossett, A. (1979). *Working with the parents of handicapped children.* Columbus: Charles E. Merrill.

MacMillian, D.L. (1969). Motivational differences: Cultural-familial retardates versus normal subjects on expectancy for failure. *American Journal of Mental Deficiency, 76,* 185–189.

MacMillian, D.L., and Knopf, E.D. (1971). Effect of instructional set on perceptions of event outcomes by EMR and nonretarded children. *American Journal of Mental Deficiency, 76,* 185–189.

McDowell, C.F. (1976). *Leisure counseling: Selected lifestyle processes.* Eugene, Oregon: University of Oregon, Center of Leisure Studies.

Montessori, M. (1967). *Spontaneous activity in education.* New York: Schocken.

Musselwhite, C.R. (1986). *Adaptive play for special needs for children: Strategies to enhance communication and learning.* San Diego: College Hill.

Neill, A.S. (1960). *Summerhill: A radical approach to child rearing.* New York: Hart.

Niles, S., Ellis, G., and Witt, P. (1982). Attribution scales: Control, competence, intrinsic motivation. In G. Ellis and P. Witt (Eds.), *The leisure diagnostic battery: Background conceptualization and structure.* Texas: North Texas State University.

Reynolds, R., and O'Morrow, G.S. (1985). *Problems, issues and concepts in therapeutic recreation.* Englewood Cliffs, NJ: Prentice-Hall.

Spivack, G., Platt, J.J., and Shure, M. (1976). *The problem-solving approach to adjustment.* San Francisco: Jossey-Bass.

Vellman, R. (1979). Serving physically disabled people. New York: R.R. Bowker.

Wehman, P. (1977). *Helping the mentally retarded acquire play skills.* Springfield, IL: Charles C Thomas.

Wehman, P. (1979). *Recreation programming for developmentally disabled persons.* Baltimore: University Park Press.

Weiner, B. (1972). Attribution theory achievement motivation and the educational process. *Review of Educational Research, 42,* 203–215.

Weiner, B. (1985). *Human motivation.* New York: Springer.

Weiner, B. (1986). *The attributional theory of motivation and emotion.* New York: Springer.

Weisz, J.R. (1982). Learned helplessness and the retarded child. In E. Zigler and D. Balla (Eds.), *Mental retardation: The developmental difference controversy* (pp. 27–39). Newark, NJ: Lawrence Erlbaum.

Chapter 9

FUTURE TRENDS AND CONCLUDING REMARKS

AUBREY H. FINE

Children are the world's most valuable resource and its
best hope for the future.

JOHN F. KENNEDY

One of my favorite and recently acquired hobbies is magic. I became interested solely for professional purposes. As a mental health provider, magic provided me an avenue for enhancing rapport with children. Curiosity is aroused and, in most cases, inhibition is lowered and a comfortable environment is created. Magic is a tremendously creative pursuit (Tarr, 1976). Magicians are always conjuring new ways to do things. They dream up their tricks and write their own script to accompany the act and thus ensure each illusion's success.

Why this introduction to the chapter? My response is simple. If I were a sorcerer, I would be able to tell what the future would be like. My simple illusions, while they have an entertainment value, cannot shed any light on years to come. However, I believe that we can all make educated assumptions of what may occur. We will never know how accurate our predictions will be until time passes. So let us enter the future and peer into what may transpire.

Peering into the immediate future, one may not see marked improvements, partially because we may not see the forest from the trees. Developments are ongoing, incremental, and cumulative. Service provisions for children with disabilities have changed significantly over the past decades. Today, there are more programs more readily available than ever before, and their content is becoming increasingly sophisticated.

Toeffler (1980) noted that in today's fast-paced world, we are presently experiencing overwhelming and rapid changes in our society. How does one respond to and prepare for change? Archaeologists are constantly unearthing the remains of ancient societies that once existed but ultimately vanished because they could not cope with the upheaval of

282

change. What makes a social system, whether it be an entire society or just one component, willing to adapt to the demands of the future? It appears that the most effective systems are flexible, fluid, and willing to take risks. They are also cognizant of the personality of their constituents and strive to recognize what needs must be met to ensure continued viability.

Just like infants and children, productive systems are usually open, curious, and receptive to trying new things. Being prepared for the future entails incorporating a framework where continuous innovation, renewal, and rebirth can occur (Gardner, 1981). How does recreation and the disabled fit into the system? Flexibility to accommodate change means that service providers must be sensitive to the current needs of special populations. So let us begin by first discussing the importance of services being rendered.

IMPORTANCE

Over the past few decades, providing structured-play opportunities for exceptional children has undergone a metamorphosis. While more children are being served in a more efficient manner, services may be limited and inadequate in certain geographic regions. However, progress has been made. Benefits should not only be measured by the quantity of growth but also by the quality of the experiences gained by the children. Children play for the pleasure attained from it. They are not concerned about or even aware of the therapeutic value of their experiences but rather of the quality of their interaction.

PUBLIC AND COMMUNITY EDUCATION

Children with disabilities have long been denied the right to participate in recreation activities. This was partially due to societies' difficulty in understanding and accepting persons with disabilities. The nondisabled have gradually learned to recognize that there are more similarities between them and those with disabilities than there are differences. Nevertheless, while progress has been made, I do not feel that the barriers of handicappism have been totally eliminated. Although studies have been conducted concerning integration, I sometimes wonder if we are promoting more tolerance by society rather than acceptance.

A girl with a birth defect told her dad how frustrated she felt being made to feel so different. At one point in her conversation, she looked helplessly at her father and, with tears in her eyes, she said: "You know, life is not a fairy tale, Dad." Although his daughter had made significant progress, she was still viewed as different and this bothered him very much.

Kenneth Kriegel (1969) discussed his frustrations on the social implications of disability. He recounts a situation in which he engaged in an argument with another boy in his neighborhood. After great verbal abuse, Kriegel finally challenged the boy to a fight. The boy agreed reluctantly. "Fighting a cripple" would not reflect credibly in the neighborhood. True to the obligations of adolescence, he knew that to not accept would be a sign of weakness and sentiment. So the fight began and Kriegel lost. Immediately after the confrontation, he forgot momentarily about his disability. He was able for the shortest time to meet with an individual as an equal. However, his feelings of being ordinary were shattered when he overheard the other boy's mother instructing him to never fight with a "cripple." Kriegel was experiencing discrimination or, in this case, handicappism.

The first step in preparing for the future is to educate today's population to this important segment of society. The population as a whole must be educated to understanding that persons with disabilities are entitled to the same provision of services and rights of access as the rest of us.

Biklen (1985) suggests several principles which logically impact the integration of disabled persons. He proposes that as long as we view integration as an experiment, the process is truly tenuous. Rights must be viewed as constitutionally guaranteed. Pity, compassion, and benevolence foster discrimination.

In our conscious society, it is amazing how few people understand why recreational provisions are just as important for the disabled person. Those involved in the community sector often do not recognize the value of recreational therapy. Some have a limited awareness of the meaning of recreational therapy and are ignorant of the types of services that can be made available. Consequently, these people need to be educated not only in understanding the disabled but, additionally, in becoming familiar with the applications of therapeutic recreation. Recreation therapy is not merely the process of conducting recreational experiences for the disabled; rather, it is the integration of specific content and the application of various processes that cause change to occur.

A poignant story of Eli Wiesel, the 1986 Nobel Peace Prize recipient, comes to mind. Wiesel was the keynote speaker at an annual dinner of 600 survivors of the holocaust in January 1987. At the reception, he shared his insightful perceptions on the struggles of humanity to provide equal access to all its citizens. The audience was moved by an anecdote which captured his feelings. When Wiesel was a student, he once came across a man carrying a bird in a cage. The man was bringing a friend a birthday gift. "Does your friend like birds?" Wiesel asked. "I do no know," replied the man, "but come with me and see what happens." As the man was about to give his friend the gift, the friend asked him to open the cage and set the bird free. The wish was granted, and the man immediately beamed with internal joy. That was his gift. Wiesel went on to explain that there is no greater joy, no greater reward, or act of faith, than setting another creature free or at least promoting its salvation or welfare.

In the introductory chapters of this book, examples illustrated the frustration that some children have encountered in attempting to access their leisure time. For some of these children, their feelings of captivity are similar to the bird in the cage. These are feelings that we hope will be eliminated in the future. The goal is to have a society with an increased knowledge and commitment to change, as well as a spirit to promote equal access so all children will have the freedom to engage in constructive-play opportunities.

The following section outlines some futuristic perspectives that will eventually allow us to attain this goal. Three broad categories—professional preparation and impact, programming, and direct benefits—are discussed.

PROFESSIONAL PREPARATION

Over the years, I have watched the field of therapeutic recreation develop. It has reached the point in its growth where recreation therapy is recognized as a valuable field. In the past many had inaccurate perceptions or were totally unaware of this professional field. These problems are now being resolved. Our proficiencies are being upgraded so that the services provided are better. For example, the National Council for Therapeutic Recreation Certification has recently made significant changes in improving the national certification of trainees as specialists within the field. It is anticipated that in the future, the certification process will become ultimately mandatory for practicing individuals and recognized by a wider circle of professionals. The standards have become more stringent and they appear to be more specific than earlier versions. Test construction is now underway to develop a certification exam. I highly commend the council for its present efforts and encourage the council's continued monitoring of the professional community. I believe that in the future we will begin to train more specialists rather than generalists.

I have found that many graduating recreational therapists are not provided the opportunity to participate in an in-depth study in pediatrics as it pertains to exceptional children. In the past, it was believed this lack of specificity occurred as a necessity because the field had not developed to the point where it could afford to be divided in so many ways. However, the time has now come to reexamine this issue. A significant proportion of recreational personnel are working with children. To deal with the complexities of working with children with disabilities, our undergraduate and graduate training programs should offer more course work or incorporate it into existing classes (i.e. special education, developmental psychology, movement) that prepare the student in working with exceptional children. There is also a need for new offerings in therapeutic recreation curriculums, for students as well as existing professionals, in the areas of specific interventive strategies and age-appropriate activities that can be applied with children.

I am not saying that we abandon the idea of preparing a generalist at the entry level. Just like most professional preparation programs, undergraduate training should provide a general overview of the field, through a full array of classes. This orientation should allow the student to successfully enter the profession. The more specialized training opportunities should occur at an advanced level with a more in-depth examination of an area of specialization and a detailed account of therapeutic techniques. I would hope that several curriculums throughout the nation would begin offering at least one class that exposes students to the applications of therapeutic recreation with children.

As we become more effective in developing our prescriptive programs for children, other disciplines will begin to turn more often to recreational personnel for consultation and collaboration. They will become more enlightened regarding the social, physical, and clinical value of involving children with disabilities in therapeutic recreation programs. I feel this is more likely to occur if our educational standards are raised so that recreators can be treated on equal ground to other disciplines. The fact remains that we can dramatically enrich the lives of children while also providing a great deal of growth and development. As a professional body, we must refine our assets while also recognizing our limitations. We should consciously and deliberately become our own monitors of quality assurance and should try to alleviate and enhance our present image. The following represents a brief overview of some areas that may be improved.

An in-depth examination of the underlying elements that relates to providing services for the disabled child should occur. Some of these variables include understanding the needs of a child (assessment), accurate programming strategies, as well as management skills. Prospective therapists should take course work in motor development, psychology, therapeutic interventions for children, and behavior management. Furthermore, within the core of the recreation therapy curriculum, several courses should assist students in synthesizing the previously presented theoretical information so that it can be applied in a practical level. I have recently attempted to incorporate such a design at the university where I am presently employed. With such a concentration of courses, some of our trainees would have the opportunity to be prepared globally as recreational therapists while also having the opportunity to specialize in working with exceptional children.

There is also a need to make continuing-education alternatives available for retraining professionals in practice. Kennedy, Austin, and Smith (1987) suggest that universities and consulting firms may find it beneficial to make available various educational classes that will update the professional community on current trends and practices. These classes will complement existing workshops on similar topics at local, state, and national conventions. It is anticipated that we will see more in-depth workshops presented at these meetings.

I also believe that it will be to the advantage of the field to train others (e.g. parents, educators, other allied health professionals) in some of the theoretical and practical underpinnings of recreation therapy. By doing so, we can enrich the possible opportunities for the therapeutic applications of recreation with special populations. It is important that we take the time to help others as they learn to utilize recreation in a multitude of environments. Through continuing education we should be charged with the responsibility of helping parents understand how to provide recreation and play experiences for their children at home. This, coupled with our professional services, will no doubt have a greater impact on the child.

Furthermore, it seems logical for trainers of therapeutic recreators to

develop classes for individuals from other disciplines who may want to incorporate some prescriptive recreation programs as interventive strategies.
For example, how can we assist in the application of recreational experiences in the child's school? Although we would like to see more recreational
therapists employed in the schools, I feel that the fiscal conditions today
will not permit the necessary changes to occur that would allow this to
happen. Since the funding potential from P.L. 94-142 has never materi-
alized, school systems appear ambivalent about expending additional
funds on related services such as recreation therapy. The most that we
can realistically contribute at this time is consultation with the school
districts. There are, however, two other alternatives. First, courses could
be offered for teachers concerning how they could incorporate recreational
alternatives as teaching strategies within their classrooms. It is presently
more likely that this will fit in classes serving the severely handicapped.
These educators could be taught principles of recreational therapy and
shown their direct relevance to education. Consequently, teachers in the
future would be more sensitized to therapeutic recreation and become
ambassadors for the field. This could directly impact the feasibility of
the following suggestions.

Second, a more direct link between community therapeutic recreation
and education would also be beneficial. In this way, services can be
provided to schools by trained personnel. These professionals could
develop goals and objectives that reflect the targeted behaviors outlined
in the child's Individualized Education Plan (I.E.P.). It is unlikely that
all children in special education classes could be initially involved, but if
the program was pushed and was promoted by the educators (who have
some basic training in therapeutic recreation), the potential impact would
be substantial. The cost of such services could eventually be shared
between the community-based program and the school system. Although
the initial fees would likely be considered costly, the end product would
be worth the initial investment.

For these goals to be realized, appropriate ties with the educational
system must be developed. We will have to establish clear arguments and
evidence that documents why recreational experiences should be provided within the schools. The purpose of education is to prepare children for their future lives. Their lives include a substantial amount of
time outside of school and work. Consequently, educators must realize
that they also have the responsibility of providing guidance to individuals so they can develop skills that can be applied in an individual's

daily life. To get this basic idea across to our school will not be an easy task, but in my opinion it can be done. Advocates will have to include the profession as a whole, plus the assistance of allies from other disciplines and parents. If appropriate networks are established with respective state departments of education, as well as with the chairs of special education programs at various universities, the barriers to the resolution of these educational alternatives could be overcome. The efforts should also be coupled with direct contacts between local recreational and school boards. A realistic time line should be established, incorporating the contributions of all parties involved.

PROGRAMMING

We have only begun to tap into the multitude of programming resources made available to children. As our training becomes increasingly targeted toward youngsters, one should anticipate more sophistication in assessment and direct programming for this young population. Techniques presently applied will be refined and research will be conducted to develop more specificity in the alternatives made available to our field. While informal involvement in play should lead to change, it is not enough. We must know not only what it takes to provide a learning atmosphere but also the ingredients necessary to enhance developmental growth. For example, I may be a great chef. However, my skills are not valuable when I am not consistently capable of putting together the ingredients necessary to prepare that specific dish. The same is true when providing therapeutic activities. One must be aware of what it is that one must do for any consistency to occur. When providing the medium of activities, the teaching strategies need to become more articulated. This is how the approaches of recreational interventions can become recognized (i.e. when we can begin to accurately describe specific interventions, then our status will be assured). It would be advantageous if we were capable of determining the types of activities that could be useful in treating specific problems and being able to match them with the most effective facilitation techniques. In this manner we could begin to apply recreational services in a more prescriptive manner. It boils down to having a clearer understanding of various intervention strategies and knowing how to promote change in the most effective fashion in different situations.

Up to this present time, there has been an inability or a possible unwillingness to sequence skills in recreational training. Although techniques such as activity analysis and games analysis have allowed individuals to adapt programs, it is believed that many practitioners arbitrarily select starting points to train self-directed leisure. Furthermore, this problem is compounded by the fact that under the rubric of recreation programming lie various specific recreation domains (i.e. community-based leisure skills, table games, sports and gross motor recreational skills, art). Decisions need to be made concerning which area should be given more attention and, for that matter, in what kind of order. One might feel that all of these areas deserve equal attention. Perhaps decisions need to be made in light of the severity of each child's disability (Fine, Welch-Burke, and Fondario, 1985).

As suggested in Chapter 6, there are a multitude of recreational alternatives that have not been employed in traditional settings. I feel that in the future we will begin to see some diversity in programming and the incorporation of more psychotherapeutic play strategies. Unfortunately, these approaches (e.g. play therapy, bibliotherapy, horticultural therapy) are underutilized. With their professional application, we may be more capable in reaching targeted goals and maximizing our potential as service providers.

One area that has received some attention over the years pertains to leisure guidance. As children begin to develop avocational skills, it becomes necessary to educate the children as to the importance of leisure and how to apply their newly developed skills (Fine et al., 1985). Mundy and Odum (1979) point out that the "ultimate outcome of the leisure education process is to enable individuals to enhance the quality of their lives in leisure" (p. 3). Professionals should not be investing energies in merely providing recreational services or teaching skills but rather in showing individuals how and where they can apply these skills. We must also take it upon ourselves to train self-initiated play behaviors. It is not useful to develop skills that will only be generated in the presence of a leader or only within the confinements of the group process. Although the growth and the experience gained may be considered beneficial in reality, the most important benefit of the process is to allow the child to develop skills that can be used in his/her free time.

This dilemma of lack of self-initiation in play appears to occur with many exceptional children. In fact, over the years of working with children, this has been one of the major complaints that I have heard from parents. They indicate how frustrated they are that their child does not spontaneously initiate play. Most of the time, these are the children who sit around their home either watching television or being dependent on others to provide them with alternatives to engage in. As was discussed in Chapter 8, perceived competence also causes lack of leisure involvement. Research by Seligman (1975) suggests a theory of helplessness that is learned by environmental encounters. Seligman (1975) indicated the consequences of learned helplessness are motivational, cognitive, and emotional. In essence, by reducing perceived control (cognitive), helplessness hinders the person from believing s/he can perform a task successfully (Iso-Ahola, 1980). It appears that many children with disabilities are confronted with this obstacle and, thus, perceived incompetence may prevent self-initiated play. Consequently, it is argued that attention in programming should not only reflect an emphasis on activity involvement but also should attempt to enhance a child's perceived competence toward play experiences in addition to educating children to applications of leisure in their lives.

RESEARCH

More research attention should be given to the therapeutic effects of recreation on children with disabilities. Thacker (1978) and Sessoms (1979) point out that although intuitively many believe that recreational activities can contribute to a positive change in the development of individuals, there is a minimal amount of scientific evidence to support this assumption. Thacker (1978) points out that several of the studies conducted in the field of recreation have been flawed in their research design and that a major weakness is seen in a lack of replication of studies to confirm or contest initial findings.

Furthermore, Lewdo and Crandall (1980), while investigating trends in research related to leisure with special populations, stated that the second most researched area in therapeutic recreation is related to leisure/recreation activities as a treatment tool. They further state that leisure with special populations is an emerging concern for many researchers with diverse academic orientations.

What I anticipate in the future is an attempt to empirically investigate several elements of recreational services that pertain to exceptional children. Areas of concentration can vary from studies that evaluate the effectiveness of specific treatment programs, to studies evaluating various staff training issues. Kennedy et al. (1987) also points out that local recreational agencies appear to be collaborating more often with university faculty in an attempt to provide some answers to applied research questions. I would concur with Kennedy and his associates and would suggest that this bond will be further strengthened in the future. Recently, a task force has been developed by the National Therapeutic Recreation Society as well as many state affiliates (e.g. California State Parks and Recreation Society, T.R. section) to encourage collaboration between community and university sectors.

DIRECT BENEFITS

It has been suggested from the writings of Crawford and Mendell (1987) that therapeutic recreation can have lifelong benefits to the person with a disability. The experiences can assist in removing roadblocks that prohibit the person's environmental freedom. Probably the most noteworthy accomplishment is therapeutic recreation's ability to facilitate and enhance the quality of life of children with exceptionalities.

Structured free time has allowed children to feel a sense of belonging, in addition to recognizing their accomplishments. Furthermore, with recreation opportunities as an option, children and their families can explore several viable and productive options for the child to engage in. This is extremely important, because it allows the child the freedom of getting involved. It is not uncommon for children to bond with certain programs and stay involved for a long time. In most situations, these programs become an important element of a child's life.

Unfortunately, if many of the previous suggestions are not initiated, especially the assurance of availability of services, the diversity of opportunity may never come into existence. Responsively, we need to investigate how we can make the opportunities available. Logically, community-sponsored activities should be our first choice; however, there are several religious and private organizations who would be willing to expand their services but lack the education of where and how to proceed. To accomplish this goal, we must be forceful in our campaign to educate and advocate. If we do not demonstrate our advocacy roles, we will significantly diminish the opportunity for success. An example will be used to illustrate this point.

I recall Terry Fox, a Canadian, who became an amputee due to cancer. In the early eighties, Terry was one of the first persons with a disability to try and run across a nation. He called his mission "The Marathon of

Hope." Others considered his mission as a run of courage to dispel perceptions about the disabled. He ran to raise money for cancer research, but what he actually accomplished was a heightened level of curiosity and possible acceptance towards persons with disabilities. We, too, must enlighten those responsible for creating new opportunities. With their assistance, we then can proceed and develop a multitude of structured recreational alternatives. Advocacy should take place not only at national and state levels but in local cities. Education begins at home. It is here that the actual services are rendered. We must help community members recognize the necessity for developing recreational programs so that all children may have an opportunity.

For too long we have ineffectively utilized our efforts. As rehabilitative professionals, we need to expand our energies in educating our fellow citizens about the disabled person. For too long this area has been neglected. Consequently, although we have placed an enormous amount of energy on the habilitation/rehabilitation process of our clients, our efforts will never be reached unless the rights of persons with disabilities are guaranteed. We must demand that human services be considered a right, not a privilege. Morally, as well as ethically, we should be responsible for promoting this change.

Robert Carkhuff (1982), a noted humanistic psychologist, expresses his dismay and frustration with our civilization with its inability to meet the needs of the children of our universe. Millions of children die each year due to starvation and neglect. Many of us become so engaged with our own hardships that we face that we cannot appreciate the warmth shared through the sounds made by children. He wrote:

> Whatever personal struggles we have, whatever obstacles we must overcome, our concerns are dwarfed by these final consequences of our neglect. Each civilization will be judged by how it treats those of its members who are most vulnerable. We cannot yet call ourselves a civilization. Perhaps we simply cannot hear the music. . . . We only hear the noise. (P. 1.)

Certainly the same joys and sounds of life are elicited by all children, including those who are disabled. We cannot discount their needs simply because they may differ from ours.

Therefore, to assure a barrier-free life-style for exceptional children, we must continue our concentrated advocacy roles. Unfortunately, formalized recreational experiences represent only one facet of growth. Our efforts must also be directed toward ensuring informal experiences at home, within the parks, and on the streets. Within our range of services, we should take it upon ourselves to educate parents on how they can develop a climate within their home that encourages individual and family play experiences. Some parents may feel inadequate in providing these opportunities. Some may not feel they have the time. I suggest that for the time being, we do not worry about how many will carry out these suggestions, but rather concern ourselves with improving the quality of life for those who wish to make the concentrated effort. Suggested strategies were discussed in Chapters 1, 7, 8, and Appendix III.

CONCLUDING REMARKS

What more can be said? We have provided the reader with our perspectives and ideas for providing recreational and play opportunities for exceptional children. We have provided an overview of the rationale for providing specialized services for the disabled as well as some insight to how this monumental task can be accomplished. We have drawn from personal experiences encountered by both children and their families whom we have worked with. We have attempted to present a balanced picture of both positive and negative situations and outcomes. Some children have been able to receive optimal services, while others have been significantly deprived or underserved. Unfortunately, some of the children who are underserved may reach a ceiling on how much they could gain from existing programs. The intent of this writing was to lift the ceilings and to orchestrate more positive opportunities. Children and their families have been led astray for too long by our unwillingness to assume some responsibility for these consequences. Human beings deserve opportunities to enhance their quality of life. For this reason, we were inspired to write this document.

Of course, good intentions do not always lead to positive results. The growing interest in pediatric recreational therapy will hopefully inspire professionals to develop the unique skills necessary to provide more dynamic and viable services to young persons of special populations. With this comes a stronger need for us to master the strategies and content necessary to intervene and cause change. There are significant differences between working with children versus adults. Furthermore, there are a multitude of subgroups within the classification of exceptional. Therefore, we must become sensitive to each population's specific needs and treatment objectives.

Most of all, we have to remember why all of this is important. All children have the right to be active and contributing members of our society. By assisting children, we will begin to unlock many doors and become a contributing factor to their well-being. We must not continue to look at differences between others and ourselves and to point out the multitude of reasons for their distinctions. Rather, we must try and become bridge builders and open up as many avenues as possible for their growth. By doing so, we remove barriers and promote access.

What does this access represent? Access is an element of freedom, the right to participate in meaningful experiences including those in free time. Social growth was not a priority in the past. Parents were forced to expend much of their energies on areas related to the physical well-being of a child. However, as time changes, so do human values and conditions. Today, we recognize the merits of social experiences. As the climate for rehabilitation has become accepted in Western society, we have developed an appreciation that all persons must find a purpose in their life.

Recreation and leisure fill a significant need in the lives of many children. Channa is a 12-year-old girl who lives in Israel. Although she has been blind since birth, she is a creative musician who has shared her talents with many. I heard a piece of music she had written describing her impressions from a recent trip to a cave. She was able to visualize what she felt through her music. She has used music as a mode of expression and a method to overcome her visual impairment.

Then there is Peter, a young lad with a mild developmental disorder. I met Peter in Europe as he was about to embark on a sixteen-day guided tour of Europe. There were eighteen other members in his group, mixed only in gender and abilities but not in enthusiasm. Twenty years ago, a trip such as this was unheard of. But today, the dreams of people like Peter are coming true and are provided an opportunity to explore the world like the rest of us.

Finally, there is Loretta. When she was in high school, she was not allowed to run on the track team. Ability was not the problem, she noted, attitude was. Loretta, now a grown woman, was in special education and diagnosed as mentally retarded. She was told that because she was in special education, she could not be on the team. Loretta had a difficult time understanding why she was being judged before anyone knew her abilities. In 1983, Loretta showed them all. She won a gold medal in the International Special Olympics in the mile run, setting a record of 5 minutes, 42 seconds. She also won the standing long jump event. These milestones were extremely memorable for Loretta and her family.

Peter, Channa, and Loretta are just a few of the human examples that demonstrate the impact of recreational experiences. There are still many unlike these three who have not experienced the inner joy that play promotes. For these children, we must continue our efforts to move forward and unlock more doors. If this book will assist some of our readers in fulfilling this milestone, then we have accomplished our goal.

Hopefully, in the near future, none of us will go to the gates of a park and silently hear children calling, "Let me in!"

REFERENCES

Biklen, D. (1985). Integration in school and society. In D. Biklen (Ed.), *Achieving the complete school.* New York: Teachers College, Columbia University.

Carkuff, R. (1982). *The noise.* McLean, Virginia: Bernice Carkuff.

Crawford, M., and Mendell, R. (1987). *Therapeutic recreation and adapted physical activities for mentally retarded individuals.* Englewood Cliffs, NJ: Prentice-Hall.

Fine, A., Welch-Burke, C., and Fondario, L. (1985). A developmental model for the integration of leisure programming in the education of individuals with mental retardation. *Mental Retardation, 23*(6), 289–296.

Gardner, J. (1981). *The individual and the innovative society.* New York: W.W. Norton.

Iso-Ahola, S. (1980). *The psychology of leisure and recreation.* Dubuque: Wm. C. Brown.

Kennedy, D., Austin, D., and Smith, R. (1987). *Special recreation: Opportunities for persons with disabilities.* Philadelphia: Saunders.

Kriegel, L. (1969). Uncle Tom and Tiny Tim: Some reflections on the cripple as negro. *The American Scholar, 38,* 412–430.

Lewdo, J., and Crandall, R. (1980). Research trends in leisure and special populations. *Journal of Leisure Research, 12*(1), 69–79.

Mundy, J., and Odum, C. (1979). *Leisure education: Theory and practice.* New York: Wiley.

Seligman, M. (1975). *Helplessness: On depression, development and death.* San Francisco: W.H. Freeman.

Sessoms, D. (1979). Organized camping and its effects on the self-concept of physically handicapped children. *Rehabilitation Literature, 13,* 39–43.

Tarr, B. (1976). *Now you see it, now you don't.* New York: Vintage.

Thacker, R. (1979). The effect of a two week camping experience on the self concept of physically handicapped children (Doctoral Dissertation, the University of North Carolina 1978). *Dissertation Abstracts International, 39*(7-A), 4113.

Toeffler, A. (1980). *The third wave.* New York: Bantam.

APPENDICES

OUTLINE OF THE ACTIVITY ANALYSIS PROCEDURE

JESSE T. DIXON

I. The Activity: Describe the objective or the nature of participation, e.g. group or individual, competitive or non-competitive.

II. Rationale: Indicate the intended benefits for programming the activity.

III. Equipment: Indicate any materials necessary for participation or teaching the activity.

IV. The Composite Learner: Briefly provide objective and subjective information about the child, e.g. prosthetic equipment, motivational preferences.

V. The Method of Participation: Briefly describe the way the activity is to be performed or demonstrated.

VI. Criterion: Indicate how the child will be evaluated and the level of independent participation necessary for terminating instruction.

VII. The Content of Participation: Briefly identify the steps or behaviors in the activity. Consider how each of the steps can be made informational rather than judgmental.

VIII. The Process: Planning the teaching interaction. Identify the motivating feedback from participation, consider teaching cues, and select an appropriate format for presenting information to the child.

IX. Conclusion: Summarize your insights into participation and consider alternative teaching cues and motivational preferences for the child.

X. Data Sheet: List the steps of the activity content and indicate whether the child has:
- failed to meet criterion

- met the criterion with strong teaching cues
- met the criterion with light teaching cues
- met the criterion identified for terminating instruction (a level of independence) for each of the steps.

AN OVERVIEW OF BEHAVIORAL MANAGEMENT STRATEGIES

AUBREY H. FINE

Specialists devising activities must incorporate strategies that will enhance outcomes as well as productivity. This appendix will present an overview of applied management and appropriate strategies for specific special populations.

UNDERSTANDING BEHAVIOR; DREIKURS'S PRACTICAL EXPLANATION OF HUMAN DRIVES

Dreikurs in his writings (Dreikurs and Soltz, 1964; Dreikurs, Grunwald and Pepper, 1971) points out that there is a force behind every human behavior. He also stresses that most human behavior is goal oriented. This is a perspective that was first espoused by Alfred Adler, a pioneer in the field of psychology. Followers of Adlerian psychology contend that a child's behavior will reflect an attempt to achieve constructive goals first. Children will usually progress to the more destructive aspects of behavior when they are not achieving the desired goal (Dreikurs et al., 1971).

Table I lists four categories that describe purposes of behavior (both positive and negative). The goals were formulated by Dreikurs in his quest to explain the rationale for most overt-elicited behaviors. These behavioral goals appear to be germane to most age periods in life, although they do not provide an adequate explanation for severe pathological disorder.

Attention-getting behavior can be positive or negative. The negative behavior that is directed at attention getting is generally some type of inappropriate behavior or misbehavior.

A second goal for misbehavior is power. Power-seeking children believe they are only significant when they are in control (Dinkmeyer and McKay, 1982).

TABLE I
FOUR GOALS OF BEHAVIOR

Goal	Purpose
Attention	Recognition and Acknowledgment
Power	To display control
Revenge	To get even
Inadequacy	A call for help

This brings us to the third goal of behavior, which is revenge. The goal of revenge is extremely complex. Children who pursue revenge usually feel rejected. They believe they are not accepted and feel the need to be spiteful and get even with others (Dreikurs et al., 1971). Finally, the fourth goal of behavior is applied to children who misbehave due to a sense of inadequacy. Some children misbehave to protect their sense of self. These problems could be circumvented by planning activities for the children where they experience success.

Suggested Disciplinary Alternatives

Dreikurs et al. (1971) stress that the teaching of discipline should be considered an ongoing process, not something to resort to only in times of stress or misbehavior. Discipline should not be confused with punishment. Children learn self-discipline through the setting of clear-cut limits, as well as obtaining approval or disapproval from significant others. For children who do not have severe cognitive or emotional disabilities, discipline may be interpreted as teaching children a set of inner controls that will allow them to become productive members of society.

Dreikurs et al. (1971) in their text **Maintaining Sanity in the Classroom** list 27 effective disciplinary procedures. A synthesis of these 27 procedures will be presented in Table II rather than each individual one.

TABLE II
DISCIPLINARY PROCEDURES FOLLOWING DREIKURS APPROACH

1. A leader must always try first to recognize the purpose of behavior. As discussed earlier, attention must be given to why a child is misbehaving prior to determining a more reliable solution for the dilemma.
2. Do not emphasize past behaviors of children. Be more concerned in regards to the future.
3. Give children the opportunity to either discontinue their behavior or else potentially face a specific consequence. The consequence should relate to the behavior at hand. Two general forms of consequences can be applied; natural or logical. Dreikurs and Gray (1970) define natural consequences as representing the natural flow of events without the interference of an adult. For example, the child who refuses to go to sleep usually will be tired the next morning. This represents the natural consequence. On the other hand, a logical consequence is correlated directly to the act. For instance, the child who continually does not clean up after a snack may lose his/her privileges. In this way, the consequence is directly related to the act.
4. Always give a child a choice to either cooperate or else to leave the environment.
5. All children have their strengths and limitations. Attempt to accentuate the strengths.
6. Consistency is of critical importance. Too often our inconsistency in managing children confuses them. We need to show children that we do not change our disciplinary actions arbitrarily. We must respond consistently so children clearly understand our expectations.
7. Allow children the opportunity to be involved in planning future goals, as well as solving their own problems. Too often, it is for our own convenience that we provide solutions for problems. By involving a child in the problem-solving process, s/he may become more committed in carrying out the solutions. Problem ownership is essential in getting a child committed to following through applying the selected alternatives. Furthermore, children may learn from these situations and become more cognizant of how they can internally solve and cope with problems.
8. We must allow children the opportunity to take greater responsibility for their actions. To learn to take responsibility does not occur unless avenues for growth are provided.
9. Children need direction and guidance. We need to recognize however that our major goal is to assist a child in becoming as self-sufficient as possible.
10. Finally, children see adults as role models. They watch and learn from us. When we are wrong, we need to admit this to children. They will usually respect us more for honesty and realize that we are only human.

DEFINITIONS OF VARIOUS PRINCIPLES OF APPLIED BEHAVIOR MANAGEMENT

What is Behavior Management?

Behavior management represents a process in which some overt behavior is changed by the systematic application of techniques which are based on learning theory (O'Leary and O'Leary, 1977; O'Leary, 1972; O'Leary, 1978).

The A.B.C.'s of Behavior Management

The tenets of behavior management pertain to the relationship between behavior and environmental events. Another way of explaining this relates to the antecedents and consequences that influence the occurrence of a behavior.

It has only been recently that attention has been given to enhance the antecedents preceding the occurrence of behavior. The word **antecedent** relates to the multiple factors that constitute the situation preceding the occurrence of a behavior. Relevant antecedents may be critical in understanding the roots of a behavior problem. On the other hand, consequences are usually responsible for determining how frequently as well as how long a behavior will occur. Consequences refer to the multiple factors that constitute the situation that follows a behavior. There are three major principles that may be applied as contingencies to alter behavior: (a) reinforcement, (b) punishment, and (c) extinction. A brief description of each will follow.

REINFORCEMENT. A reinforcer is a contingency that increases the frequency of a behavior. Basically, it can be defined as a consequence that increases the likelihood that a specific behavior will recur. There are several different types of positive reinforcers that can be applied.

Three of the most common categories of positive reinforcers are tangible rewards, activity rewards and social rewards. Tangible rewards represent such items as food, stickers, small trinkets, check marks, and certificates. On the other hand, favorite games and activities represent a sound alternative for increasing behavior. The final form of reinforcer is social rewards. Social reinforcers are sometimes the most effective rewards for increasing behavior. Social rewards can be communicated in a variety of ways, ranging from a simple hug or a pat on the back to an actual statement of recognition (e.g. "Good job!" "Excellent work!"). Social reinforcers are usually the most preferred reward, since they occur more naturally in the living environment (Foxx, 1982a).

NEGATIVE REINFORCEMENT. Negative reinforcement is the removal of an aversive stimuli in an effort to increase the frequency of a desired behavior.

PUNISHMENT. Punishment is usually understood as a procedure that causes a decrease in the future probability of a behavior occurrence. Ayllon and Azrin (1968) point out that in everyday terms, punishment is understood as being applied for performing a specific act or at least for retribution. Punishment's main purpose is to decrease the frequency of a specific act.

There are two types of punishments (aversive and removal). The most common form is when one applies an aversive event following an unacceptable behavior. On the other extreme is the form of punishment that involves withdrawing positive reinforcers following an unacceptable behavior.

Time-out and social disapproval are both examples of this form of punishment (removal). Time-out represents the temporary withdrawal from a rewarding situation following the occurrence of an undesirable behavior. The term **time-out** means time away from the event that seems to be reinforcing the behavior.

EXTINCTION. Extinction is the technical term for the procedure in which a reinforcer that has been applied to sustain an undesirable behavior is withheld. Technically, extinction is a behavioral weakening procedure that involves the consistent failure to deliver a reinforcer following a behavior that had previously produced that reinforcer. Most commonly, this procedure is the most applied of all behavioral processes which attempt to weaken a behavior. Extinction typically involves the removal of attention that appears to be maintaining the behavior under focus. It seems logical that if one ignores a behavior, the behavior will eventually subside.

METHODS TO INCREASE POSITIVE BEHAVIOR

PREMACK PRINCIPLE. This is a procedure in which the behavior that a child frequently performs is used to reinforce a behavior that is seldom displayed (Premack, 1965).

SHAPING. Shaping is the process of gradually altering the quality of a behavior. Becker (1969) suggests a simple response is required initially, and the criteria for reinforcement is gradually made more stringent so as to produce more complex or refined behavioral responses. Martin and Pear (1983) stress that it is impossible to increase the frequency of nonexistent behavior by waiting until it occurs and then reinforcing it.

Shaping is frequently referred to as a method of applying successive approximations. New behaviors can be shaped by the successive reinforcement of closer approximations. Successive approximations are accepted for reinforcement because they resemble the terminal behavior that is being molded and shaped. In essence, the instructor continually modifies his/her expectations.

CHAINING. To apply the principles of shaping, a determination must occur of the sequence of skills necessary to perform the act. This sequence is defined as a chain. Chaining is the process in which simple behaviors already in the repertoire of an individual are reinforced in a particular fashion so they eventually form a more complex behavior. There are two feasible chaining methods. Forward chaining is where the first response in a behavior chain is taught first and the last response is taught at the end. However, when the child does not possess any of the prerequisite skills necessary to complete the desired response, teaching using forward chaining may not be effective. It therefore has been argued that when working with individuals who do not possess the prerequisite skills, it may be helpful for the facilitator to instruct the chain backwards. In essence, the components that comprise the task are taught in reverse order. This means that instruction begins with the last behavioral component in the chain. The logic behind the decision to apply this procedure is simple. The final step in the chain continuum is the most powerful, because it is always associated with the immediate delivery of the terminal reinforcer. Most children appear more excited when they are rewarded for the completion of an entire task rather than its elements. Ironically, the first response in a chain is the weakest of all.

TASK ANALYSIS. To initiate either forward or backward chaining, a list must be formulated representing the sequence of steps necessary to accomplish the behavior. This determination is known as task analysis. Task analysis has been defined by Howell, Kaplan, and O'Connell (1979) as any set of behaviors that a learner must engage in to demonstrate the acquisition of the skills. The theoretical origin of the task analysis originates from the research of several applied behavioral analysts and educational theorists (Bijou, 1970; Bloom, 1978; Gold, 1976; Skinner, 1968; Gagne, 1974).

The primary element of the analysis is a complete and detailed description of every behavioral element within the desired behavior. The underlying aspect of this approach is the analysis of the behavior in terms of the skills necessary to accomplish the entire chain. The investigation incorporates the breaking down of the identified behavior into small specific steps. The splintered tasks which will be instructed represent all of the elements of the behavioral chain. Utilizing a task-analysis format theoretically provides the best instructional sequence in which to teach a task (Scanlon and Almond, 1981).

Once the actual task analysis has been formulated, time must be designated to develop instructional strategies. Ironically, some may blame the ineffectiveness of the process on the task analysis rather than recognizing that the deficiency may exist at the instructional level. Initially, physical guidance may be necessary to help the individual perform the subskill appropriately.

FADING. Fading is the term applied to the gradual removal of a prompt. Fading is utilized to encourage independence. This is done by reducing the control of the instructor by altering the locus of authority to the learner. Fading is incorporated to eliminate the control of the instructor in a gradual fashion. Table III lists several strategies that directly relate to the process of fading.

TABLE III
PROCEDURES WHICH CAN BE UTILIZED IN FADING

1. Verbal cueing.

1.1 Instructional cue hierarchy — Verbal cueing that is utilized with other techniques (Wehman and Marchant, 1978).

1.2 Prompter — A cue utilized after other instructional techniques have been faded out (Paloutzian, Hasafi, Streifel, and Edgar, 1971).

1.3 Indirect verbal cues — Cues which indicated a response was necessary without directly indicating the response to be performed.

1.4 Direct verbal cueing — Cues that are directly utilized to indicate the desired response (Nietupski and Svobada, 1982).

2. Physical prompting — Represents a technique (manual guidance) that is usually applied when modeling and demonstrating are ineffective. In essence, prompting is other-directed and requires little or no input from the participant. Prompting can be naturally (totally) faded so that through the shaping process, less manual guidance will be needed.

SOURCE: Fine, Welch-Burke and Fondario, 1985; Hooper and Wambold, 1978.

BEHAVIORAL CONTRACTING. A behavioral contract is a written agreement between two or more individuals. The final document specifies both the behavior that is required of an individual in addition to the consequence(s) that will be implemented contingent on the performance of those designated required behaviors.

Contracting is based on good behavioristic and humanistic principles of learning. As a procedure, it works well with elementary school-age and older children. Furthermore, this procedure is efficient with those who are capable of taking an active role in collaborating. A contract is simply a clear articulation of what is expected of an individual and how s/he will be reinforced.

Contracts should encourage and recognize successive approximations of the final outcome. In this way, the child will experience success and be motivated to work on the behavior. Furthermore, the most effective contracts are those that are generated collaboratively. It has always been understood that the more involved people are in the process, the more involved they are in generating solutions.

The classic text on how to prepare effective contracts was written by Homme, Csanyi, Gonzales and Rechs in 1969. They suggest ten basic rules. A synthesis of these basic rules and a sample contract are displayed in Table IV.

Token Economies. A token economy can be considered as a motivational system in which tokens are earned for the performance of previously defined appropriate behaviors and subsequently exchanged for previously defined rewards (known as backup reinforcers). The notion of an economy pertains to the fact that tokens are utilized in the same fashion as money in an ordinary economy. In fact, many of the basic principles of economics are directly incorporated in this behavioral technique (e.g. earnings, savings, banking systems). Kazdin (1980, 1978) defines token economy as a reinforcement system where tokens are earned for a variety of behaviors and can be used to purchase items. Within token systems, the tokens themselves have no specific value. However, their power lies within the ability to be exchanged for backup rewards such as tangibles, selecting favorite activities, and privileges.

METHODS OF DECREASING BEHAVIOR

Time-Out. Time-out involves the temporary removal of an individual from a rewarding situation following the occurrence of the undesirable behavior. Time-out is a process where a child is removed from an environment that is reinforcing to a setting that is presumably non-reinforcing. Time-out represents time away from the reinforcement. It is the least restrictive form of punishment and usually works extremely well with a variety of children. Table V represents a simplified listing of how one can apply the time-out procedure.

Satiation. Repp (1983) defines satiation as a temporary decrease in

TABLE IV
GUIDELINES FOR SUCCESSFUL BEHAVIORAL CONTRACTING

1. The contract should reward performance immediately.
2. As noted previously, contracts should be organized to develop gradually the desired behavior. It seems ridiculous to quickly expect dramatic growth, even with this procedure.
3. Contracts should provide frequent rewards in small increments as well encourage reward accomplishment rather than mere obedience. This helps the child eventually develop the behavior into his/her life-style and enhances the transfer maintenance. If we can help children recognize that they are changing for their own good, they appear more likely to comply.
4. Rewards should only be presented contingent upon the elicitation of the contracted behavior.
5. A contract should always be written in the positive and has to be clearly understood by all parties involved.
6. A contract should be developed fairly for both the child and the facilitator. It would be unfortunate if those responsible for developing the contract were not being honest with the other party. Furthermore, although it is expected that the contract's major purpose is to motivate a child externally, one should genuinely respect the integrity of the child.
7. Contracts should be negotiated, as well as agreed to by all parties involved.
8. The contract must clearly define the rewards, as well as build in a time for evaluation and renegotiation.

SAMPLE CONTRACT

Child's name _____

Instructor's name _____

Date of Agreement. Contract begins on _____ and ends on _____
                                          (Date)   (Date)

(should also have a space on the contract which identifies when the contract will be reviewed).

If (clearly identifies the expected behaviors, criteria for acceptance, as well as and where they are to occur)_____

_____

_____

By (identifies when the behavior is to be accomplished) _____

_____

Then (what is the instructor's part of the agreement in addition the rewards) _____

_____

Child's signature _____

Instructor's signature _____

the elicitation performance of a behavior due solely to the repeated presentation of the reinforcer. Satiation can also be understood as the elimination of an unacceptable behavior due to its increased reinforcement.

TABLE V
GUIDELINES FOR THE APPLICATION OF TIME-OUT

1. Time-out must be applied immediately following every occurrence of the target behavior.
2. The area that one utilizes for the time-out should not be reinforcing or rewarding to the individual.
3. There should be a prescribed limit set in advance for the duration of the time-out punishment.
4. A procedure should be formulated, articulating what behaviors must occur for the child to reenter the learning environment.
5. A procedure should be formulated describing what will occur if the undesirable behavior is reintroduced.

DIFFERENTIAL REINFORCEMENT OF OTHER BEHAVIOR (DRO). DRO is a schedule through which reinforcement is delivered at the end of a period of time during which no instances of the target behavior occurred. In essence, one is reinforcing the omission of the negative behavior, for that is what is required for reinforcement to be delivered.

DRO is understood as reinforcing a child for not eliciting the undesirable behavior. Unlike the application of other behavioral paradigms, this approach is an instructional technique that should be administered only at specific times. Prior to initiating the process, baseline data needs to be collected (Foxx, 1982b).

DIFFERENTIAL REINFORCEMENT OF APPROPRIATE (DRA) OR IN-COMPATIBLE (DRI) BEHAVIORS. Both of these two approaches are considered to be more effective than DRO. However, they are formulated primarily on the same principles. DRA is an approach where attention is given to develop alternative appropriate behaviors. The advantage of this approach is in the development of a newly learned skill. However, attention is not directly given to how the misbehavior will be diminished (a major criticism). On the other hand, DRI offers the specialist with the greatest reinforcement control over the inappropriate behavior (Foxx, 1983). Within DRI, a reinforcer is presented following the performance of a behavior which makes the negative behavior virtually impossible. This can occur because the designated requested task makes it impossible for the child to engage in a negative pattern.

SUMMARY

An understanding of behavior and its consequences is a must for persons engaged in working with others. Therefore, the initiation of effective behavior management interventions requires thorough training. It is hoped that this overview has provided the reader with a basic awareness of effective techniques used in behavior management. Throughout this appendix, I have integrated a number of procedures with considerations for their implementation, in an effort to facilitate humane, ethical and the responsible use of the techniques discussed.

The original meaning of the word **discipline** (from the Oxford definition) suggests that it is an instruction to be imparted to "disciples," two words that stem from the Latin root, which means **a learner.** The idea of imparting discipline must then be understood, not only as the management of others, but rather through the combination of teaching, mutual respect and care, an attempt to instill into our charges desirable values and the importance of self-discipline (Bettelheim, 1987). If this flavor is incorporated in our interactions with children, we will become better models and teachers.

REFERENCES

Ayllon, T., and Azrin, N. (1968). *The token economy: A motivational system for therapy and rehabilitation.* New York: Appleton-Century-Crofts.

Becker, W. (1969). In L. Homme et al. (Eds.), *How to use contingency contacting in the classroom.* Champaign: Research.

Bettelheim, B. (1987). *A good enough parent.* New York: Alfred A. Knopf.

Bijou, S. (1970). What psychology has to offer education—Now. *Journal of Applied Behavior Analysis, 3,* 65–71.

Bloom, B. (1978). New views of the learner: Implications for instruction and curriculum. *Educational Leadership, 35,* 563–575.

Dinkmeyer, D., and McKay, G. (1982). *The parent's handbook: Systematic training for effective parenting.* Circle Pines: American Guidance Service.

Dreikurs, R., and Soltz, V. (1964). *Children: The challenge.* New York: Hawthorn/Dutton.

Dreikurs, R., and Grey L. (1970). *A parent's guide to child discipline.* New York: Hawthorn/Dutton.

Dreikurs, R., Grunwald, B., and Pepper, F. (1971). *Maintaining sanity in the classroom: Illustrated teaching techniques.* New York: Harper and Row.

Fine, A., Welch-Burke, C., and Fondario, L. (1985). A developmental model for the integration of leisure programming in the education of individuals with mental retardation. *Mental Retardation, 23,* 289–297.

Foxx, R. (1982a). *Increasing behaviors of severely retarded and autistic persons.* Champaign: Research.

Foxx, R. (1982b). *Decreasing behaviors of severely retarded and autistic persons.* Champaign: Research.

Gagne, R. (1974). Task analysis—Its relation to content analysis. *Educational Psychologist, 11,* 11–18.

Gold, M. (1975). *Try another way.* The California Project.

Homme, L., Csanyi, A., Gonzales, M., and Rechs, J. (1969). *How to use contingency contracting in the classroom.* Champaign: Research.

Hooper, C., and Wambold, C. (1978). Improving the independent play of severely mentally retarded children. *Education and Training of the Mentally Retarded, 13,* 42–46.

Howell, K., Kaplan, J., and O'Connell, C. (1979). *Evaluating exceptional children: A task analysis approach.* Columbus: Charles E. Merrill.

Kazdin, A. (1980). *Behavior modification in applied settings.* Homewood: Dorsey.

Kazdin, A. (1977). *The token economy: A review and evaluation.* New York: Plenum.

Martin, G., and Pear, J. (1983). *Behavior modification: What it is and how to do it.* Englewood Cliffs, NJ: Prentice-Hall.

Nietupski, J., and Svoboda, R. (1982). Teaching a cooperative leisure skill to severely handicapped adults. *Education and Training of the Mentally Retarded, 17,* 38–43.

O'Leary, K.D., and O'Leary, S. (1977). *Classroom management: The successful use of behavior modification.* New York: Pergamon.

O'Leary, K.D. (1972). Behavior modification in the classroom: A rejoinder to Winett and Winkler. *Journal of Applied Behavior Analysis: 5,* 505–510.

O'Leary, K.D. (1978). The operant and social psychology of token systems. In A.C. Catina and T.A. Brigham (Eds.), *Handbook of applied behavior analysis: Social and instructional processes.* New York: Irvington.

Paloutzian, R., Hasazi, J., Streifel, J., and Edgar, D. (1971). Promotion of positive social interaction in severely retarded young children. *American Journal of Mental Deficiency, 75,* 519–524.

Premack, D. (1965). Reinforcement theory. In D. Levine (Ed.), *Nebraska symposium on motivation.* Lincoln: University of Nebraska Press.

Repp, A. (1983). *Teaching the mentally retarded.* Englewood Cliffs, NJ: Prentice-Hall.

Scanlon, C., and Almond, P. (1981). *Task analysis and data collection.* Portland: ASIEP Education Co.

Skinner, B.F. (1968). *The technology of teaching.* New York: Appleton-Century-Crofts.

Wehman, P., and Merchant, J. (1978). Improving free play skills of severely retarded children. *The American Journal of Occupational Therapy, 32,* 100–104.

Appendix III

THE ROAD TO SUCCESS

NYA FINE

The games of children are their most serious business.
MONTAIGNE

Participation in activities is an important aspect of a child's life — disabled or non-disabled. The riches one can bring to a child and the quality of them will be treasures he/she draws on for the rest of their lives (Kelly and Peterson, 1985). One can do many things with children, if one only plays with them. Having fun also enhances other avenues of learning — avenues that can appear unobtainable to parents of disabled children. How can one determine the role of activities in a child's life? Some children may need to learn how to play, while others may need to acquire other skills. How does one teach a child to play? How does one determine what skills should be taught?

SELECTION OF AN ACTIVITY

It is imperative that activities are appropriately selected for the child. Activities need to be adapted to the child's level of skill so that the child enjoys the activity, feels the success, and is motivated to participate again. Sometimes, recreation activities can be utilized without the child really enjoying the activity and, thus, the child does not want to participate in any activity.

If a child does not possess the necessary skills to engage in a certain activity, one must not involve the child in that activity. For example, John is a seven-year-old educable mentally retarded child who is about to engage in a board game of Chutes and Ladders. The skills one must possess are number recognition, concepts of numbers, and concept of up and down. John does not possess the skills of counting and number recognition. Therefore, is the purpose of the game for another person to count and move the game piece so that John can enjoy the game? Since

313

John does not possess the skills for this board game, one must look at the skills that he does possess. Since John can identify colors, select a board game or an activity based on John's abilities. Candyland/Candyland Bingo are just two board games that John could utilize his abilities and have fun while participating. There are numerous games one could utilize based on colors, and there are many more that one could create.

One needs to be sensitive to the child's likes, dislikes, strengths, capabilities, and experiences. Two very important skills come into action when determining the selection of an activity. One must observe and listen to the child. Watch the child and learn from the child. What is the child capable of doing, what makes the child happy, when is the best time for the child to engage in an activity, what is the best position for participation? Listen to the child. It is easy for one to select an activity based on what one thinks is the best activity for the child. It may not be. A child should be involved in the selection of the activity as much as possible. Children also have marvelous insight on the ways to modify activities to meet their needs. Another important fact is not to exclude the siblings when discussing modifications. Siblings have wonderful ideas of creating and adapting activities. It is imperative that parents learn what is the best way to help their child.

Now let us examine the skill components that will assist in the selection of an activity.

1. What skills are required to engage in this activity?
   a. cognitive
   b. physical
   c. social
   d. emotional
2. Is the activity age appropriate?
3. Can the activity be adapted to the skill level of the individual?

When one is examining an activity and determing what component of the activity needs to be modified, do only the amount of adaptation that is absolutely necessary. A common mistake when adapting activities is that the activity becomes "overly" adapted which results in a non-challenging experience. The purpose of the adaptation is to allow the child to participate and experience the activity. Remember: Modifications have to be based on the child's abilities.

Here are some elements to consider when one is planning the activity session.

1. Activity should be fun.
2. Start with a short period of time and increase the time as one progresses.
3. Make directions clear and concise—Demonstrate what is to be done.
4. Get involved with the activity and express enthusiasm.

It is important to remember that activities can be enjoyed by the entire family. Families should incorporate fun activities into the daily family life. All family members can benefit from the interaction, and it may promote awareness of the values of family experiences. The benefits in participating in activities together are limitless. Activities are fun, and learning can occur. The efforts that one does, whether it is to teach a child how to play or how to develop interests, is a very important and necessary task. According to Doctor Wayne Dyer, "Once you see a child's self image begin to improve, you will see significant gains in achievement areas, but even more important you will see a child who is beginning to enjoy life more." To live and enjoy life—What better gift could be given to a child than to give them the gift to enjoy their lives?

RESOURCES

Recreation Organizations

American Athletic Association
3916 Lantern Drive
Silver Springs, MD 20902

American Camping Association
5000 State Road
Martinsville, ID 46151

Disabled Sportsmen of America
P.O. Box 5496
Roanoke, VA 24012

Handicapped Scuba Association
1104 El Prado
San Clemente, CA 92672

American Blind Bowling Association
c/o Gilbert Baqui
3500 Terry Drive
Norfolk, VA 23518

American Wheelchair Bowling
Association
N54 W15858 Lakspur Lane
Menomonee Falls, WI 53051

Boy Scouts of America
Scouting for the Handicap
Camping for the Handicapped
830 Third Avenue
New York, NY 10002

International Foundation for
Wheelchair Tennis
2203 Timberlock Place
Suite 126
Woodlands, TX 77380

National Association for Sports
Cerebral Palsy
66 E. 34 St.
New York, NY 10016

National Handicap Sports and
Recreation Association
P.O. Box 33141, Farragut Station
Washington, DC 20033

National Wheelchair Basketball
Association
P.O. Box 737
Sioux Falls, SD 57101

Special Olympics
Kennedy Foundation
1350 New York Ave.
Washington, DC 20005

U.S.A. Toy Library Association
104 Wilmont
Suite 201
Deerfield, IL 60015

National Foundation of
Wheelchair Tennis
15441 Redhill Ave.
Suite A
Tustin, CA 92680

International Wheelchair
Road Racers Club
16578 Ave. N.E.
St. Petersburg, FL 33702

National Archery Association
1750 E. Boulder St.
Colorado Springs, CO 89090

National Handicapped Sports and
Recreation Association
Capitol Hill Sta.
P.O. Box 18664
Denver, CO 80218

National Park Service
Division of Special Programs and
Populations
Dept. of Interior
18th & C. St. N.W.
Washington, DC 20240

National Wheelchair Racquetball
Association
c/o AARAA
815 Weber
Suite 203
Colorado Springs, CO 80903

North American Riding for the
Handicapped
111 E. Wacker Drive
Chicago, IL 60601

Ski for Light
c/o Bud Keith
737 North Buchanan St.
Arlington, VA 22203

World Recreation Association
of the Deaf
P.O. Box 7894
Van Nuys, CA 91409

SUMMARY

It was the intent of the writer to expose the reader to the process of selecting appropriate activities and adapting activities based on the child's needs. Activities are an important aspect in everyone's lives, especially children. Activities and recreation organizations were given as a resource to the reader. Activities are fun learning experiences that can open new doors for children as well as families.

REFERENCES

Kelley, M., and Parsons, E. (1975). *The mother's almanac.* New York: Doubleday.

NAME INDEX

319

SUBJECT INDEX